BRUTALITY GARDEN

BRUTALITY GARDEN

TROPICÁLIA AND THE EMERGENCE OF A BRAZILIAN COUNTERCULTURE

CHRISTOPHER DUNN

THE UNIVERSITY OF NORTH CAROLINA PRESS

CHAPEL HILL & LONDON

Manufactured in the United States of America

Designed by Richard Hendel

Set in Quadraat, Spontan, and Lithos types

by Tseng Information Systems, Inc.

The paper in this book meets the guidelines for
permanence and durability of the Committee on
Production Guidelines for Book Longevity of the
Council on Library Resources.

Library of Congress Cataloging-in-Publication Data

Dunn, Christopher, 1964–

Brutality garden : Tropicália and the emergence of a
Brazilian counterculture / Christopher Dunn.

p. cm.

Includes bibliographical references and index.

ISBN 0-8078-2651-0 (cloth : alk. paper) —
ISBN 0-8078-4976-6 (pbk. : alk. paper)

1. Tropicália (Music) — Brazil — History and criticism.
2. Counterculture — Brazil — History — 20th century.

I. Title.

ML3487.B7 D86   2001

306.4'84 — dc21   2001035148

05   5 4 3 2

The publication of this book was supported by generous contributions
from the Roger Thayer Stone Center for Latin American Studies,
the Dean of Liberal Arts and Sciences, and the
Graduate School of Tulane University.

THIS BOOK WAS DIGITALLY PRINTED.

For my parents,
John and Gwenn Dunn,
with admiration, gratitude,
and love

CONTENTS

ILLUSTRATIONS

A section of color plates follows page 112

ACKNOWLEDGMENTS

I have a vague sense that the remote origins of this book can be traced to a moment in 1985, when I was visiting the home of Peter Blasenheim, my professor of Latin American history at The Colorado College. We spent an evening listening to his favorite Brazilian songs collected during several extended research trips, including João Gilberto's sublime distillations of bossa nova, Elis Regina's jazz-bossa hits, Chico Buarque's plaintive sambas, Roberto Carlos's romantic ballads, and several protest anthems from the 1960s. At the time, I was barely conversant in Spanish, much less Portuguese, the wonderfully sonorous language I first heard on those albums in Colorado Springs. I was captivated by the sound of the language combined with the music and fascinated with his explanations of each song. At one point, Peter pulled out a copy of *Tropicália, ou panis et circencis*, a strange "concept album" from 1968, during which time Brazil was entering the most repressive phase of military rule. While most of the other albums he played that evening seemed relatively comprehensible given my limited knowledge of Brazil, this one seemed ambiguous and utterly confusing to me. Was it a patriotic celebration of life in the tropics? Or was it a wicked satire? Was it an apology for modernization under military rule? Or was it a protest album?

I later found out that the album I heard that evening was the "album-manifesto" of a movement known as "Tropicália" or "Tropicalismo." In 1992, I had the opportunity to interview key participants in this movement, Caetano Veloso, Gilberto Gil, and Tom Zé, for a National Public Radio program dedicated to the twenty-fifth anniversary of Tropicália produced by Sean Barlow and Ned Sublette for Afropop Worldwide. At the time, I was pursuing a graduate degree in Portuguese and Brazilian Studies at Brown University and I realized that Tropicália was a compelling topic for further study. With help from a Fulbright student grant, I was able to return to Brazil and carry out the research for my Ph.D. dissertation, "The Relics of Brazil: Modernity and Nationality in the Tropicalista Movement," which provided the basis for this book. I will forever be indebted to Nelson Vieira, Luiz Valente, and Thomas Skidmore, who formed my dissertation committee. Each of them contributed in distinct ways to my understanding of Tropicália within the context of modern Brazil. I also wish to thank Anani Dzidzienyo, Onésimo Almeida, and Neil Lazarus, who greatly enriched my intellectual experience at Brown University.

I would like to express my profound gratitude to all of the Brazilian artists who generously shared their insights with me, including Caetano Veloso, Gilberto Gil, José Celso Martinez Corrêa, Augusto de Campos, Rogério Duarte, Gilberto Mendes, Júlio Medaglia, and Waly Salomão. My deepest thanks are for Tom Zé and Neusa Martins, who have been particularly helpful and generous.

In Brazil I was very fortunate to meet with scholars whose work has enriched my understanding of Tropicália. I would like to thank Carlos Calado, Celso Favaretto, Carla Gallo, Marcelo Ridenti, Hermano Vianna, Durval Muniz de Albuquerque Jr., Roberto Schwarz, Heloísa Buarque de Hollanda, Silviano Santiago, Sérgio Miceli, Renato Ortiz, Evelina Hoisel, and Liv Sovik. I would also like to send *aquele abraço* to my friends in Brazil who helped me in different ways before and during the development of this project: Pedro and Roberto Amaral, Adilea, Helena, and Susana de Castro, Denise Cavalcanti, Fernando Velloso, Edgard Magalhães, Eliana Stefani, Fátima and João Farkis, Teresa and Dan Nakagawa, Eulália dos Santos, Ceres Santos, Cícero Antônio, Silvio Humberto, and Ismael Mazza. I am especially grateful for the friendship and hospitality of Vitória Aranha and Paul Healey.

I wish to thank several scholars of Brazilian culture in the United States, including Leslie Bary, Barbara Browning, Leslie Damasceno, David George, Randal Johnson, Emanuelle Oliveira, and Robert Stam, who have contributed in different ways to the development of this book. I am especially indebted to Charles A. Perrone, a leading authority on Brazilian popular music, who has been a great friend and an insightful critic of my work. J. Lorand Matory read an early draft of the manuscript and has been a great source of encouragement and inspiration since I first entered graduate school. Special thanks to friends Nick Nesbitt, Richard Schuler, Robert Arellano, and T. R. Johnson, who have, at one stage or another, shared their thoughts on Tropicália, popular music, and the 1960s with me. These friends and colleagues deserve credit for the strengths of this book but bear no responsibility for its shortcomings.

During the last five years, Tulane University has provided a most collegial and stimulating environment for the development of this project. I would like to thank my colleagues from the Department of Spanish and Portuguese, especially Harry Howard, Maureen Shea, Henry Sullivan, and Nicasio Urbina. I am particularly indebted to my friend and colleague Idelber Avelar. He has foregrounded the "task of mourning" in his own work but has also reminded me of the primacy of *alegria* with great affection and intellectual generosity. I am also grateful to my friends and colleagues of the African and African Diaspora Studies Program, particularly Rosanne Adderley, Michael Cunningham, Gaurav Desai, Adeline Masquelier, Supriya Nair, and Felipe Smith. Special thanks are in order for all of the graduate students at Tulane University who have challenged and inspired me in myriad ways during the last five years.

I feel most fortunate to have had the opportunity to teach and conduct research at a university with a first-rate Latin American Studies program. I wish to thank the Roger Thayer Stone Center for Latin American Studies at Tulane University, its director, Thomas Reese, and associate director, Gene Yeager, for generously providing funds to support the production of this book. Guillermo Nañez and Paul Bary have done a splendid job in developing the Brazil collection at the Latin American Library of Tulane University and have been most helpful in procuring relevant materials. I have had the great pleasure of codirecting the Brazilian Studies program with Anthony Pereira, who generously read a previous draft of this book and offered marvelous insights. I would also like to acknowledge personal, organizational, and intellectual debts to other members of the Brazilian Studies Council, including William Balée, Bill Lennon, Ana Lopez, and Timmons Roberts.

I gratefully acknowledge the support of Teresa Soufas, Dean of Liberal Arts and Sciences, and Kay Orrill, Assistant Dean of the Graduate School, who provided subvention grants for the production of the color plates in this book. The reproduction of these splendid works of art would have been impossible without this kind of institutional support.

I wish to thank Rubens Gerchman, Glauco Rodrigues, and Hélio Eichbauer for graciously authorizing the color reproduction of their works. In Brazil, I also received helpful assistance from photo archivists Ana Vidotti, Bias Arrudão, Marcos Massolini, and Fabiana Dorighello of Abril Imagens, and Luiz Fernando Brilhante and Tatiana Constant of Agência JB. Thanks also to César and Cláudio Oiticica of Projeto Hélio Oiticica and Alda Baltazar of Universal Records in Rio de Janeiro.

I wish to acknowledge permission to reprint material that previously appeared elsewhere in abridged form. An earlier version of Chapter 4 appeared as "In the Adverse Hour: The Denouement of Tropicália," in *Studies in Latin American Popular Culture* 19 (2000): 21–34. Portions of several chapters contained here appeared as "Tropicália, Counterculture, and the Diasporic Imagination in Brazil," in a volume of essays I coedited with Charles Perrone, titled *Brazilian Popular Music and Globalization*, published by the University Press of Florida in 2001.

It has been a pleasure to work with the editorial staff of the University of North Carolina Press. With a keen eye for detail and consistency, Mary Caviness did a splendid job of editing. I am especially indebted to Elaine Maisner, who took an early interest in this project and then guided me through various stages in the preparation of the manuscript with patience and enthusiasm.

This book is dedicated to my parents, John and Gwenn Dunn, who have always taken a keen interest in my work. I also wish to thank my sister, Susan Dunn, who has offered her insights to this project over several years. I have been blessed with the affection and patience of Alyse Njenge Ntube, who has offered constant support and encouragement. Finally, I wish to send um *beijo grande* for my son, Luango, with whom I have shared many pleasurable hours listening to Brazilian music.

ABBREVIATIONS

AI-5   Ato Institucional 5 (Fifth Institutional Act)
CPC   Centro Popular de Cultura (People's Center for Culture)
DOPS   Departamento de Ordem Política e Social
        (Department of Political and Social Order)
FIC   Festival Internacional da Canção (International Song Festival)
IBGE   Instituto Brasileiro de Geografia e Estatística
        (Brazilian Institute of Geography and Statistics)
IBOPE   Instituto Brasileira de Opinião Pública e Estatística
        (Brazilian Institute of Public Opinion and Statistics)
ISEB   Instituto Superior de Estudos Brasileiros
        (Advanced Institute for Brazilian Studies)
MNU   Movimento Negro Unificado (Unified Black Movement)
MPB   Música Popular Brasileira (Brazilian Popular Music)
TUCA   Teatro da Universidade Católica
UNE   União Nacional dos Estudantes (National Student Union)

BRUTALITY GARDEN

INTRODUCTION

Every cultural complex has specific forms of consecration and adulation for its artistic luminaries. For Brazilian singer-songwriter Caetano Veloso, perhaps the supreme moment of popular and official canonization came on February 20, 1998, as he surveyed a crowd of five thousand carnival celebrants in Salvador, Bahia, while he was perched on top of a *trio elétrico*, a moving soundstage that transports electric dance bands through the city's streets. Since the early 1970s, he has made annual guest appearances on *trios elétricos* on the morning of Ash Wednesday to perform his songs that have become standards of the Bahian carnival repertoire.

This time, however, Veloso was there to receive the title of Doctor Honoris Causa from the Federal University of Bahia for the "grandiosity of his oeuvre and his renowned wisdom." [1] In the past, the university had awarded the title to famous Bahian artists like novelist Jorge Amado, composer Dorival Caymmi, and filmmaker Glauber Rocha, but this was the first time the title had been conferred in the streets during carnival. For the rector of the university, it was a democratic gesture: "We want to integrate the university into society. For this reason we opted to pay homage to Caetano in the streets, together with the people celebrating carnival." Despite some editorial grumbling that the ceremony made the university look ridiculous, the event was a public relations success for the institution and its honored guest, an artist who has been at the forefront of musical innovation and cultural transformation since the late 1960s. As the carnival ceremony would suggest, Veloso is an artist who enjoys mass popularity as well as critical acclaim among intellectuals.

Veloso came to national attention together with Gilberto Gil, his friend and colleague from the University of Bahia, as leading figures of Tropicália, a short-lived but high-impact cultural movement that coalesced in 1968. They worked collectively with other artists from Salvador, including vocalist Gal Costa, singer-songwriter Tom Zé, and poets Torquato Neto and José Carlos

Capinan. The so-called *grupo baiano* (Bahian group) had migrated to São Paulo, where they forged a dynamic artistic relationship with several composers of the vanguard music scene, most notably Rogério Duprat and the innovative rock band Os Mutantes (The Mutants). This alliance between musicians from Bahia, a primary locus of Afro-Brazilian expressive culture, and from São Paulo, the largest, most industrialized Brazilian city, proved to be a potent combination and has had a lasting effect on Brazilian popular music and other arts. Although Tropicália coalesced as a formal movement only in the realm of popular music, it was a cultural phenomenon manifest in film, theater, visual arts, and literature. The dialogic impulse behind Tropicália would generate an extraordinary flourish of artistic innovation during a period of political and cultural conflict in Brazil.

The year of 1968 has special historic resonance for several nations around the world. Of course, significant events occurred on both sides of 1968, but in several national contexts the year serves as a generational watershed. In the United States, 1968 marked a public turning point against the Vietnam War, widespread antiwar student protests, the assassinations of Martin Luther King Jr. and Robert Kennedy, and the emergence of the Black Power movement. In France, radical Maoist students and workers forged a brief and ultimately failed alliance against the postwar Gaullist State. The Soviets invaded Czechoslovakia, putting an end to the democratic and liberationist aspirations of the Prague Spring movement. In Mexico City, student protests against high unemployment and repression of political dissent ended when hundreds of unarmed demonstrators were massacred by army and police detachments.

The symbolic density of 1968 is particularly evident in Brazil, especially for artists, intellectuals, students, workers, civilian politicians, and activists who opposed a right-wing military regime that had seized power in 1964. In 1968, broad sectors of civil society coalesced in opposition to the regime. Factory workers in São Paulo and Minas Gerais carried out the first strikes since the inception of military rule. Leftist students engaged in pitched battles with the military police and ultrarightist allies in the universities. Meanwhile, more radicalized groups of the opposition went underground and initiated armed struggle against the regime. The government responded to civil protest and incipient armed resistance with a decree known as the Fifth Institutional Act (AI-5), which outlawed political opposition, purged and temporarily closed congress, suspended habeas corpus, established blanket censorship over the press, and effectively ended the protest movement. Thereafter, opposition to the regime would be expressed primarily through disparate movements of armed resistance, which were ultimately liquidated. The generation reaching adulthood at that time would subsequently be called the "geração AI-5," an emblematic reference to this draconian decree that initiated a period of intense repression.²

Cultural conflicts also came to a head in 1968, primarily within a largely middle-class urban milieu that opposed military rule. Artists and intellectuals began to reevaluate the failures of earlier political and cultural projects that sought to transform Brazil into an equitable, just, and economically sovereign nation. Tropicália was both a mournful critique of these defeats as well as an exuberant, if often ironic, celebration of Brazilian culture and its continuous permutations. As its name suggests, the movement referenced Brazil's tropical climate, which throughout history has been exalted for generating lush abundance or lamented for impeding economic development along the line of societies located in temperate climates. The tropicalists purposefully invoked stereotypical images of Brazil as a tropical paradise only to subvert them with pointed references to political violence and social misery. The juxtaposition of tropical plenitude and state repression is best captured in the phrase that serves as the title for this book, "brutality garden," which was taken from a key tropicalist song discussed in Chapter 3.

The musical manifestations of Tropicália did not propose a new style or genre. Tropicalist music involved, instead, a pastiche of diverse styles, both new and old, national and international. On one level, tropicalist music might be understood as a rereading of the tradition of Brazilian popular song in light of international pop music and vanguard experimentation. In Brazil, the tropicalists elicited comparisons with their internationally famous contemporaries, the Beatles, a group that also created pop music in dialogue with art music as well as with local popular traditions. The tropicalists contributed decisively to the erosion of barriers between música erudita, for a restricted audience of elite patrons, and música popular, for the general public. Tropicália was an exemplary instance of cultural hybridity that dismantled binaries that maintained neat distinctions between high and low, traditional and modern, national and international cultural production.³

On a discursive level, the tropicalists proposed a far-reaching critique of Brazilian modernity that challenged dominant constructions of national culture. Instead of exalting the povo (masses) as agents for revolutionary transformation, their songs tended to focus on the quotidian desires and frustrations of "everyday people" living in the cities. Ultimately, the tropicalists would give impetus to emerging countercultural attitudes, styles, and discourses concerning race, gender, sexuality, and personal freedom. These issues were becoming increasingly salient in countercultural movements in the United States and Europe but were manifested in distinct ways in Brazil during the period of military rule.

As with any cultural object or practice, the significance of Tropicália is not produced solely by the artists themselves. As Pierre Bourdieu has shown, the "symbolic production" (i.e., production of value and meaning) of art depends on a wide range of agents, including managers, producers, critics, and consumers.[4] A considerable body of journalistic and scholarly literature on Tropicália has accumulated in Brazil during the last thirty years. Cultural critics in the mainstream press of São Paulo and Rio de Janeiro published the earliest articles about the movement. As the movement unfolded, the concrete poet and theorist Augusto de Campos wrote a series of enthusiastic articles that praised Veloso and Gil for their brazen critiques of musical nationalism.[5] From the outset, several journalists were supportive of the movement, although other critics expressed anxiety over its unabashed enthusiasm for electric instrumentation, Anglo-American rock, and mass media exposure.

In 1970, the literary critic Roberto Schwarz published a watershed essay about contemporary Brazilian culture and politics that became a fundamental reference for subsequent scholars of Tropicália.[6] Working within a tradition of Marxist criticism, Schwarz was the first critic to draw attention to the allegorical nature of Tropicália, noting its frequent allusions to anachronistic cultural emblems filtered through the "white light of ultramodernity" so as to convey the disjunctures of capitalist development in Brazil.[7] While recognizing the critical potential of the tropicalist allegory, he was troubled by its propensity to advance a fatalistic "atemporal idea of Brazil" that seemed to negate any potential for social transformation.[8] Several other critics revisited the question of allegory in Tropicália during the 1970s but with different conclusions. Celso Favaretto, for example, argued that the tropicalist allegory derived its critical effect precisely by leaving historical contradictions unresolved, thereby generating an indeterminate and fragmentary image of Brazil that could then be activated to satirize official culture.[9] Silviano Santiago critiqued Schwarz for privileging dialectical reason (indebted to a European Hegelian-Marxist theoretical tradition) over other artistic and theoretical practices grounded in the cultural and historical specificities of Brazil. Santiago was not attempting to delineate a pure space of irreducible difference in relation to the West but rather to suggest ways in which Brazil and Latin America generally confound metropolitan models of historical transformation.[10] Heloísa Buarque de Hollanda further contributed to the critique of Schwarz's position in her account of cultural politics during the sixties and early seventies. She asserted that Tropicália proposed a "new critical language" that refused the redemptive claims of more orthodox leftists yet intervened directly on the level of individual attitudes and behavior, thereby paving the way for countercultural practices and discourses.[11] Veloso and Gil also contributed to debates surrounding Tropicália with their own volumes of collected interviews and articles from the mainstream and underground print media.[12]

Tropicália has become the subject of a growing body of literature on contemporary Brazilian culture produced for a general reading public. Included in this category are didactic pocket books, secondary education texts, and lavishly illustrated coffee-table volumes.[13] In the 1990s, the music critic Carlos Calado published two meticulously researched narratives relating to Tropicália—one that focuses on the rock group Os Mutantes and the other that recounts the history of the movement.[14] Since the late seventies, Tropicália has been regularly revisited in the national press, usually in five-year intervals. The commemorative surge grew considerably in 1992–93, when Veloso and Gil celebrated their fiftieth birthdays and recorded *Tropicália 2*, an album that reinterprets the movement within a contemporary context.

A wave of memorialist writing about the sixties in Brazil has also contributed to ongoing debates around the tropicalist experience. Most of the earliest memoirs were written by former urban guerrillas and tended to ignore cultural debates.[15] Subsequent memoirs have focused more broadly on the existential crises, political disputes, and cultural conflicts of artists and activists. In 1997, Caetano Veloso published *Verdade tropical* (Tropical truth), a hefty tome that primarily focused on his personal experience in the tropicalist movement. Veloso offered a fascinating account of the sixties, political and cultural conflicts, and the lasting importance of Tropicália. His memoir provoked yet another round of debate in the national press over the value and significance of Tropicália and, more importantly, how it relates to contemporary culture.

The corpus of English-language literature relating to Tropicália is relatively small in light of its centrality to contemporary Brazilian culture. Drawing on the early formulations of Augusto de Campos, the ethnomusicologist Gerard Béhague first introduced tropicalist song to a North American academic audience. Situating the movement within the context of post–bossa nova Brazilian popular music under military rule, Béhague argued that Tropicália had the effect of "liberating Brazilian music from a closed system of prejudices and giving it conditions of freedom for research and experimentation."[16] In the first scholarly book in the United States on Brazilian popular music, Charles Perrone explored the tropicalist poetics of Veloso and Gil, drawing attention to their "refined parody, sociocultural allegory, and structural experimentation." [17] In some ways, Perrone's book is a companion to Randal Johnson's study of Cinema Novo and David George's study of modern Brazilian theater, which discuss how Tropicália was manifested in these two artistic fields.[18] Following the resurgence of interest in Tropicália in Brazil and abroad, the journal *Studies in Latin American Popular Culture* dedicated an entire issue to the movement in 2000.

To fully appreciate the significance of Tropicália it is necessary to first examine preceding literary movements and musical phenomena that contributed decisively to what was understood to be a "national culture." The first chapter of this book discusses *modernismo*, a literary and cultural movement that began in the 1920s. Two basic imperatives guided the modernist generation, one oriented toward formal literary experimentation informed by European vanguards and the other concerned with the articulation of what was distinctive about Brazil. I focus on two major modernist writers, Oswald de Andrade and Mário de Andrade, who both outlined projects for the renovation of Brazilian arts and letters that would have a sustained impact on subsequent generations.[19] Mário's pioneering work in musicology is particularly relevant to this book since it constituted a foundational statement of musical nationalism that would profoundly influence succeeding generations of composers and critics. Oswald is noted for his humorous and ironic interpretations of Brazilian history and culture most famously expressed in two manifestos. In his "Brazilwood Manifesto" (1924), he exhorted his colleagues to create a "poetry for export" that was neither deferent to, nor ignorant of, metropolitan literary currents. Oswald further radicalized his project in the "Cannibalist Manifesto" (1928), which advanced a model for critically "devouring" cultural inflows from abroad. Cannibalism proved to be a compelling and controversial metaphor for artists and critics of subsequent generations. Forty years later, Veloso would claim that Tropicália was a form of "neo-cannibalism" relevant to the cultural context of the 1960s.[20]

The vanguardist energies of Brazilian *modernismo* waned in the 1930s and 1940s, during the nationalist, populist, and ultimately authoritarian rule of Getúlio Vargas. The free-verse poetry, experimental prose, and provocative manifestos of the 1920s gave way to realist novels and social histories oriented primarily toward the "discovery" and documentation of Brazilian culture. Of particular salience was the articulation of a *mestiço* paradigm, which extolled cultural and racial hybridity as the foundation for a unified national identity. As elsewhere in the Americas, popular music would play a central role in the "invention," dissemination, and international projection of national culture.

The samba singer and Hollywood film star Carmen Miranda played a particularly important role in this process, and the tropicalists would later reference her with gleeful irony. The final part of this chapter examines the eclipse of Miranda and other radio stars and the emergence of a cosmopolitan and internationalist aesthetic in the late 1950s, during a period of optimism regarding Brazil's prospects for democratic modernization and development. In the realm of popular music, the cool sophistication of bossa nova was emblematic of this period.

In the early 1960s, young artists who aspired to raise political consciousness among urban and rural working classes became increasingly disaffected with the introspective sentimentalism of early bossa nova. Chapter 2 discusses the populist and nationalist critique of bossa nova and the development of an urban protest culture following the coup of 1964. At this time, artists who were identified with an eclectic post–bossa nova category, which would later be denominated MPB (Música Popular Brasileira), were generally opposed to military rule. Like many other societies around the world, Brazil also had a homegrown rock movement known as the Jovem Guarda (Young guard), which attracted a large urban audience who were attracted to the consumer-oriented "youth culture" disseminated globally by the American culture industry. Many Brazilians associated rock with U.S. cultural imperialism and championed the MPB camp as the most appropriate musical expression of Brazilian modernity. The young Bahians were devotees of João Gilberto, the musical innovator of bossa nova, yet had become increasingly frustrated with an artistic community that defined aesthetic priorities according to the imperatives of cultural nationalism. In response, Gil and Veloso developed what they called the "universal sound," which they first performed during a televised music festival in 1967.

This event is generally considered to be an inaugural moment of the tropicalist movement together with manifestations in film, theater, visual arts, and literature. Chapter 3 begins with a discussion of key cultural productions from other fields that converged with the musical project of the Bahian group and its allies in São Paulo. Of particular salience was Glauber Rocha's 1967 film *Terra em transe* (Land in anguish), a watershed in Brazil's Cinema Novo movement that allegorized the collapse of populism and the ascension of authoritarian rule in Brazil. Veloso has noted that the film represented a "traumatic moment" for left-wing artists, creating the conditions for what would soon be called "tropicalismo."[21] It dramatized a historical moment of crisis for progressive artists and intellectuals living under a right-wing military dictatorship. Rocha's films directly influenced the "guerrilla theater" of

São Paulo's Teatro Oficina, which was subsequently identified with the tropicalist movement. Around the time that Gil and Veloso presented their "universal sound," Teatro Oficina staged "O rei da vela" (The candle king) (1933), Oswald de Andrade's modernist farce about the Brazilian elite, reconfigured for the present context. As shown in the color plates on this book, Tropicália also found expression in the visual arts, including album cover graphics, paintings, theater scenes, and installations from the late 1960s.

The story behind the naming of the movement suggests the degree of dialogic cross-fertilization among several artistic realms. After hearing one of Veloso's untitled compositions in late 1967, the cinematographer Luís Carlos Barreto detected affinities with an installation called Tropicália by the visual artist Hélio Oiticica. Despite Veloso's initial reluctance, he agreed to use "Tropicália" as the title of his song, which subsequently became a key song-manifesto of the movement. Tropicália would eventually serve as the name for the entire movement, although "tropicalismo" was more commonly used during the 1960s and 1970s. Veloso has expressed some ambivalence regarding the designation "tropicalismo" since it seemed to reduce the movement to a repertory of clichés about "life in the tropics" and evoked a remote affiliation with "Luso-tropicalismo," a theory of Portuguese colonial adaptability first advanced by Gilberto Freyre in the 1940s. The term "Tropicália," on the other hand, seemed to suggest a cosmopolitan and vanguardist attitude to which the Bahians aspired.[22] Like the 1920s avant-garde movement dada, the name Tropicália resists association with a succession of "isms." At the time of the movement, one critic argued that as a designation, "Tropicália" was preferable since "all 'isms' connote an extensive program with principles and norms, and all 'alias' are composites intertwined with disparate and heterogeneous elements."[23] Although there is some merit in using "tropicalismo" to refer to the entire movement (as opposed to Oiticica's installation and Veloso's song), I have opted to use "Tropicália," or the "tropicalist movement," except when quoting directly from a source in which "tropicalismo" was originally used.

The remainder of Chapter 3 is dedicated to the exploration of several representational strategies and themes developed extensively in individual efforts and a collective tropicalist "concept album" from 1968. I revisit the question of national allegory in the two tropicalist song-manifestos "Tropicália" and "Geléia geral." This discussion is followed by sections relating to the representation of urban migration, mass culture, political violence, and Third World marginality in tropicalist song.

Although censors largely ignored tropicalist recordings, their public performances aroused suspicions among agents of the regime, who were disturbed by their caustic and irreverent attitude toward authority. Chapter 4 focuses on the conflicts and controversies surrounding tropicalist performances in music festivals, nightclubs, and televised programs. Soon after the promulgation of the Fifth Institutional Act in December 1968, Veloso and Gil were arrested and subsequently exiled to London. This chapter also discusses the brief "aftershocks" of the movement as represented by the tropicalist recordings of 1969, following the formal end of the movement. Of particular salience here were Gilberto Gil's recordings and press statements, which suggested a turn toward black cultural politics, which would become central to his musical production in the following decade.

Following AI-5, many well-known Brazilian artists emigrated abroad, for both political and professional reasons. While most previous accounts of the tropicalist movement end with the late 1960s or early 1970s, I have extended my analysis to 1979, when the military regime passed an amnesty bill that allowed for the return of political exiles. Chapter 5 follows the artistic trajectory of the tropicalists after the formal movement had ended. Gil and Veloso spent two and a half years in England, where they participated in the vibrant countercultural scene of "swinging London," revolving around the rock music scene, and interacted with the Caribbean immigrant community, absorbing emerging Afro-diasporic styles such as reggae. Upon their return, the former leaders of the tropicalist movement were celebrated as icons of a Brazilian countercultural movement. In the latter part of the 1970s, Gil and Veloso also became enthusiastic proponents of emerging Afro-Brazilian cultural movements associated with soul, reggae, and the Afro-Bahian carnival in Salvador. These phenomena were to varying degrees connected to a broader movement calling for the end of military rule.

The final chapter discusses the various revisitations and homages relating to Tropicália since the restoration of civilian rule in the mid-1980s. Throughout the 1990s, Tropicália received several public tributes during carnival, both in Rio and in Bahia. In 1992, Veloso and Gil produced a recording titled Tropicália 2, which commemorated the movement and attempted to update its political and aesthetic concerns. This chapter highlights the work of Tom Zé, an artist who launched his career with Tropicália but then fell from public view as he continued to develop more experimental pop music. In the 1990s, he regained visibility with the international release of a compilation of his work from the 1970s and two innovative albums featuring new material. Together with the other tropicalists, Tom Zé found new audiences outside of Brazil, especially following a brief tropicalist vogue in the United States and Europe during the late 1990s. Attracted to the ironic and decentered pastiche aesthetics of Tropicália, international singer-songwriters drew attention to the movement and its principal figures. More importantly, the tropicalist movement has had a lasting impact on the production of popular music in Brazil. I will discuss the impact of this legacy on some contemporary artists who have claimed affinities with the tropicalist project.

This book provides both a diachronic and a synchronic analysis of the tropicalist movement. Chapters 4 and 5 focus exclusively on tropicalist cultural production during 1968. In each of the chapters, I have expounded on key issues that serve as thematic or theoretical detours from the narrative. Otherwise, it is structured chronologically so as to historicize Tropicália and to follow the trajectories of some of its key proponents after 1968. Instead of including long transcriptions and translations of entire song texts, I have highlighted phrases and stanzas that are particularly important to my arguments and observations. For readers who would like to hear audio samples and consult complete transcriptions and translations of lyrics, I highly recommend the CD *Tropicália Essentials* (Hip-O/Universal, 1999), a compilation of some of the most important tropicalist songs, many of which have since become standards of the Brazilian songbook. Well-crafted translations of several key tropicalist songs may also be found in Charles Perrone's *Masters of Contemporary Brazilian Song* and in the appendix to Gerard Béhague's essay "Bossa and Bossas." Readers of Portuguese who are particularly interested in the work of Gilberto Gil should consult his annotated book of lyrics, *Todas as letras*, organized by Carlos Rennó. Musicians may consult the two-volume songbooks of compositions by Caetano Veloso and Gilberto Gil that feature lyrics and musical annotations of important works from the mid-1960s to the late 1980s. By the turn of the millennium all of the key figures of the tropicalist movement had also set up personal websites on the Internet that may be easily found using any search engine. There are presently several informative websites dedicated to Tropicália in Brazil and in the United States.[24]

At the turn of the new millennium, over thirty years after the emergence of Tropicália, most of its key participants are alive and continue to produce in their respective fields. Tropicalist musicians are particularly active and influential, having established what is in many ways the dominant model for popular music in Brazil. Indeed, it would be difficult to find popular musicians of other national contexts with comparable sustained influence. The significance of their work extends beyond the field of popular music, having impacted on other realms of artistic production. Robert Stam has argued that popular music has been more successful than any other area of Brazilian culture in generating syntheses that are simultaneously local and cosmopolitan, popular and experimental, pleasurable and political. In his view, Brazilian music "has been the least colonized and the most Africanized branch of Brazilian popular culture, as well as the most successful in disseminating itself not only within Brazil but also around the world."[25] This particular combination of qualities and strengths in contemporary Brazilian popular music owes much to the tropicalist project and its artistic legacy.

1
POETRY FOR EXPORT
MODERNITY, NATIONALITY, AND INTERNATIONALISM IN BRAZILIAN CULTURE

ne of the most remarkable aspects of the tropicalist movement of the late 1960s was its sustained dialogue with several trends in Brazilian literary and cultural production of the twentieth century. The group of young singer-songwriters and their interlocutors in film, theater, visual arts, and literature responded to long-standing polemics over modernity and nationality, as well as to specific dilemmas of cultural production under military rule. Tropicália intervened in a constellation of debates surrounding popular culture and national identity that, as Renato Ortiz has argued, constitutes an evolving "modern tradition" in Brazil.[1]

The most salient point of reference for this modern tradition is *modernismo*, a heterogeneous literary and cultural movement that emerged in the 1920s. *Modernismo* brought together artists who were broadly committed to the aesthetic renovation of Brazilian arts and letters and the articulation of a national culture that was at once "original" (i.e., rooted in the popular cultures of Brazil) and "modern" (i.e., informed by contemporary literary trends in the international sphere). The synthesis of native originality and cosmopolitan technique would generate, as one modernist writer proposed, a "poetry for export" that could have international impact. Brazil would no longer simply import and passively consume metropolitan culture; it would be an exporter of culture. By the 1930s, the spirit of irreverent rebellion against literary conventions had subsided as *modernismo* was institutionalized under the aegis of an emergent nationalist and populist political regime. During this period, key artists and intellectuals sought to explain the originality of Brazilian civilization in terms of its racial and cultural hybridity, thereby establishing a paradigm for a mestiço national identity.

Throughout the twentieth century, Brazilian popular music has been the most important vehicle for the affirmation of this mestiço national identity both at home and abroad. As early as the mid-1920s, several modernist artists and intellectuals regarded popular music as a prime exemplar of authentic national expression and a source of inspiration for art music. Aided by the expansion of radio in urban centers, African-derived forms, most notably samba, were becoming popular among Brazilians of all races and classes. Samba would eventually be heralded as Brazil's "national music" and play a key role in the projection of Brazilian culture abroad. In the 1950s, samba would also provide the foundation for bossa nova, a sophisticated new style that gave expression to the cosmopolitan aspirations of Brazil's cultural elite during a phase of democratic modernization and industrial development. This period of national optimism and confidence was short-lived, but it produced lasting cultural achievements, such as bossa nova, that demonstrated to emerging artists that a poor and unevenly developed country could still produce a "poetry for export" and receive international acclaim.

BRAZILIAN MODERNISM

Launched formally in February 1922 during the Modern Art Week in São Paulo, Brazilian modernismo was a movement with important manifestations in several areas of cultural production.[2] The so-called heroic phase of modernismo (1922–30) primarily involved a group of writers, visual artists, and composers from São Paulo and Rio de Janeiro. Although a heterogeneous group, both in terms of aesthetic values and political ideologies, the modernists were generally committed to the critique of belles lettres aesthetics, most identified with Parnassianism, a movement of French origin that had great influence on the previous generation of Brazilian literati. In their attack on literary and artistic conventions, the modernists appropriated avant-garde practices and techniques from European movements such as futurism, cubism, surrealism, and Dada. At the same time, they denounced the acritical imitation of metropolitan forms and the use of continental Portuguese as stylistically removed from Brazilian reality. Even more than other Latin American vanguard movements, Brazilian modernismo was concerned foremost with articulating a project of cultural nationalism. *Modernismo* signaled transformations in Brazilian cultural, political, and economic life that eventually culminated in the nationalist-populist Revolution of 1930, led by Getúlio Vargas.

The Modern Art Week of São Paulo coincided with the centennial of Brazil's political independence from Portugal and was articulated as an event to herald the nation's cultural independence. Although vanguardist literary and artistic activities had been going on for several years before the event, the Modern Art Week marked the moment in which diverse intellectuals coalesced to advance a national cultural project. Established and emergent figures of the literary and artistic milieus of São Paulo and Rio de Janeiro participated in the Modern Art Week, including writers Mário de Andrade, Oswald de Andrade, Menotti del Picchia, and Plínio Salgado; painters Anita Malfatti and Emilio Di Calvancanti; and composer Heitor Villa-Lobos. By the mid-1920s, *modernismo* had fragmented into separate, often antagonistic subgroups.

Alfredo Bosi identified two imperatives of European avant-garde movements that were manifest in Brazilian *modernismo*: a futurist imperative calling for formal experimentation, engagement with technology, and the representation of urbanity; and a primitivist imperative with its emphasis on the quotidian experience and cultural practices of the Brazilian people. The modernists were divided, according to Bosi, between a futurist imperative to keep pace with modernity and a primitivist imperative to express "Brazilian roots."[3] This binary may be understood, on one level, as a tension between the simultaneously local and cosmopolitan orientations of the Brazilian modernists. International vanguardism, urbanity, and industrialization were foregrounded in the futurist tendency. A renewed interest in the colonial experience, myths of national foundation, linguistic vernaculars, and the cultural practices of the *povo* (people or masses), especially Afro-Brazilians and indigenous peoples, oriented primitivist concerns. The modernists appropriated cultural materials of Brazil's nonwhite population in order to advance the project of cultural nationalism. By interpreting the "primitive" within a framework of vanguardist poetics, the modernists sought to delineate both the specificity and the universality of Brazilian culture. Artistic production that was simultaneously autochthonous and cosmopolitan could be readily "exportable" as an original intervention in the international sphere.

In Brazil, as elsewhere in Latin America, local contexts and concerns mediated these two imperatives. Enthusiasm for Franco-Italian futurism, for example, had already subsided by 1922, when *modernismo* was formally articulated. Later in the decade, Brazilian modernists would also express ambivalence toward the primitivist vogue, in which they detected a metropolitan fascination with the exotic. Primitivism was often an expression of the West's own fantasies and anxieties about racial others.[4] These two vanguardist tendencies appeared as traces in aesthetic practice and not as programmatic directives. This binary was also not mutually exclusive in modernismo, nor did it necessarily inform for all writers and artists of the modernist generation. It did generate, however, a dominant tension in Brazilian artistic production and cultural debates throughout the twentieth century.

THE FOREST AND THE SCHOOL

Of all the modernists, the poet, novelist, dramatist, and literary provocateur Oswald de Andrade had the greatest impact on the tropicalist movement. He authored the most radical gestures of modernismo, including two of its most celebrated and cited manifestos. Published in 1924, his "Manifesto da Poesia Pau-Brasil" (Manifesto of Brazilwood Poetry) called for a "poetry for export" that would be informed by international literary vanguards but also grounded in the cultural context of Brazil. As the first extract product for international export during the early period of Portuguese colonial rule, Brazilwood was a suggestive metaphor for a "native" cultural project informed by contemporary international trends. Some critics have argued that the notion of a "poetry for export" based on the Brazilwood metaphor merely reaffirms Brazil's historical role as an exporter of cheap raw materials to the metropolis.[5] Yet there is a heavy dose of irony in the Brazilwood metaphor since the manifesto is ultimately about subverting the European colonial legacy while fomenting a modern, technologically informed Brazilian culture. Following a visit to Paris in 1912, Oswald de Andrade had returned to São Paulo with Felippo Tomaso Marinetti's "Futurist Manifesto" (1909), a dramatic call for the violent destruction of art and institutions of the past and the elaboration of a new project exalting the velocity and technology. In the "Brazilwood Manifesto," he proposed that futurism served to "reset the Imperial clock of national literature" and that it was time to be "regional and pure in our time."[6]

Oswald de Andrade's "Brazilwood Manifesto" is structured around a binary tension between "the forest and the school" in the genesis of Brazilian culture. In his formulation, the school connotes lettered society, with its formal institutions and technological resources, and the forest serves as a natural metaphor for that which was excluded or marginalized from the economic, political, and cultural centers of power and prestige. Oswald denounces the twin legacy of colonial exploitation and academic pretense represented in the figures of the *profiteur*, with his will to dominate nature for commercial ends, and the *doutor*, with his moralizing and phony erudition useful only for marking and reproducing social distinction. As an antidote to these historical types, Oswald calls for more inventors and engineers to produce and implement new forms of modern technology, as well as for new artists to create "agile and candid" poetry using Brazilian street vernacular "without archaisms, without erudition." Against any programmatic imperatives for artistic production, he simply exhorts his audience to "see with free eyes."

Oswald de Andrade located popular culture at the center of his poetry for export: "Carnival in Rio is the religious event of our race. *Pau-Brasil*. Wagner is submerged under the carnival groups of Botafogo. Barbarous and ours. Rich ethnic formation. Vegetal riches. Ore. Cuisine, *Vatapá*, gold, and dance." Like precious commodities of the national patrimony, local cultural practices—cuisine and dance—are set alongside Brazil's iron ore, gold, and botanic splendor. During the annual pre-Lenten festival, neighborhood carnival groups even overwhelm the operas of Wagner, the epitome of European high culture consumed by the local elite. These popular manifestations, which overwhelm imported metropolitan culture with insurgent glee, are claimed as emblems of nationality.

Implicit in this formulation was a celebration of racial and cultural diversity, which provided the necessary conditions for the emergence of a distinct and original culture in the tropics. Romantic writers, artists, and composers of the mid-nineteenth century exalted the Brazilian Indian as a symbol of nationality, a literary motif that was common to many new nations of the Americas. In most cases, the celebration of Indians was possible only after they had been exterminated in large numbers, geographically isolated, or socially marginalized. Oswald eschewed bucolic nostalgia for victims of colonialization, emphasizing instead their agency in the creation of modern Brazil. His reference to *vatapá*, a traditional Afro-Bahian dish, underscored the centrality of Afro-Brazilians in the formation of national culture. In a critique of Europhilia in Brazilian letters, he satirized Rui Barbosa, a famous white scholar-diplomat from Bahia, labeling him "a top hat in Senegambia." For Oswald de Andrade, Barbosa's buttoned-down formality seemed so out of place in this exuberant New World profoundly influenced by indigenous and African cultures.

In the "Brazilwood Manifesto," the forest and the school, the primitivist and the futurist, the natural and the technological, the local and the cosmopolitan, and the past and the present exist simultaneously. Silviano Santiago has noted the ubiquitous presence of the conjunction "and" in which contradictory or opposing phenomena cited in the manifesto "contaminate" each other.[7] On the horizon there is a suggestion of synthesis in which the affective qualities of the Brazilian people would be fused with modern rationality: "A mixture of 'sleep little baby or the bogey-man will get you' and equations." The tension between the two poles never quite reaches dialectical resolution, generating a poetics of playful contradiction. The "Brazilwood Manifesto" invokes a multiplicity of cultural referents that hold promise for future synthesis that could serve as the foundation for an original "poetry for export."

THE CANNIBALIST GESTURE

Oswald's project was further radicalized with a second declaration of principles, "Manifesto Antropófago" (Cannibalist Manifesto), first published in the *Revista de Antropofagia* in 1928.[8] A cohort of associates coalesced around the cannibalist group, including Oswald's second wife, Tarsila de Amaral, who gave visual expression to *antropofagia* in her tropical surrealist paintings. By this time, *modernismo* had fractured into a field of competing projects and movements.

The most contentious exchange involved Oswald's cannibalist group and the ultranationalist movement, Verdeamarelismo (Green-yellowism), later constituted as *Anta* (Tapir), led by Menotti del Picchia, Cassiano Ricardo, and Plínio Salgado. Originally articulated as a critical response to Oswald's *Pau-Brasil*, their nationalist project was based on the mythic history of precolonial native Brazilians. In their 1929 manifesto, the *Anta* group exalted the Tupi Indians, who had been driven from the high plains to the coast by a rival group, the Tapuias, "in order to be absorbed" by the Portuguese colonists.[9] This was a "historic fatality" in which the Tupi "disappeared objectively" in order "to live subjectively and be transformed into a prodigious force of goodness in the Brazilian." They eulogized the Tupi as a "race that transformed the races" precisely for their putative lack of resistance to the foreign invaders, which paved the way for the genesis of a peace-loving nation. According to the *Anta* manifesto, there was no racial prejudice among Brazilians thanks to an unconscious substratum of "Tupi nationalism." The *Anta* group acknowledged the cultural heterogeneity of Brazil but maintained that "Tupi nationalism" was reducible to an immutable "essence of feeling" that was impervious to exogenous influence.

In marked contrast to the *Anta* manifesto, Oswald de Andrade's "Cannibalist Manifesto" proposes the figure of a defiant and aggressive Indian who violently resists colonial incursions. For Oswald, there was no national "essence," only a dynamic and conflict-ridden process of critical assimilation, or "deglutition," of various cultural influences. The manifesto is structured as a series of short, telegraphic aphorisms that refer to Brazilian history, Enlightenment philosophy, indigenous religions, psychology, and anthropology. The brevity and humor of the manifesto has made it one of the most quotable texts in Brazilian literature, and it is frequently cited in song lyrics, poems, and epigraphs. Forty years after its publication, it became a key text for the tropicalists.

While "Brazilwood Manifesto" suggested the possibility of synthesis, however unresolved or contradictory, between the "forest and the school," the "Cannibalist Manifesto" negates the harmonious fusion of cosmopolitan and native elements. The guiding metaphor for Oswald's manifesto was the native Brazilian cannibal, the antithesis of the noble savage nostalgically exalted by nineteenth-century Romantic Indianists such as José de Alencar and later by *Anta* modernists. In one aphorism, Oswald satirized the literary invention of the deferent Indian "performing in Alencar's operas, full of worthy Portuguese sentiments." [10] His project took inspiration from the Tupinambá and other coastal Indians who were believed to ritually cannibalize vanquished enemies in order to absorb their physical and spiritual powers. This was a potent metaphor for elite Brazilian intellectuals who were indebted to European literary trends yet also sought cultural autonomy anchored in national reality.[11] For Oswald, cannibalism served as the master trope of an anticolonialist project for critically and selectively absorbing cultural products and technologies from abroad. He inveighed against the "importers of canned consciousness" but also heralded the modern golden age of American cinema. Metropolitan cultures were to be neither slavishly imitated nor xenophobically rejected but simply "devoured" for the purposes of elaborating an autonomous cultural project in Brazil.

In the manifesto, Oswald inverted the relationship of dependency, noting that Montaigne's seventeenth-century description of the noble savage inspired the Enlightenment discourse of natural right: "Without us, Europe wouldn't even have its meager declaration of the rights of man." The Portuguese colonial project was stripped of its foundational status as a civilizing endeavor: "But those who came here weren't crusaders. They were fugitives from a civilization we are eating, because we are strong and vindictive like the Jabuti." [12] Benedito Nunes has argued that cultural cannibalism functions simultaneously in several registers: as an organic metaphor that links ritual cannibalism of Brazilian natives with the modernist quest for intellectual autonomy from Europe; as a diagnostic of a society traumatized by colonialism; and as a therapy for counteracting the legacy of this trauma through satire and humor.[13]

In the "Cannibalist Manifesto," Oswald introduced a new set of binaries related to but not entirely coterminous with the forest and the school. Adopting the oedipal terms of Freud's *Totem and Taboo*, Oswald describes the genesis of Brazilian civilization as a struggle to subvert the colonial legacy of Catholicism and patriarchal power in order to restore a utopian "matriarchy of Pindorama." [14] Yet the manifesto was not a nostalgic appeal for the return of a premodern Brazil, unsullied by colonial contact. The matriarchal restoration would be consummated by the "technicized barbarian," who utilizes the instruments of modernity in order to establish a socially and psychologically liberated society based on a "primitive" cosmology.

As a cultural metaphor attuned to historical contingency and change, cannibalism proposed an allegory of Brazil, a strategy revived by the tropicalists in the late 1960s. In modern criticism, allegory is distinguished from the symbol, a mode of representation preferred by nineteenth-century Romantics as an aesthetic ideal best suited for representing the universal (i.e., the idea) and the particular (i.e., the object) as a unified totality. Allegorical representations, on the other hand, acknowledge the effects of time as an inevitable process of decay, fragmentation, and loss of meaning. Lúcia Helena has detected an "allegorical impulse" in the cannibalist project since it "undermines the 'official' version of Brazilian culture that seeks to project an image of unity in the integration of our formative elements." [15] In contrast with Romantic representations of the Indian as a *symbol* of national cohesion and identity, which were later recycled by the *Anta* group, Oswald's manifesto renders the Indian as an *allegory* of what was lost with the violent imposition of European civilization. The Indian ceases to represent an idealized and unchanging national "essence." Any sense of national unity can be produced historically only through collective practice, as implied in the first line of the manifesto: "Only cannibalism unites us. Socially. Economically. Philosophically." In other words, Brazilians are not defined by who they are but rather by what they do, which, in Oswald's formulation, is to "digest" myriad cultural influences.

Oswald de Andrade's cultural cannibalism has provoked extensive critical debate, especially since the late 1960s, when artists and scholars revisited his work. At issue in many of these debates is the formation of national culture in relation to dominant metropolitan cultures of Europe and, later, the United States. One critical position celebrates the cannibalist project as a radical rupture with cultural dependence on imported models, creating instead a "dialogical and dialectical relationship with the universal," in the words of Haroldo de Campos.[16] In his view, Oswald undermined Eurocentric binaries (i.e., civilization vs. barbarism, modern vs. primitive, original vs. copy) and their implicit assumptions about linear progress in which the colonized world can at best develop into an inferior imitation of Europe.

Detractors allege that the cannibalist model merely sidesteps or "leapfrogs over" the vexed problem of economic and cultural dependency.[17] Roberto Schwarz, for example, has argued that the philosophical destruction of the original/derivative binary does little to address this dilemma in practical terms. For Schwarz, cultural cannibalism was an imaginary solution for elite intellectuals that obscured their own social alienation from the laboring classes: "How can we fail to notice that the cannibalist subject . . . is the abstract Brazilian, with no class specification?"[18] In this view, cultural cannibalism functions as a sort of ideology of national identity that elides class inequality and ignores power differentials between metropolitan centers and peripheries.

Oswald de Andrade's "Cannibalist Manifesto" remains one the most provocative and suggestive texts in Brazilian literature. The continuous recycling of the cannibalist metaphor suggests that it remains a viable, though hardly uncontroversial, model for negotiating local and cosmopolitan imperatives in Brazilian cultural production.

MACUNAÍMA AND MUSIC

Mário de Andrade, perhaps the most important artist and intellectual of *modernismo*, was an accomplished and prolific poet, prose fictionist, literary critic, musicologist, folklorist, teacher, and culture administrator. Whereas Oswald authored the most radical gestures of *modernismo*, Mário is widely credited to be a central force behind the canonization and institutionalization of the modernist program. In the international sphere, Mário de Andrade is best known as the author of the experimental prose "rhapsody" *Macunaíma: Um herói sem nenhum caráter* (Macunaíma: A hero without character) (1928). As Gilda de Mello e Souza has shown, *Macunaíma* is a bricolage of myths, songs, rituals, and texts taken from indigenous, African, Portuguese, and Brazilian sources. As in a rhapsody, they constitute a series of narrative fragments based on a unifying principle or theme.[19] Although Mário remained aloof from the cannibalists, *Macunaíma* was claimed by the group as an exemplary cannibalist work in prose fiction. Forty years later, it would also be reinterpreted on film by Joaquim Pedro de Andrade, which is regarded as an important statement in tropicalist cinema.[20] It tells the story of a lazy and mischievous trickster figure born in the Amazon forest. The central plot involves Macunaíma's zany quest to retrieve his *muiraquitã*, a sacred amulet that represents his affective and cultural links to his traditions, from the hands of a monstrous bourgeois villain in São Paulo. Unlike the medieval Arthurian legends in which a cavalier hero typically attains heightened self-knowledge in his pursuit of the Holy Grail, Macunaíma's story ends on a pessimistic note when the Brazilian hero is devoured by a lake siren after returning to the jungle with the amulet. Macunaíma's sloth, deceit, greed, and naive fascination with the modern metropolis contribute to his demise, which allegorized Brazil's own frustrated search for cultural autonomy at the time.[21] As in Oswald's "Cannibalist Manifesto," Brazilian culture, represented in the figure of Macunaíma, is not a coherent totality. He is an allegorical personage with no fixed racial or cultural identity. Macunaíma was born black to an Indian mother, but after bathing in a magic puddle he becomes white. Many elite intellectuals regarded racial and cultural *branqueamento* ("whitening") as a desirable and necessary process for modernizing Brazil. Yet Macunaíma is even more irresponsible after his racial transformation, becoming a womanizing and slothful "hero without any character" who lacks reliability and virtue.

Macunaíma lacks character in another sense as well; his origins are vague and irreducible to Brazilian nationality. Mário's rhapsody was based on legends collected by a German ethnologist in the border region between Brazil and Venezuela. Macunaíma's organic link to Brazil is tenuous at best. In this sense, *Macunaíma* can be read as a parody of foundational fictions such as Alencar's Indianist novels *O Guaraní* (1857) and *Iracema* (1865), which portray mythic encounters between natives and Portuguese colonizers as originary instances of Brazilian nationality. The foundational status of the story is further compromised by the fact that it was told to the anonymous and unreliable narrator by a parrot that had heard the story from Macunaíma before he died.[22] By playing with the hero's lack of "character" he ironically subverts notions of identity and originality.

Mário de Andrade's representation of an ill-defined and polymorphous Brazilian identity in *Macunaíma* contrasts sharply with the programmatic nationalist imperatives advanced in his musical scholarship. He opened his *Ensaio sobre a música brasileira*, also published in 1928, with a remarkable affirmation: "Until recently, Brazilian art music (música artística) was divorced from our racial identity. It had to be this way. The Brazilian nation predates our race."[23] If, in Macunaíma, the idea of a unitary and stable Brazilian "race" is confounded by the hero's constant mutations, in the Ensaio it denotes a fixed identity in need of expression. According to Mário, nationhood predated the formation of a unified "Brazilian race." In terms of cultural identity, there were no Brazilians during the first century of national sovereignty, only Indians, blacks, and Europeans, all of whom, in his estimation, were "still very pure." In other words, Brazil existed as a political entity but not as cohesive cultural unit. It was incumbent upon artists and intellectuals of the modernist generation to give expression to this emerging national "race," presumably a hybrid of the elements cited above.

To advance this project, Mário de Andrade exhorted Brazilian composers to draw on popular elements to create a distinctive national art music: "The current period of Brazil, especially in the arts, is that of nationalization. We are seeking to bring artistic production of the country in line with national reality." To this end, he attempted to set guidelines for musical production and criticism in order to determine what was and was not authentically Brazilian. He rejected the reductive position that true Brazilian music only could be rooted in Amerindian music. He also inveighed against European visitors in search of the "amusing exoticism," who would delight in hearing a hot batuque (percussive Afro-Brazilian music) while disparaging the modinha (a type of lyrical ballad) as "Italian music" that was not authentically Brazilian. This kind of reductive thinking, according to Mário, impoverished Brazilian music.

Yet in the same essay, Mário de Andrade also denounced "so-called universal music" as "antinational," "individualistic," and "disinterested" and therefore inappropriate for the phase of nationalist construction. In his estimation, the criterion for defining Brazilian music should be socially, not philosophically, grounded—a "criterion of combat" that unmasks "antinational and falsifying forces" in Brazilian culture. In an attempt to ground this standard of authenticity, he proposed its site of production: "The present historical criteria for Brazilian music are musical manifestations which, being made by Brazilians or naturalized individuals, reflect the characteristics of the race. Where are they to be found? In popular music."

The idea of using popular material in the composition of art music was not a radical proposition. By the late 1920s, when Mário de Andrade wrote this essay, it had become standard practice by modernist composers throughout the Americas.[24] In Brazil, the consecrated composer Heitor Villa-Lobos had been mining popular music for his compositions since the early 1910s. What is novel about the *Ensaio* is its ideological and programmatic intentions that make it seem like a musical manifesto.[25] The other striking feature of the text is its constant invocation of a homogeneous "race" that is coterminous with the nation. Despite regional variations, Brazil was, according to Mário, a "racial totality" whose most distinguishing attribute was its music: "Brazilian popular music is the most complete, most totally national, most powerful creation of our race so far."

José Miguel Wisnik has called attention to Mário's privileging of rural folklore in his conception of popular music.[26] Although Mário recognized that there were authentic urban forms, he expressed some anxiety about Brazilian popular music that evidenced the "deleterious influences of urbanism." In the study of urban folklore, therefore, it would be necessary to distinguish music that was "traditionally national" from music that was "influenced by international fashion."[27] According to Wisnik, Mário de Andrade and other modernist intellectuals regarded emergent forms of urban popular music as commercial banalities that impeded the didactic project of cultural nationalism. In the elaboration of a nationalist cultural project, two musical phenomena were regarded as obstacles: commercial popular music and international vanguard music.[28]

Mário de Andrade established a modern foundational discourse on Brazilian musical nationalism. The issues he raised in *Ensaio sobre a música brasileira* were revisited often in debates regarding the direction of Brazilian music, both art and popular, during the twentieth century. In the field of art music, nationalistic approaches would remain dominant for several decades, despite the emergence in the 1940s of composers associated with the *Música Viva* group, who experimented with duodecophonic technique and defended musical internationalism. In subsequent decades, the polemics surrounding nationalism and cosmopolitanism in art music would find curious parallels in debates over popular music.

POPULAR MUSIC AND THE MESTIÇO PARADIGM

Mário de Andrade's manifestolike statement in his *Ensaio* suggests the centrality of race in the modernist formulation of Brazilian culture. What he means by "our race," however, ultimately remains unclear in the text. Implicit in his formulation of cultural nationalism, however, is the centrality of the racial and cultural hybrid, the *mestiço*. Mário de Andrade was himself a person of European, African, and indigenous descent, whereas most of his modernist colleagues belonged to the traditional white elite. Another young intellectual of the modernist generation, Gilberto Freyre, was more explicit in linking nationality with mestiçagem.

Freyre occupied a distinct position within Brazilian modernismo. He was from northeastern Brazil, an economically and politically marginalized region that was nevertheless regarded as the colonial crucible of Brazilian civilization. His first and most influential book, Casa Grande e Senzala (The Masters and the Slaves), published in 1933, is largely devoted to the circumstances and consequences of interracial cultural, social, and sexual contact, primarily between Portuguese colonizers and their African slaves. Freyre argued that intimate links between the big house and the slave quarters on colonial era sugar plantations in the Northeast laid the foundations for Brazilian civilization writ large. While acknowledging the coercive and often sadistic nature of these relationships, he also argued that they involved sincere affection and reciprocity that would generate a racially and culturally miscegenated society. Freyre was ultimately most concerned with affirming the centrality of Afro-Brazilians to the formation of a national mestiço culture.

At the time, his celebration of a mestiço Brazil was a bold and relatively progressive endeavor. Many elite intellectuals were beholden to racist theories of biological determinism that located Africans at the bottom of a racial hierarchy. Some scholars expressed anxiety about the supposedly degenerative effects of racial mixing. Others believed that racial mixing would progressively lead to the "whitening" of Brazil.[29] In either case, the Afro-Brazilian population was widely regarded as an impediment to modernization and progress. Against this racial pessimism, Freyre advanced the idea that the multiracial formation of Brazil was a great asset and that Africans in particular had made indispensable contributions to the development of a unique tropical civilization.

Hermano Vianna has suggested that Freyre's exuberant view of racial and cultural hybridity in Brazil may have been inspired in part by his encounter with Afro-Brazilian samba musicians while visiting Rio de Janeiro in 1926. He documents one particularly notable night of samba music involving Pixinguinha, Donga, and Patrício Teixeira of the seminal group Os Oito Batutas and members of the cultural elite including Freyre and Villa-Lobos. Freyre later wrote an enthusiastic article that exalted the black musicians for revealing "the great Brazil that is growing half-hidden by the phony and ridiculous official Brazil."[30] The emergence of urban samba as a distinct style roughly coincided with the first radio broadcasts in Rio de Janeiro. Via the radio, white performers such as Francisco Alves and Carmen Miranda popularized highly stylized and richly orchestrated sambas. Meanwhile, large percussion-based ensembles known as *escolas de samba* (samba schools) emerged in the working-class neighborhoods and *favelas* (shantytowns) in Rio de Janeiro and quickly became the dominant force in carnival. Once stigmatized and even subject to official repression, urban samba gradually became consecrated as the most exemplary musical expression of the nation.

According to Vianna, this process depended largely on "transcultural mediators," including musicians, intellectuals, and politicos of diverse social origins. For some composers and musicians, the ascension of samba brought them a measure of prestige within and beyond their communities and provided them with opportunities to earn money. For modernist artists and intellectuals, samba could be embraced as a vibrant popular expression that authenticated their nationalist cultural project and provided the "raw material" for their own creative endeavors. For political leaders, samba was particularly useful as a conduit for expressing the interests of an emergent nationalist and populist regime.

The vanguardist "heroic" phase of *modernismo* and the emergence of samba as a popular musical form in the cities came in the waning years of the First Republic, a political system established in 1889, following the ouster of the second Brazilian emperor, Pedro II. The decentralized political system established during the First Republic favored the interests of a small but economically powerful coffee planter elite of São Paulo state and its oligarchical allies in other states, most notably Minas Gerais. A nascent urban middle class and sectors of the military were increasingly dissatisfied with political arrangements that favored regional agrarian interests. The late 1910s and 1920s saw a wave of labor strikes in the cities and a series of military revolts led by reform-minded and nationalistic *tenentes* (lieutenants) of the Brazilian army. In 1930, the former governor of Rio Grande do Sul, Getúlio Vargas, led a final *tenente* uprising that succeeded in overthrowing the fractured Republican government of Washington Luis. The Vargas revolution received broad support, including that from the coffee planters who were reeling from the effects of the world economic crisis of 1929.

The Vargas regime sought to centralize federal authority, integrate new urban social groups into the political process, develop the nation's industrial base, and foment a sense of social cohesion. The so-called Revolution of 1930 exemplified what Antonio Gramsci called a "passive revolution," since it was carried out from above with little popular participation.[31] It preempted more radical transformations by instituting basic labor rights and forging a populist alliance with urban workers. The regime's official promotion of *brasili-dade* (Brazilianness) served to mitigate tensions and conflicts based on social, racial, ethnic, and regional differences. Vargas's nationalist-populist regime also had to manage the contentious political environment of the early thirties in which Communists, fascistic Integralists, and liberal constitutionalists were vying for power. Raising the specter of political chaos and national fragmentation, Vargas and his military allies abolished party politics in 1937 and instituted the authoritarian Estado Novo (New State) regime, which lasted until 1945, when Vargas was deposed.[32]

The nationalist Revolution of 1930 created new professional opportunities for artists and intellectuals committed to cultural nationalism, initiating the institutionalization of *modernismo*.[33] During the Vargas years, the experimental, vanguardist imperatives of the "heroic phase" receded, as modernist intellectuals became increasingly engaged in political and institutional activities. Oswald de Andrade joined the Communist Party in 1931, renouncing the vanguardism of *antropofagia* and pledging to be a "stalwart of the Proletarian Revolution."[34] Plínio Salgado of the *Anta* group emerged as leader of the Integralists. Mário de Andrade participated in the foundation of a state-sponsored institution for the promotion of Brazilian culture and the preservation of the national patrimony. Heitor Villa-Lobos directed massive civic choirs organized to sing paeans to the nation.[35] Following the implantation of the Estado Novo regime, several modernist intellectuals went to work for the government's propaganda machine or served in the diplomatic corps.

What had begun primarily as an artistic project extended into other fields of intellectual production in the 1930s. A new generation of historians and social scientists, including Gilberto Freyre, Sérgio Buarque de Hollanda, and Caio Prado Junior, engaged in the "rediscovery of Brazil."[36] Chief among their concerns was the social, economic, and cultural life during the colonial period and the meaning of this legacy for modern Brazilian society. This emerging generation of scholars was particularly interested in the social and cultural impact of slavery and the plantation economy on national formation.

The "rediscovery of Brazil" required new definitions of national identity. As noted above, Freyre was at the forefront of a general trend to undermine biological determinism with its racist implications and celebrate Brazil's unique *mestiço* culture. During this period the formerly maligned cultural practices of the urban black poor were legitimized as authentic expressions of nationality. Racial and social differences were subsumed by a unitary concept of national culture based on *mestiçagem*. Renato Ortiz has summarized this process in these terms: "The ideology of *mestiçagem* had been imprisoned within the ambiguities of racist theories. Having been reelaborated, it could be socially articulated and become common sense, ritually celebrated in quotidian relations or in grand events like carnival and soccer matches. That which was *mestiço* becomes national."[37] The articulation of a *mestiço* nationality coincided with the construction of the *povo* (masses) as a social and political category. Under the Estado Novo, this process entailed the co-optation of urban labor through state-controlled unions and the symbolic appropriation of popular expressive cultures as emblems of nationality. The confluence of *mestiçagem* and nationalist populism in the 1930s generated a new dominant paradigm for Brazilian culture.

During Vargas's authoritarian Estado Novo, samba composers and musicians were mobilized to sing the praises of a unified and hard-working nation. Themes of racial harmony and natural splendor were especially prominent in songs associated with a subgenre known as *samba-exaltação* that exalted the Brazilian nation. The most famous example of this subgenre was Ary Barroso's "Aquarela do Brasil" ("Brazil"), a samba that celebrated the sensuality and natural beauty of Brazil. In 1943, it was popularized internationally as the theme song to "Saludos Amigos," Walt Disney's first Latin American cartoon adventure, which introduced the wily Brazilian parrot Zé Carioca to American audiences. This cartoon was part of a larger American effort, under the aegis of the Good Neighbor Policy, to foment Pan-American solidarity in order to develop lucrative export markets and to bring Latin America into the allied fold during World War II. The Estado Novo government had realized that Brazilian popular music was not only a useful vehicle for encouraging patriotism within the country but also a potentially effective means for projecting a positive national image abroad.

POETRY FOR EXPORT:
FROM CARMEN MIRANDA TO TOM JOBIM

In 1924, Oswald de Andrade had called for a "poetry for export" that would be simultaneously rooted in local popular cultures and engaged with modern international trends. Although Oswald was referring to literary production, this trope can also be read as synecdoche for all forms of cultural production. Popular music stood out as the most exemplary form of Brazil's "poetry for export" in the twentieth century.[38] This is not to suggest that the aesthetic and social value of Brazilian popular music is merely a function of its exportability and international acclaim. Rather, the use of Oswald's trope in this context acknowledges, as do several other critics, the literary credentials of Brazilian popular music, its significant contribution to the articulation of cultural identities, and its key role in projecting Brazilian national discourse in the international sphere.

Carmen Miranda, although not the first Brazilian entertainer to perform abroad and gain international recognition, was the first to create a lasting impression. Having begun her career in radio and film as a performer of stylized urban sambas, she came to the United States under contract to perform on Broadway in 1939 and later became the highest paid woman in Hollywood with her dynamic performance style, flamboyant gestural vocabulary, and extravagant sartorial accoutrements. The turbans, the tutti-frutti headgear, the jangling bracelets were camp stylizations of attire used by Afro-Brazilian market women of Salvador, the *baianas*. Although born in Portugal, she symbolically embodied the image of a *mestiço* Brazil.

Carmen Miranda was widely adored in her own country but was also a source of embarrassment for some Brazilians because her Hollywood persona epitomized the uneven nature of cultural flows between Brazil and the United States. When Miranda returned to Rio de Janeiro for a brief visit in 1940, she received a cold reception from upscale audiences who found her performance too "Americanized."[39] Although Carmen Miranda had become Brazil's most famous cultural product abroad, her repertoire and performance style seemed anachronistic and stereotypical to many musicians and cultural critics. By the time of her death in 1955, bossa nova, a new musical form, was ready to emerge in the predominantly middle-class South Zone of Rio de Janeiro. The significance of bossa nova in terms of self-perception and self-fashioning among the Brazilian elite and urban middle class cannot be overestimated.[40] One might even argue that bossa nova was the first musical movement to produce Brazilian culture "for export" in the way Oswald de Andrade had imagined.

The musicians who developed bossa nova were relatively unconcerned with issues of nationalism and authenticity that had defined the cultural imperatives of the thirties and forties. They were avid connoisseurs of American vocalists, especially Frank Sinatra, Billy Eckstine, and Sarah Vaughn, West Coast jazz artists such as Chet Baker, Stan Getz, and Gerry Mulligan, and the cool jazz luminary Miles Davis. Bossa nova has often been regarded as a simple fusion of samba and jazz, although several observers have also noted its debt to earlier Brazilian crooners such as Mário Reis and Orlando Silva.[41] In contrast to *samba-canção*, a melodramatic vocal style influenced by the Cuban bolero, bossa nova introduced a cool, understated vocal style, in which the words were almost whispered. The creation of bossa nova involved dozens of young musicians, but the most acclaimed figures were composer-pianist Antônio Carlos Jobim (a.k.a. Tom Jobim, 1927–94), poet-diplomat Vinícius de Moraes (1913–80), and the singer-guitarist João Gilberto (b. 1932), who invented the distinctive *batida* (guitar rhythm) and vocal delivery that defined the style. Gilberto's 1958 recording of the Jobim-Moraes composition "Chega de saudade" ("No More Blues") initiated the movement and had a tremendous impact on Brazilian popular music. In his history of the bossa nova movement, Ruy Castro refers to the song as the "one minute and fifty-nine seconds that changed everything." [42]

The lyrics of the first phase of bossa nova (1958–62) foreground the subjective, private life of the individual, while references to the public sphere (i.e., popular festivals, social conflicts, and political crises) are almost entirely absent. These songs typically feature a high degree of lyrical and musical integration in which the existential concerns of the artist or imagined protagonist correspond to the harmonic logic of the song. David Treece has characterized this tendency in early bossa nova songs as a form of "ecological rationality," in which the protagonists and their natural surroundings "converge toward an equilibrium of intimate communion and understanding." [43] This aesthetic effect is most explicit in "Desafinado" ("Off Key") (Tom Jobim–Newton Mendonça), which serves as a kind of musical manifesto for bossa nova. In this song, discord between two lovers finds musical correspondence in dissonant chords. The source of conflict is then transferred into the realm of musical polemics as the lover classifies the protagonist's behavior as "unmusical," which elicits a plea for comprehension: "this is bossa nova / this is quite natural."

In the late fifties and early sixties, bossa nova musicians enjoyed official support from the governments of Juscelino Kubitschek and his successors, Jânio Quadros and João Goulart. The Ministry of Foreign Relations, Itamaraty, was involved in the first bossa nova excursion to the United States in 1962. An entourage of musicians, including Tom Jobim, João Gilberto, Carlos Lyra, Carmen Costa, and Sérgio Mendes, performed a historic concert at Carnegie Hall that further consolidated bossa nova's growing success and prestige in the United States. By that time, tenor saxophonist Stan Getz and guitarist Charlie Byrd had already popularized bossa nova with their recording *Jazz-Samba*. Jobim, Gilberto, and Getz later recorded *Getz/Gilberto*, featuring an English version of "The Girl from Ipanema," which stayed at the top of the pop charts for several months in 1964. Dozens of bossa nova compositions, most notably those written by Tom Jobim, have been canonized as jazz standards. With the advent of bossa nova, Brazilian popular music was primarily received abroad as a jazz-related idiom.

The bossa nova movement might be regarded as a cultural expression of what Thomas Skidmore calls "the years of confidence." [44] The style emerged during the presidency of Juscelino Kubitschek (1956–60), who promised "fifty years of progress in five" and to prove his point presided over the construction of Brasília, a futuristic, utopian capital located in the central plains. The government followed a policy of developmentalist nationalism, introducing a new phase of import substitution to attract international and domestic capital investment, promote infrastructural modernization, and address social and regional inequalities. [45]

Before returning to bossa nova, it is worth briefly discussing significant intellectual and literary trends related to developmentalist ideology in Brazil. Throughout the 1950s, the most influential institutional base for social and cultural theory was the Instituto Superior de Estudos Brasileiros (ISEB, Advanced Institute for Brazilian Studies), whose affiliates were ideologically diverse but were broadly committed to promoting infrastructural development and national consciousness. One ISEB thinker, Roland Corbisier, argued that Brazil was a victim of a "colonial situation" since it was subordinate to the imperialist interests of metropolitan nations such as the United States. Corbisier invoked the concept of "alienation" to describe the lack of historical consciousness necessary for the development of an autonomous national culture. He argued that colonial and neocolonial societies were "globally alienated" and therefore condemned to cultural inauthenticity. [46] Corbisier understood the relationship between the metropolis and the colony in terms of the Hegelian dialectic between master and slave. [47] In Hegel's formulation, the slave could only comprehend his/her reality as a reflection of the master's will and therefore lacked historical subjectivity and agency. By understanding this relationship dialectically, Corbisier and his colleagues at ISEB suggested that cultural alienation could be overcome through the development of an anti-imperialist national consciousness.

The ISEB group was particularly invested in the idea of a nationalist bourgeois revolution that would undermine the economic and political power of the mercantilist elite, a landed, export-oriented class that perpetuated Brazil's neocolonial dependence on international capital. Another ISEB thinker, Nelson Werneck Sodré, argued that the "Brazilian revolution" would be carried out by the *povo*, which, in his formulation, was a heterogeneous group comprising the urban proletariat and rural peasants, as well as progressive, nationalist sectors of the bourgeoisie.⁴⁸ The ISEB group understood Brazil's dilemma dialectically but without the sort of class analysis one would expect from this type of historical view. Its anti-imperialist critique failed to account for the conflicting interests among diverse groups that supposedly constituted the *povo*. In the early 1960s, ISEB would be critiqued for underestimating class conflict, but key concepts of the ISEB project, such as "national consciousness" and "alienation," would continue to be relevant for more radical cultural projects discussed in Chapter 2.

In many ways, the supreme expression of developmentalist ideology was the construction of Brasília, designed by urban planner Lúcio Costa and architect Oscar Niemeyer. A bold monument to high modernist architecture, Brasília signaled the advent of Brazil's optimistic future. Brasília was more than just a symbol of modernization; it was regarded as a means for transforming society and achieving modernity. Brasília would integrate the vast expanses of territory and become a "pole of development" for the nation.⁴⁹ Costa and Niemeyer were politically progressive (the latter belonged to the Brazilian Communist Party) and sought to build a city that would engender equality and harmony by designing standardized residential areas where people of diverse social classes would interact. At the beginning of construction, Kubitschek proclaimed: "From this central plateau, from the solitude which will shortly be converted into a center of high national decision-making, I look once again into the future of my country, and see this dawning with firm faith and boundless confidence in its great destiny." Lúcio Costa's "plano-piloto" (pilot plan) of the city resembled an airplane; two main residential sectors were divided into wings, government bureaucracies formed the fuselage, and the Plaza of the Three Powers (executive, legislative, and judicial) were located at the tip of the fuselage. Brazil, it seemed, was ready for takeoff.

The modernist architecture of Brasília shared clear affinities with the concrete poets, members of an emergent literary vanguard based in São Paulo. In 1958, they published a literary manifesto in their journal, *Noigandres*, titled "Plano-piloto da poesia concreta," a direct reference to Costa's pilot plan for Brasília. The instigators of *poesia concreta*, Augusto de Campos, Haroldo de Campos, and Décio Pignatari, situated themselves on the cusp of an experimental tradition descended from Stéphane Mallarmé, Ezra Pound, James Joyce, and e. e. cummings. Within the national literary field, concrete poetry was a critique of poets associated with the Generation of 1945, a neo-Parnassian reaction to the use of free verse, colloquialisms, and popular themes by the previous modernist generation.⁵⁰ In the international sphere, concrete poetry was articulated as a midcentury avant-garde from a peripheral nation. There was no need to "reset the clock" of national literature in order to be up to date with metropolitan trends. The São Paulo vanguard was on the cutting edge of formal experimentation and therefore constituted a form of "poetry for export." In following years, concrete poetry would attract disciples from around the world but also elicit trenchant critiques from critics at home who regarded it as overly formalistic and impervious to the "national exigencies" of underdeveloped countries such as Brazil.[51]

The project of concrete poetry was a multidimensional critical, theoretical, and aesthetic intervention that went through several phases. Calling for a poetic language devoid of conventional syntax, the concrete poets proposed the use of functional "object-words" that would instantly communicate meaning. They sought to create a "product-poem" that, unlike lyric poetry, could be a "useful object." By using the communication technologies of industrial society, such as advertisement graphics, they sought to revolutionize poetic language. They were particularly interested in rapid communication made possible by mass media. Décio Pignatari explained this idea in "nova poesia: concreta" (1956):

> a general art of language. commercials, press, radio, television, cinema. a popular art
> the importance of the eye in the fastest communication: from luminous advertisements to cartoons. the ideogram as a basic idea.

The concrete poets' dialogue with visual arts opened up new semantic possibilities outside of discursive or metaphoric expression. By linking avant-garde experimentation to developments in mass media, the concrete poets attempted to restructure the relationship between "high" and "low" art. They regarded the culture industry not as an unwelcome encroachment but as a means to produce and disseminate artistic production.

The three principal instigators of the movement have maintained a ubiquitous presence in Brazilian cultural life as experimental poets, music critics, literary theorists, and translators. In the 1960s and 1970s, they were instrumental in the critical reevaluation of Oswald de Andrade. Augusto de Campos has been active as a music critic and scholar, producing numerous articles about popular and experimental music. His vigorous promotion and defense of bossa nova (and later Tropicália) yielded important insights into the relationship between experimental poetry, popular music, and national culture.

BOSSA NOVA AND DEVELOPMENTALISM

By the late 1950s, the conflicting imperatives of economic nationalism, which was regarded as the key to sovereignty and social progress, and industrial development, which depended on massive foreign investment, became increasingly difficult to reconcile. The eventual fallout of Kubitschek's developmental strategies (an inflationary crisis) finds a curious parallel in subsequent debates about bossa nova. Cultural nationalists reasoned that bossa nova was excessively dependent on foreign music (especially jazz), just as industrial modernization had relied heavily on foreign loans and investments. Its most severe critic, José Ramos Tinhorão, argued that bossa nova "constituted a new example (not consciously desired) of alienation among the Brazilian elite, who are subject to the illusions of rapid development based on paying royalties to foreign technology." [52] In his view, bossa nova was merely a novel form of jazz that mirrored unequal economic relations between the periphery and the center. Bossa nova was a musical form in which "the raw material was Brazilian and the form was North American." [53]

According to Tinhorão, the white bourgeoisie and middle class that resided in the South Zone of Rio de Janeiro had become alienated from the mostly black working class that lived in the hillside *favelas* and in the North Zone. Social distance had led to the development of a young, middle-class milieu that was disconnected from samba, the musical tradition of the urban poor. For Tinhorão, the new music of Tom Jobim, João Gilberto, and others was a betrayal of tradition, not a creative innovation or commentary based on tradition. He denounced the "incapacity of the boys, disconnected from the secrets of popular percussion, to feel in their own skin the impulses of black rhythm." [54] Previously, white middle-class artists had maintained contact with popular music of the *favelas* in order to learn the "secrets of black rhythm." Their distance from this site of authenticity led them astray to the foreign world of jazz. In one article, Tinhorão interprets this transgression as a family crisis: "Child of secret adventures with American music, which is undeniably its mother, bossa nova today lives the same drama of many children from Copacabana, the neighborhood in which it was born: It doesn't know who its father is." [55]

Ultimately, Tinhorão arrived at a stagnant and even paternalistic position with regard to Brazilian popular music. He lamented the continuous flow of mass culture consumed by the middle class but was heartened that the poor had remained valiant guardians of cultural authenticity: "Meanwhile, the people, calm in their cultural unity established by semi-illiteracy, and social unity, determined by poverty and lack of opportunities to ascend, continue to create and happily sing their carnival sambas, beating the drum to a vigorous $\frac{2}{4}$ rhythm." [56] In the mid-1960s, his critique of bossa nova would elicit an ironic rejoinder from Caetano Veloso: "Judging from the book of hysterical articles by Mr. José Ramos Tinhorão . . . only preservation of illiteracy will assure the possibility of making music in Brazil." [57]

The nationalist critique of bossa nova was by no means hegemonic. The new style enjoyed popular success, and the cultural elite embraced it as an expression of cultural modernity. Early bossa nova enthusiasts included the concrete poets and composers associated with the São Paulo musical vanguard. Like Tinhorão, Augusto de Campos also used metaphors of international trade and global economics to analyze bossa nova, but with very different conclusions: "Bossa nova had a sensational impact on Brazilian music, allowing it to influence jazz just as it had been influenced by it. With this, Brazil began to export finished products and not just musical raw material (exotic rhythms), 'macumba for tourists,' to use the expression of Oswald de Andrade." [58]

According to dependency theory, poor countries suffer a structural disadvantage in relation to developed nations. [59] Brazil depended on First World nations to supply capital, technology, and "finished products," including industrial machinery and consumer items. In exchange, Brazil could only sell "raw materials" (agricultural products and mineral resources) that were subject to the vicissitudes of the international market. Since the price of raw materials increased at a slower rate than that of finished products, Brazil would inevitably fall behind even though it participated in world trade. In cultural terms, dependency meant that Brazil consumed "finished" (that is, refined and complex) cultural products from abroad but exported "raw" (that is, exotic and picturesque) items for metropolitan consumption. Campos hailed bossa nova for producing a "finished product" for domestic and international consumption.

Forty years after the advent of bossa nova, Augusto de Campos's developmentalist analysis would reappear in a song by tropicalist singer-songwriter Tom Zé. [60] The song opens by noting that in early 1958, "Brazil only exported raw material / that elixir / this is the lowest level of human capacity." By the end of the same year, Brazil had made a massive leap forward: "With bossa nova, Brazil exported art / the highest level of human capacity." With calculated hyperbole, the song claims a foundational role for the genre, proposing in the refrain that "bossa nova invented Brazil." Indeed, for Tom Zé's social and cultural milieu, which came of age in the late 1950s, the advent of bossa nova had an enormous impact. Many of the artists who gained national recognition in the 1960s, most notably the tropicalists, would remember the first time they heard João Gilberto's version of "Chega de saudade" on the radio as something of an epiphany.

For the generation of artists and intellectuals that reached adulthood in the late 1950s and early 1960s, the era of bossa nova is invariably remembered with fondness and nostalgia. Bossa nova is still identified with a "golden age," or an "age of innocence," especially in the middle-class imagination. Ronaldo Bôscoli, a composer of several bossa nova standards, would later refer to the bossa nova era as "a great national holiday." [61] Its association with a time of democracy, prosperity, and national pride became more pronounced in subsequent decades of political repression under military rule. Bossa nova also came to epitomize the cultural prestige of Brazilian popular music in the international context. Following Tom Jobim's death in 1994, one journalist eulogized: "He is the great Brazilian artist. He's our Borges, our Picasso, our Beethoven. . . . In popular music, Argentina, Spain, and Germany never had a Tom Jobim." [62]

CONCLUSION

In an article published in the New York Times, Caetano Veloso related the story of a benefit concert at Carnegie Hall in 1989 on behalf of environmental action in the Amazon rain forest that featured Elton John, Sting, and Tom Jobim.[63] Before the concert, it was rumored that when Jobim and his band started to play "The Girl from Ipanema," Elton John would appear on stage in drag dressed as Carmen Miranda. Out of respect for Jobim, the plan apparently was aborted because it was feared that the American audience would fixate on the identity that linked Jobim and Miranda, without understanding the significant differences between them. For cosmopolitan Brazilians, bossa nova was sophisticated music deserving of international respect, while Carmen Miranda invoked a vulgar exoticism that conformed to stereotypes of "Latin" sensuality. For Veloso, the mere idea of this impromptu performance in that particular context was highly suggestive because it pointed to the presence of Carmen Miranda hovering like a specter over Brazilian musicians whenever they perform abroad.[64] He was not suggesting that contemporary Brazilian music resembles the sambas of Carmen Miranda, nor that foreigners necessarily think of her when they hear Brazilian music. Rather, he sought to point out ways in which the cultural diversity of Brazil has often been flattened out into consumable stereotypes for foreign consumption. Yet it was precisely the vulgar iconography of Carmen Miranda that later inspired Veloso's irreverent attacks on musical propriety during the tropicalist movement.

Oswald de Andrade's injunction to produce a Brazilian "poetry for export" was most successfully consummated in the realm of popular music. It became apparent, however, that international cultural prestige did not necessarily herald economic and social modernization. At the same time that bossa nova was enjoying critical and popular success overseas, artists in Brazil were turning their attention once again to the social contradictions of their country in an attempt to mobilize the masses in the service of revolutionary transformations.

2

PARTICIPATION, POP MUSIC, AND THE UNIVERSAL SOUND

The tropicalist movement coalesced toward the end of a tumultuous decade marked by the intensification of left-wing activism and a reactionary military coup in 1964 aimed at preempting any movement for radical social transformation. Debates over the proper role of the artist in relation to progressive social and political movements oriented much of the cultural production during this period. The 1960s also witnessed the consolidation of a national culture industry that sought to tap into consumer markets primarily in the urban areas. With the advent of military rule, the state invested heavily in mass media technologies in an attempt to exert ideological influence throughout the national territory.

These transformations led to conflicting perceptions and definitions of the "masses" in Brazilian society. Political and cultural activists of the Left often identified this exploited and oppressed majority as *o povo* (the people or masses), a designation with both populist and revolutionary resonances based on the conviction that the masses were potential agents in social transformation. On the other hand, media technocrats of the culture industry tended to regard the masses as *o público* (the public), a designation that focused on their potential as cultural consumers. These conflicting definitions underscored a tension within the artistic community between artists who positioned themselves as professionals working in increasingly competitive cultural industries and those who defined themselves foremost as political activists. Renato Ortiz has summarized this tension as "a dichotomy between cultural work and political expression."[1]

This dichotomy was not unique to Brazil during the 1960s. Néstor García Canclini has described a sort of double consciousness among artists throughout Latin American who were working within the culture industry during this time:

> A confrontation occurs between the socioeconomic logic of the growth of the market and the voluntaristic logic of political culturalism, which was particularly dramatic when it was produced inside a particular movement or even within the same persons. Those who were carrying out the expansive and renovating rationality of the sociocultural system were the same ones who wanted to democratize artistic production. At the same time that they were taking to the extremes the practices of symbolic differentiation—formal experimentation, the rupture with common knowledges—they were seeking to fuse with the masses.[2]

Two basic and frequently intersecting tensions oriented the work of Latin American cultural producers engaged with mass communication: between market rationality and political commitment, and between formal experimentation and mass appeal.

Of course, professional and political motivations were not always mutually exclusive. Many of the artists discussed in this chapter thought simultaneously in terms of career advancement, political activism, and formal innovation. The tropicalist musicians were unique, however, in making explicit the competing imperatives of civic-minded participation, professional success, and aesthetic experimentalism in an emerging market for pop music. This tension was central to their aesthetic approach to Brazilian popular music as well. The musician-critic Luiz Tatit has shown that in 1967–68 Caetano Veloso had a dual project committed simultaneously to radical aesthetic innovation and to the legacy of the great pre–bossa nova radio singers, such as Orlando Silva and Nelson Gonçalves, who were among the first modern media celebrities in Brazil. According to Tatit, Veloso had, on the one hand, an "explicit and noisy project dedicated to rupturing and desacralizing the dogmatic norms of MPB during that time" and, on the other, an "implicit and patient project that sought to recover the ethos of radio song for the new era."[3] This dual project would necessarily have to confront another productive tension between nationalism and cosmopolitanism in Brazilian culture. In an attempt to synthesize these competing and often contradictory imperatives, Caetano Veloso and Gilberto Gil proposed what they called the "universal sound," which was the prelude to Tropicália.

CULTURE AND SOCIAL ACTION IN THE EARLY 1960S

In one of several memoirs written by Brazilian intellectuals who reached adulthood in the early 1960s, Luiz Carlos Maciel stated that the principal belief of the youth of his generation was that "art had a transforming function in society."[4] It is important to remember that what Maciel understands as his generation is circumscribed by social class, educational experience, and to some extent geographical location. The generation to which Maciel refers primarily encompasses urban middle-class students and young professionals, especially those involved with cultural production or political activism, such as musicians, filmmakers, playwrights, actors, visual artists, educators, journalists, student leaders, and labor organizers. This sector constituted a minority even within its own generation, but it was a minority with disproportional access to electronic and print media outlets and other institutional networks, such as universities, museums, cultural centers, and governmental agencies.

The developmentalist project had yielded ambiguous results. Infrastructural and industrial development had made considerable advances, artistic movements such as bossa nova and concrete poetry achieved international recognition, and the nation had a new federal capital that symbolized for many the advent of modernity in Brazil. At the same time, Brazil continued to be a country of great regional disparities and social inequalities. The modernizing imperatives that were characteristic of the Kubitschek years increasingly ceded to calls for more profound social transformations. The Cuban Revolution of 1959, with its nationalist and socialist objectives, profoundly inspired progressive artists and intellectuals throughout Latin America. In Brazil, the Cuban example contributed to new cultural projects emphasizing "participatory" art that would directly engage the masses. Drawing on conceptual categories outlined by Michael Löwy and Robert Sayre, Marcelo Ridenti has argued that most left-wing artists in Brazil during the 1960s embraced an ethos of "revolutionary romanticism" characterized by a search for national "roots" and a radical critique of capitalist modernity.[5]

It is customary in Brazil to refer collectively to left-wing or progressive political parties, social movements, and cultural groups in the plural as *as esquerdas* (the lefts). This term acknowledges not only that progressive forces in

Brazil are divided into frequently antagonistic groups but also that somehow they are imagined relationally as a collective force with common adversaries and similar goals. In mainstream politics of the 1950s, the Brazilian Labor Party (PTB) functioned as a nationalist and populist organization with a significant working-class constituency. Although it was officially proscribed, the Brazilian Communist Party (PCB) had emerged as the dominant left-wing party and advocated a nationalist bourgeois revolution as a cautious first step toward more radical transformations. In addition to several smaller left-wing parties, such as the Brazilian Socialist Party (PSB) and the Maoist Communist Party of Brazil (PC do B), several progressive nonparty organizations, including labor unions, peasant leagues, progressive Catholic groups, and student movements, were active in local, regional, and national politics.[6]

The first few years of the decade seemed to hold great promise for those who hoped for, or were actively involved in, the progressive transformation of Brazilian society. At the forefront of this struggle was the Centro Popular de Cultura (CPC, People's Center for Culture), a left-wing cultural organization with national scope that was founded in 1962 under the aegis of the União Nacional dos Estudantes (UNE, National Student Union). It was modeled in part after the Movimento de Cultura Popular (MCP, Popular Culture Movement), a state-sponsored literacy program in the poor northeastern state of Pernambuco, which used the methods of renowned Brazilian educator Paulo Freire. Prominent artists participated in the CPC, including dramatist Oduvaldo Vianna Filho, filmmaker Carlos Diegues, poet Ferreira Gullar, and musicians Carlos Lyra, Sérgio Ricardo, and Geraldo Vandré. Like the ISEB theorists, the intellectual leaders of the CPC denounced Brazil's dependency on foreign capital and advocated a more nationalist economic policy. They criticized the influx of cultural products from developed nations, particularly from the United States, as a cause of political alienation. In general, CPC activists perceived themselves as a cultural and political vanguard that could lead rural and urban masses toward social revolution. The CPC was founded during the presidency of João Goulart, a champion of labor rights who was deeply mistrusted by conservative civilian and military leaders. The historic moment seemed to be with the Left during his presidency, and Goulart increasingly turned to radical grassroots organizations for political support.[7]

It is worth examining the theory and practice of the CPC during this brief period under Goulart when progressive forces were gaining momentum. The CPC saw its mission as raising political consciousness through mass-based cultural and educational activities while seeking to forge a broad alliance of workers, peasants, intellectuals, artists, and radical nationalists within the military. Working on several fronts, the CPC staged agitprop plays at factory gates and in working-class neighborhoods, produced films and records, and published pedagogical books for popular consumption. The CPC project was predicated on the idea that revolution could not be achieved simply through union activism and electoral politics. Social and political transformations would only follow a revolutionary change in the mentality of the *povo*, and popular culture would be the vehicle for this struggle. One critic has characterized the CPC experiment as "a dress rehearsal for the socialization of culture" that sought to set the stage for collective social transformation.[8] Against folkloric conceptions of popular culture as timeless practices of the "folk" to be preserved and protected, the CPC advanced the idea that popular culture could be an agent for raising consciousness and resisting the alienating effects of cultural imperialism. Drawing heavily from the cultural program of the Brazilian Communist Party, CPC artists and intellectuals advocated a national-popular paradigm for cultural production based on the conviction that only that which was "popular" was authentically national.[9]

The definition of what was "popular" became a central concern for CPC artists and intellectuals. One leading theorist, Carlos Estevam, distinguished between three general categories of non-elite or popular culture: *arte do povo* (people's art), *arte popular* (popular art), and *arte popular revolucionária* (revolutionary popular art).[10] People's art denoted the cultural practices that were organically linked to the quotidian material life of communities, such as folk music, traditional dances, crafts, and popular religion. In Estevam's view, people's art was no more than a "rough and clumsy attempt to express trivial facts" and merely "satisfied ludic necessities." He was equally disdainful of popular art that was created and distributed by professionals of the culture industry such as radio music, *novelas* (soap operas), and films based on romance, adventure, and light comedy. Estevam rejected popular art as "inconsequential" and "escapist" entertainment for the masses.

For Estevam, these two categories of artistic expression were ultimately not even truly popular, as suggested in his maxim: "Outside of political art, there is no popular art."[11] In his analysis, popular does not refer to culture produced by the people but rather to culture oriented toward social and political activism. The only authentic manifestation of popular culture was revolutionary popular art that could mobilize the masses. Estevam believed that the Brazilian masses were unable to produce revolutionary popular art because they were politically and culturally alienated from national reality. A revolutionary vanguard of intellectuals was needed to raise the consciousness of the masses and incite them to action. The neo-Leninist orientation of the CPC proved to have serious limitations since it was based on paternalistic and ethnocentric value judgments regarding the category of the "popular." The basic assumption that popular culture must be generated by an enlightened cultural elite and then brought to the masses contradicted the grassroots pretensions of the CPC movement.

In his program for the CPC, Estevam also criticized the artistic vanguards, represented foremost by the concrete poets. While he acknowledged that artistic vanguards, such as the concrete poets, produced "de-alienated" or nonconformist art that undermined traditional bourgeois aesthetics, they were not revolutionary because they failed to communicate with a mass audience. In his view, artists must always privilege communication over formal experimentation or else the masses would never be able to comprehend their work. The communicative imperative of the CPC is most apparent in the *Cadernos do povo* (People's notebooks), a series of didactic booklets that included a three-volume anthology of *engagé* poetry titled *Violão de rua* (Street guitar). Calling for content-centered poetry, CPC-affiliated writers positioned themselves in relative opposition to the concrete poets, the dominant literary vanguard in Brazil.[12] For the concrete poets, formal experimentation with nonverbal syntax and new media did not preclude mass communication, whereas for the CPC poets, communication with the people was necessarily based on discursive clarity.

Similar artistic values guided the production of the LP *O povo canta* (The people sing), which eschewed the sentimentalism and musical sophistication of bossa nova in favor of simple folk tunes that addressed the experience of working people. The liner notes to the LP affirm that the songs represent a "new experience in popular music" in which "the authentic elements of collective expression are utilized in order to achieve an efficacious form of communication with the people [in order to] enlighten them."[13] This programmatic and paternalist approach hindered the success of the CPC project, and many of its events failed to attract much attention from working-class audiences. Most critics, including former leaders of the CPC, would later admit that CPC productions were politically naive, aesthetically retrograde, and in some cases condescending to target audiences.[14]

Despite these limitations, the CPC project was a bold experiment in cultural activism that raised important issues regarding the role of intellectuals in transforming society, the efficacy of art in political mobilization, and the value of formal experimentation. For the most part, it was not merely populist demagoguery but rather a concerted effort to overcome social barriers and collectively produce politicized art. Some observers have fondly recalled the early 1960s as a period of great promise for social transformation. Later in the decade, during the height of military repression, Roberto Schwarz would remember: "The pre-revolutionary winds were decompartmentalizing the national consciousness and filling the newspapers with talk of agrarian reform, rural disturbances, the workers' movement, the nationalization of American firms, etc. The country had become unrecognizably intelligent." [15] The country may have become more "intelligent" in some respects, but it was not sufficiently mobilized to bolster the Goulart government and effectively resist a right-wing military coup. The military conspirators who set in motion an armed movement against the government on April 1, 1964, met with little popular resistance. The coup ushered in an authoritarian, procapitalist military regime, marking the end of Brazil's democratic experiment between 1945 and 1964. The culture of left-wing populism, however, proved to be more resilient than the political system from which it emerged. The utopian energies of the CPC experiment were transferred to new arenas.

CONSERVATIVE MODERNIZATION AND CULTURAL PRODUCTION

Far from a mere hiatus in the popular struggle for political power, the military coup of 1964 initiated a prolonged period of authoritarian rule. The United States served as the regime's most important foreign ally, immediately recognizing its legitimacy and helping it to secure loans with the International Monetary Fund and the World Bank. Meanwhile, the new military government of General Humberto Castelo Branco established austerity measures designed to control inflation and attract foreign investment. Under the preceding civilian governments, modernization was conceived broadly as a dual process of infrastructural development and social transformation. The military regime pursued a policy of conservative modernization dependent on foreign investment, which intensified the former and suppressed the latter.

With the military takeover, archaic and reactionary social and cultural values gained ascendancy. Initial public demonstrations in support of the military suggested a reaffirmation of facile patriotism, traditional Catholicism, patriarchal family values, and vigorous anticommunism. The most urgent matter for the regime immediately following the coup was the suppression of the radical Left and the demobilization of grassroots social and cultural movements in the cities and countryside. For progressive artists and intellectuals, one of the gravest consequences of the coup was the proscription of the UNE and the CPC. Meanwhile, labor and peasant movements were swiftly suppressed and their leaders were detained, tortured, and, in some cases, executed. The regime initiated a series of purges in the civil service, armed forces, and elected offices yet also tried to maintain a facade of democratic rule, allowing the formation of two civilian political parties, the progovernment Aliança Nacional Renovadora (ARENA) and the opposition Movimento Democrático Brasileiro (MDB), in 1966.

During the early years of military rule there was a relative degree of artistic freedom, and protest culture flourished in the principal urban centers. This led to a curious situation in Brazilian culture that Roberto Schwarz later described in the following terms: "Despite the existence of a right-wing dictatorship, the cultural hegemony of the Left is virtually complete." [16] It must be kept in mind that the cultural hegemony of the Left was limited within a relatively small urban social milieu. If left-wing artists had occupied a hegemonic position in Brazilian society as a whole, there would have been greater resistance to the coup.[17] The regime tolerated protest culture as long as it was produced for a limited audience of middle- and upper-class progressives. State violence and legal repression were also mitigated by questions of social class, reflecting what one observer has called the "liberal elitism" of the military regime.[18] Whereas the CPC experiment sought to bridge cultural gaps between progressive intellectuals and workers, the postcoup period was characterized by a conspicuous separation of social classes. Protest culture during this period was produced primarily for an audience that was relatively small but well connected with media networks.

The Castelo Branco regime ushered in a return to archaic, conservative social values, but it was also committed to capitalist modernization under the guidance of technocrats. Military authorities encouraged private sector development of the communication industry but submitted it to state control. The expansion and modernization of the communication networks, especially radio and television, were part of a larger effort to achieve "national integration" and ideological control over civil society, a strategy codified in the 1967 Law of National Security.[19] Military authorities regarded the mass media networks as an essential tool for fomenting patriotism and promoting allegiance to the regime. Under the aegis of the military regime and with financial and technical support from the American Time-Life media conglomerate, a new television station, TV Globo, emerged in 1965. By the end of the decade, Globo had become the largest television station in Brazil and the first to establish a national network.

Social advances did not accompany technocratic modernization. Figures from the Instituto Brasileiro de Geografia e Estatística (IBGE, Brazilian Institute of Geography and Statistics) show that important indices of social development failed to keep pace with the modernization of the communication industry.[20] IBGE figures suggest relatively modest advances in literacy and infrastructure (i.e., access to running water and electricity) together with dramatic increases in household ownership of cultural appliances such as radios and televisions. The number of radio stations grew rapidly in the 1950s (nearly a 225 percent increase), then slowed considerably in the 1960s (roughly a 37 percent increase). During the 1960s, the number of television stations registered a 250 percent increase, from fifteen to fifty-two. During the same period, private ownership of television sets grew exponentially. According to one estimate, there were 4.5 million television sets in Brazil in 1970, up from a mere 78,000 in 1958.[21] The process of modernization evidenced stark regional asymmetries in terms of human, infrastructural, and technological development. In 1970, the literacy rate of Bahia remained just above 40 percent, while over 75 percent of the population of São Paulo state could read and write. Only 12.8 percent of all Bahian households had running water, 22.8 percent had electricity, and 36.6 percent owned radios, while the same indices for São Paulo were 58.5 percent, 80.4 percent, and 80.5 percent, respectively. By 1970, nearly half of all Paulista households owned televisions, compared to only 3.3 percent in Bahia. The infrastructure of Brazil was developing rapidly but unevenly. The regime had abandoned the doctrine of developmentalism, with its abiding concern for social progress, and adopted a program of conservative modernization, which privileged the concentration of capital and technological advances.[22]

THE NORTHEAST, BAHIA, AND MODERNITY

The statistics cited above are significant given that the artists who would later articulate the tropicalist movement hailed from small towns of Bahia in northeastern Brazil. The Northeast is regularly cited in official statistics as the poorest region of Brazil. It is divided into three geographical zones: a lush coastal region, or litoral, the arid sertão, and an intermediary zone known as the agreste. As the site of the largest and wealthiest colonial era sugar plantations, the northeastern littoral was the privileged locus of Gilberto Freyre's Casa Grande e Senzala (discussed in Chapter 1), which made a case for understanding social relations between the big house and the slave quarters as a transhistorical template for Brazilian culture and society. Urban coastal dwellers typically perceived the arid *sertão* as an impoverished hinterland, home to messianic religious fanatics, lawless bandits, ruthless *coroneis* (regional bosses), and a miserably exploited peasantry. As a regional entity, the northeastern *sertão* entered national consciousness with the publication of Euclides da Cunha's *Os Sertões* (Rebellion in the backlands) (1902), which described the violent military campaigns of the then recently installed Republican government against a monarchist and messianic religious community in the Bahian *sertão*. In the 1930s, several modernist novelists with regionalist and social realist concerns represented the rural Northeast as a site of nostalgia for a patrimonial world lost to modernization and urbanization, or as a place of abject poverty and injustice leading to social revolt. Progressive artists and intellectuals of the early 1960s, especially those affiliated with the CPC and the peasant leagues, invoked the rural Northeast as a symbol of Brazil's endemic social problems and regional disparities and also as a site of authentic folk cultures that could be useful for an anti-imperialist national-popular cultural project.[23]

The group of Bahian musicians who would later launch the tropicalist movement maintained an ambivalent relationship with the Northeast as it was imagined in the more developed southern cities. They were sensitized to the material conditions of their surroundings and motivated by the CPC project and other progressive social and cultural movements. As aspiring cosmopolitans who read magazines from Rio de Janeiro, followed national and international cinema, listened to the radio, and were inspired by bossa nova, they were also eager to participate in "modernity" and its various manifestations in Brazil.[24] After moving south in the mid-1960s, they occasionally expressed exasperation with stereotypical perceptions of the Northeast as a uniformly rustic and impoverished region.

The formative social and cultural contexts of the future tropicalists were diverse. Tom Zé (b. 1936) has described Irará, his hometown in the Bahian *sertão*, as "pre-Gutenbergian," since the exchange of information and knowledge there depended primarily on oral communication. His father owned a fabric shop where he would spend time learning from the conversations among local clients: "The counter of my father's store was the most sophisticated university that I ever attended."[25] Caetano Veloso (b. 1942) and his sister, Maria Bethânia (b. 1946), grew up in a lower-middle-class family in Santo Amaro de Purificação in the littoral region known as the *recôncavo* surrounding Bahia de Todos os Santos (All Saints Bay). In contrast with Tom Zé's evocation of Irará, Veloso has described his small hometown as a place where young people listened to bossa nova, American rock 'n' roll, and the latest boleros from Cuba and Mexico. One could also stay au courant with the trends in French and Italian cinema. According to his memoirs, Santo Amaro seemed to provide nearly everything for an adolescent Caetano Veloso: "It was there that I first experienced genital sex, I saw La strada, I fell in love for the first time . . . , I read Clarice Lispector, and most importantly, I heard João Gilberto."[26] Gilberto Gil (b. 1942) came from a relatively privileged black middle-class family (his father was a physician) and spent his childhood in the small rural town of Ituaçú before moving to Salvador, the coastal state capital of Bahia, for schooling in the early 1950s. In the 1970s, after embracing black consciousness, Gil remembered his early family life in the following terms: "I am the son of a mulatto family in every sense. My parents are mulattos of color, leaning toward whiteness in terms of consciousness and culture. The struggle for the social ascension of family and the children was always based on clientelist relations with whites in society.[27] Gil's family occupied a relatively comfortable place within the personalist, nonconfrontational socioracial order invoked in a famous samba by Dorival Caymmi, "São Salvador" (1960), which idealized Bahia as "the land of the white mulatto / the land of the black doctor." José Carlos Capinan (b. 1941) came from Esplanada Bahia, and Torquato Neto (1944–72) grew up in Teresina, the capital of Piauí, before moving to Salvador to study at the University of Bahia. Of the Bahian cohort that would later elaborate the tropicalist project, only Gal Costa (Maria da Graça, b. 1945) was born and raised in Salvador.

Since regional identity was an important dimension of the tropicalist project, it is worth discussing the specificity of Bahia vis-à-vis the rest of the nation, as well as its cultural context during the period in which these young musicians and lyricists came of age. Salvador da Bahia served as the colonial capital of Brazil from 1549 until 1763, when the Portuguese crown transferred the capital to Rio de Janeiro. Its colonial economy was based primarily on sugar production and depended on a massive labor force of African slaves. By the time Brazil became independent in 1822, sugar was no longer as central to the national economy and Bahia entered a period of slow decline, becoming increasingly marginalized from centers of political and cultural power and prestige in the South. Throughout the first half of the twentieth century, Bahia was a provincial backwater, remaining on the margins of urban-industrial modernization under Vargas. With the discovery of petroleum reserves under All Saints Bay in the 1950s, the Bahian economy picked up again, contributing to the urbanization and modernization of Salvador. For the most part, however, the city remained one of the poorest state capitals in Brazil, with marked inequalities between a mostly white minority elite and a mostly black and poor majority.

Gilberto Gil (top) and Caetano Veloso, 1968 (Paulo Salomão/Abril Imagens)

Tom Zé, 1968 (J. Ferreira da Silva/Abril Imagens)

In the national imaginary, Bahia is regarded with some ambivalence. Among inhabitants of the more developed South, racist stereotypes often cast Bahians as lazy and ill equipped for the exigencies of modern life. At the same time, Bahia is romanticized as the foundational site of Brazilian tropical civilization with magnificent examples of colonial architecture, splendid beaches, and an exuberant popular culture. Above all, it is widely regarded as the epicenter of Afro-Brazilian cultural life, where Candomblé (an Afro-Brazilian religion), *capoeira* (a dance/martial art of Angolan origin), and samba first emerged. The cultural life of Bahia, particularly its state capital, gained national and international recognition with the voluptuous novels of Jorge Amado, the watercolors and sculptures of Carybé, the photography of Pierre Verger, and the sambas and *modinhas* of Dorival Caymmi. Dozens of radio hits from the thirties and forties by Dorival Caymmi, Ary Barroso, and others exalted the natural beauty, culinary delights, and mystical powers of Bahia.

As Bahia entered a period of industrial modernization, Salvador developed a lively cultural scene revolving around the local university, producing what Antônio Risério has called an "avant-garde in Bahia."[28] The University of Bahia was founded in 1946 under the direction of Edgard Santos, who served as rector until 1961. A traditional humanist committed to national and regional development, Santos believed that the university should take a leading role in Bahia's modernization, which was understood both as urban-industrial development and as "cultural de-provincialization."[29] To this end, the rector invested heavily in the humanities and recruited artists and educators from Europe and other parts of Brazil to establish schools of music, theater, dance, and visual arts.

Veloso has singled out two events that were emblematic of the vibrant cultural life of the university while he was a student during the early 1960s. The first was the innovative production of Bertolt Brecht's *Three Penny Opera* directed by Eros Martim Gonçalves, who had been recruited by Edgard Santos to found a theater program in 1955. The production was staged in the ruins of the Teatro Castro Alves, a modern theater that had burned down on the day after it was inaugurated in 1959. Gonçalves turned the tragedy into an occasion for an innovative production in the somber, burned-out shell of the theater. The other memorable event involved David Tutor's performance of John Cage's aleatoric music for prepared piano and a radio, which was played just as a local announcer intoned "Rádio Bahia, Cidade de Salvador." The daily station identification figured into the piece by chance, thereby symbolically inscribing the city into the international musical vanguard.[30]

The events Veloso recalled were made possible by the establishment of innovative theater and music schools at the University of Bahia in the mid-1950s. These institutions brought together and trained young artists who later emerged as leading figures in Brazilian cultural life. Several of Gonçalves's students, for example, would later star in films of the Cinema Novo, a Brazilian movement that took a leading role in Third World cinema in the 1960s.

The movement's most prominent director, Glauber Rocha (1938–81), a native of Vitória da Conquista in southern Bahia, became a key figure in theater and film circles of Salvador during the late 1950s. In 1957, he founded the cultural journal *Mapa*, which featured contributions by João Ubaldo Ribeiro and Sonia Coutinho, who would later become acclaimed fiction writers. In short, during the 1950s and early 1960s, Salvador enjoyed an extraordinarily active cultural life and would produce some of the most important artists and intellectuals of that generation.[31]

In 1955, the University of Bahia also established a music school under the direction of Hans Joachim Koellreutter. A refugee of Nazi Germany, in 1937 Koellreutter had come to Rio de Janeiro, where he founded the Música Viva group, which was dedicated to the duodecophonic (twelve-tone) compositional techniques of Arnold Schoenberg. In Bahia, he trained a cadre of composers before relinquishing the position in 1963 to Ernst Widmer, who founded the Bahian Composers Group, which experimented with vanguard music and local Afro-Brazilian forms.[32] Tom Zé was a founding member of the Bahian Composers Group while he pursued an advanced degree in music between 1962 and 1967 before moving to São Paulo and embarking on a career in popular music. During this time, Tom Zé also studied with Walter Smetak, an iconoclastic Swiss emigré who established a workshop at the university for building instrument-sculptures with local materials.[33]

Caetano Veloso studied philosophy at the university and circulated among the theater milieu, accompanied by his sister, Maria Bethânia. Gilberto Gil studied business administration at the university and performed bossa nova at bars and private gatherings. Tom Zé had been locally known as a satiric balladeer ever since his appearance in 1960 on a local talent show, "Escada para o sucesso" (Stairway to success), aired by TV Itapuã, Salvador's only television station at that time. He parodied the program with a song called "Rampa para o fracasso" (Ramp to failure), a humorous reference to the ramp leading up to the presidential palace in Brasília.[34]

In relation to the more industrialized south central region of Brazil, Bahia was poor and underdeveloped but was not entirely isolated from national and international cultural developments. One of Caetano Veloso's earliest compositions, "Clever Boy Samba," suggests that Salvador was becoming a cosmopolitan city with much to offer an aspiring artist.[35] In the song, Veloso does not regard the peripheral location of Bahia with anxiety but rather with irony and self-confidence, as suggested in blithe references to a Fellini film and American popular music: "although I'm underdeveloped / I'm living the 'Dolce Vita' . . . I adore Ray Charles / or 'Stella by Starlight' / but my English / has not progressed past 'goodnight.' " The supreme emblem of cultural modernity in "Clever Boy Samba," however, is not foreign. Veloso ends the song with a tribute to Bahian native João Gilberto, which he follows with the declaration, "if it's not bossa nova / it's not for me."

Of course, by that time, bossa nova had inspired an entire generation of emerging musicians throughout Brazil. The young Bahians first coalesced as a group of young artists devoted to the innovations of João Gilberto. In August 1964, Veloso, Gil, Bethânia, and Costa participated in a musical showcase, *Nós, por exemplo* (Us, for example), at the Teatro Vila Velha, an alternative stage in Salvador founded by university students. With the success of this program, they gave a second presentation a month later, this time with the participation of Tom Zé. In November, the group produced another showcase, *Nova bossa velha, velha bossa nova*, a rereading of the tradition of Brazilian song in light of bossa nova.[36] In all of the shows, the repertoire was divided between bossa nova standards, original compositions, and classic sambas from the thirties and forties by composers such as Pixinguinha, Noel Rosa, and Ary Barroso. The shows launched these artists' professional careers, establishing them as leaders on the local music scene. One local music critic exulted that "for the first time there had been direct contact between the public and musicians who were creating a new style, in step with the times, to be sure, but also imbued with Bahianness."[37] Several months later, Maria Bethânia was invited to participate in a major cultural event in Rio de Janeiro and plans for further shows were indefinitely suspended.

OPINIÃO AND THE LEFTIST CULTURAL SCENE

In Rio de Janeiro and São Paulo, musical theater assumed a leading role in protest culture during the period immediately following the military coup. After the suppression of the CPC, several of its leading dramatists formed the Grupo Opinião as a forum for publicly articulating an "opinion" in a context of political repression. It would inspire an art exhibition, *Opinião 65*, which featured the work of young artists influenced aesthetically by pop art but decidedly committed to social and political critique. The group's first production, *Show Opinião*, was a dramatic musical directed by Augusto Boal of Teatro de Arena, featuring Nara Leão, a well-known bossa nova vocalist, João do Vale, a singer-songwriter from Maranhão, and Zé Keti, a samba musician from the *favelas* of Rio de Janeiro. The *Show Opinião* initiated a series of performances directed by Boal based on a similar format that combined popular music and dramatic narrative. Bethânia, Gil, Veloso, and Tom Zé participated in the 1965 production *Arena canta Bahia* (Arena sings Bahia), which showcased musical traditions of the Northeast.[38] These staged productions dovetailed with a revival of middle-class interest in folk music, primarily from the *sertão*, and in roots samba from the *favelas* of Rio de Janeiro. At the time, it was fashionable for middle-class artists and students in Rio to congregate at Zicartola, a downtown restaurant-bar operated by Cartola, a venerated sambista of the so-called *Velha Guarda* (Old Guard), and his wife, Zica. With the suppression of the CPC, artists and activists sought to maintain in this way contact with working-class popular culture.

The *Show Opinião* was structured around the artists' personal narratives and their opinions on culture and politics in contemporary Brazil. When it opened on December 11, 1964, it was heralded as the first cultural response of any impact to the military coup. It marked the transformation of Nara Leão from the demure "muse of bossa nova" to the new voice of protest music, signaling a conscious effort on the part of left-wing artists to reaffirm their alliance with the *povo*. By bringing together an urban sophisticate from the Carioca bourgeoisie with musicians from humble backgrounds, *Opinião* sought to recapture the spirit of the CPC experiment. The stagebill of the show proclaimed: "Popular music is more expressive when it has an opinion, when it is allied with the people in harnessing the new sentiments and values that are necessary for social evolution; when you keep alive traditions of national integration and unity." [39] *Opinião* protagonists were represented as the popular voice of the nation, implicitly foregrounding unity of the masses against the military regime while eliding class differences.[40] At one point in the script, the uncomfortable social differences that separated middle-class artists from their desired mass audience is broached but not seriously developed. After Nara Leão earnestly explains her newfound commitment to public performance as a way to confront the regime, an offstage voice sarcastically questions her sincerity, pointing out her bourgeois pedigree, her residency in Copacabana, and her ties with bossa nova. The ambiguities and complexities of the moment are quickly resolved, however, as Nara Leão begins singing "Marcha da quarta-feira de cinzas" (Ash Wednesday march) (Carlos Lyra–Vinícius de Moraes), an antiregime anthem that proclaims the collective imperative to sing.[41]

The most acclaimed song from the *Show Opinião* was "Carcará" (João do Vale–José Candido), which refers to a bird of prey indigenous to northeast Brazil. It became particularly renowned after Maria Bethânia was invited to replace Nara Leão in 1965:

Carcará, pega, mata e come
Carcará não vai morrer de fome
Carcará, mais coragem do que homem

Carcará, gets it, kills it, eats it
Carcará, will not die of hunger
Carcará, more courage than humans

The bird of prey serves as a metaphor for northeastern peasants who must constantly struggle to survive in the arid *sertão*. Failing there, they are forced to migrate to the cities. Bethânia's rendition of the song, which was featured on her first LP, *Maria Bethânia* (1965), ends in a dramatic crescendo with her indignant declamation of the percentages of outgoing migrants from the poorest northeastern states. Although the song did not refer directly to the regime in power, it advanced a forceful critique of rural poverty. That Bethânia was from Bahia and had a husky and powerful alto voice made her interpretation much more effective than that of Nara Leão. She was perceived as a rustic folk singer rather than a suave bossa nova singer from a privileged background. "Carcará" established a new paradigm for protest music yet would later prove to be burdensome for Bethânia when she pursued other artistic directions.[42]

Several critics have pointed out that the *Show Opinião* had political and aesthetic limitations since it treated audiences to romanticized and celebratory representations of the people engaged in revolutionary struggle while all but ignoring the real crisis of progressive politics. Heloísa Buarque de Hollanda has provided a revealing personal reflection of this show: "I remember seeing the show a number of times, standing, overcome with civic emotion. It was a collective rite, a festive program, an action among friends. The audience was in accordance with the stage. A ritual encounter, everyone at 'home,' secretly reflecting on the failure of '64, lived as a passing incident, an unforeseen and rectifiable error, a failure that could be overcome by the rite."[43] Another critic later described the event as a "religious rite" in which the "stage and the audience were united in brotherhood by the same faith."[44] Upbeat and redemptive "rites" like the *Show Opinião* assuaged the collective disappointment of progressive audiences.

Events such as *Show Opinião* typically attracted an urban social and cultural milieu sometimes referred to as the *esquerda festiva* (festive Left), composed mostly of young students, professors, journalists, and other artists. In generational terms, this milieu also came to be known as the "geração Paissandu" in reference to the movie theater near downtown Rio de Janeiro that was a favorite meeting place for the *esquerda festiva*. In some respects, this milieu is comparable to New Left circles that developed in the United States in the early 1960s. Despite the enormous differences in context, emergent left-wing politics in both countries were largely youth centered and highly critical of traditional leftist organizations. In Brazil, many post-1964 activists broke ranks with the Brazilian Communist Party, which was perceived as overly cautious and reformist. Having been suppressed by the military regime, the young Left turned to symbolic protest through cultural events. The *esquerda festiva* was symptomatic of the political and existential crises of a young and relatively privileged sector.

By the end of the decade, as the military regime became increasingly entrenched and repressive, a sense of anguish had replaced the redemptive optimism of the mid-1960s. In 1968, one young cultural critic, Ruy Castro, published a long piece of self-criticism about the "geração Paissandu" in a Rio newspaper: "What seems certain is that the agony of this generation is caused by the emptying of its myths. Those endless rap sessions after the film that lasted until dawn ended up resulting in a half dozen slogans which, having been used so often, lost meaning. . . . It was like always framing reality according to the formulas learned at the university. It's necessary to do something, but what? How? As long as we don't answer these questions we're going to sit there masturbating on the beer table, protesting, protesting and protesting, and nothing more."[45] In 1965, when the *Show Opinião* was attracting large and enthusiastic audiences, the coup was still widely perceived by many on the Left as a passing aberration or even as a last-ditch attempt to preempt an impending revolution. History still seemed to be on the side of progressive forces. Castro's anguished remarks suggest that three years later disorientation and disillusionment had set in as the military regime tightened its grip on civil society.

LINHA EVOLUTIVA: FROM BOSSA NOVA TO MPB

In the early 1960s, bossa nova artists developed two distinct though not always mutually exclusive tendencies: one that was oriented toward urban "roots" samba and various rural "folk" genres and another that accentuated the urbane and jazzy elements of bossa nova. Artists such as Carlos Lyra, Sérgio Ricardo, and Geraldo Vandré admired early bossa nova but felt that its lyrical content and musical form were too distant from the quotidian life and culture of the Brazilian people. These musicians developed new trends based on musical traditions from rural Brazil, especially from the Northeast. Owing to its abiding concern for social injustice, poverty, and cultural authenticity, this music was often referred to as "nationalist-participant" music. Following the military coup, this music provided a template for protest music. Other young performers such as Elis Regina, Jair Rodrigues, and Wilson Simonal, and instrumental groups like Tamba Trio and Zimbo Trio developed ensemble bossa nova that was jazzier and more ostentatious than the music of João Gilberto. Taken together, protest and jazz-bossa musicians constituted a "second generation" of bossa nova. Chico Buarque de Hollanda emerged as the most acclaimed singer-songwriter of second-generation bossa nova with well-crafted compositions that encompassed both romantic lyricism and social critique. Although eclectic and heterogeneous, these artists shared a common commitment to defend Brazilian musical traditions from the effects of imported popular music, especially rock 'n' roll. These new stylizations of bossa nova evolved into a category of song known as Moderna Música Popular Brasileira. By the late 1960s, this music was known simply as Música Popular Brasileira, or MPB.[46]

When Maria Bethânia was invited to substitute for Nara Leão in the Show Opinião, she came to Rio de Janeiro accompanied by Caetano Veloso. Gilberto Gil had received his degree from the University of Bahia and went to work in São Paulo for Gessy Lever, a multinational company that produced laundry detergent. All three continued to develop artistic careers in Rio de Janeiro and São Paulo, where they were later joined by their musical companions from Salvador, Gal Costa and Tom Zé, and by poets Torquato Neto and José Carlos Capinan. This young cohort, known as the grupo baiano (Bahian group) identified with the MPB artists, although Caetano Veloso and Gal Costa were less enthusiastic about jazz-bossa stylizations and protest music. Other members of the Bahian group had more affinities with socially oriented protest music. Gil, Capinan, and Tom Zé had participated in the musical and dramatic productions of the CPC in Salvador. They worked with musical forms and lyrical themes from the sertão, which had become standard practice in protest culture.

Of the Bahian group, Gilberto Gil was the most engaged with protest music and northeastern folk traditions. Growing up in the Bahian hinterland, his earliest musical influence was Luiz Gonzaga, the great northeastern singer-songwriter-accordionist who had achieved fame throughout Brazil in the forties and fifties with regional dance music known as the baião. In a 1968 interview, Gil called Gonzaga "the first spokesperson for marginalized culture of the Northeast."[47] Gil's first LP from 1967 featured songs about the social, cultural, and religious life of the rural Northeast, focusing especially on the inequalities and injustices perpetuated by rural landowners. His song "Viramundo" (Shackle) (Gil-Capinan) was used as the sound track to a film by the same name by Geraldo Sarno that portrayed the struggles of a northeastern migrant in São Paulo. The most strident protest song of this album, "A roda" (The wheel), pointedly warns: "Mister be careful with your exploitation / or else I'll give you as a present a pit in the ground." His song "Procissão" (Procession) both celebrates and questions the religious faith of rural peasants: "I'm also with Jesus / But I think he forgot / To say that here on earth / We have to manage a way to live." Most of the songs from this LP exalt the rural *povo* as active agents in historical transformation.

While Gil responded to social imperatives, Veloso composed songs mostly about existential dilemmas. The CPC experience, the military coup, and protest culture are entirely absent from the album. Veloso believed the second generation of bossa nova had merely added didactic political slogans to a diluted version of bossa nova mixed with rural northeastern popular music. His first album, *Domingo* (1967), recorded with Gal Costa, was a somewhat melancholic rereading of early bossa nova with its emphasis on nature, love, personal anguish, and nostalgic longing for the past. Yet Veloso also indicated that his affirmation of orthodox bossa nova was a prelude to more radical experiments. In the liner notes to *Domingo* he stated: "My inspiration does not want to depend any more on nostalgia for times and places but rather to incorporate this longing in a future project."

In a roundtable discussion titled "Que caminho seguir na música popular brasileira?" (Which way to go in MPB?), published in *Revista civilização brasileira*, an important leftist journal of the time, Veloso criticized what he considered to be an aesthetically retrograde use of musical "tradition," especially samba, in Brazilian popular music. He invoked the example of João Gilberto as an artist who had used "information of musical modernity" in order to renovate the tradition of Brazilian song. Veloso did not call for a stylistic return to the early bossa nova sound but rather a return to the *linha evolutiva* (evolutionary line) in Brazilian popular music: "If we have a tradition and we want to do something new with it, not only do we have to feel it, but we have to know it. . . . Only by retaking the evolutionary line can we establish organic criteria by which to select and evaluate. To say that samba can only be made with a frying pan, a tambourine, and a guitar, without sevenths and ninths, does not resolve the problem."[48] Years later, Veloso would distance himself from this teleological and programmatic appeal to "evolution" in Brazilian popular music.[49] At the time, however, he invoked the "evolutionary line" to critique second-generation bossa nova, which he regarded either as too folkish (i.e., protest music) or as too pretentious (i.e., jazz-bossa). His intervention attracted the attention of the concrete poet Augusto de Campos, who subsequently wrote a newspaper article praising the young Bahian musician.[50] Given that the concrete poets had presented their vanguard literary project as a "critical evolution of forms," it is logical that Augusto de Campos would find affinities with Veloso's critique.

JOVEM GUARDA: BRAZILIAN ROCK OF THE 1960S

When Veloso outlined his critique of MPB in 1966, the field of urban popular music was fraught with conflict between two competing currents. Artists of the second generation of bossa nova had positioned themselves as guardians of national culture against artists who enjoyed enormous commercial success with Brazilianized rock 'n' roll, known as iê-iê-iê (a reference to the refrain of the Beatles' hit song "She Loves You"). For many university-educated urbanites who had come of age with bossa nova, rock 'n' roll seemed comparatively unsophisticated. They regarded Brazilian rockers as pathetic and misguided imitators under the insidious influence of American cultural hegemony.

By 1965, Roberto Carlos, a working-class kid from the state of Espirito Santo who grew up in the North Zone of Rio, had become the undisputed "king of iê-iê-iê" and the leader of a rock cohort known as the Jovem Guarda (Young Guard). Augusto de Campos argued that the movement constituted a new form of "urban folklore" that appropriated modern communication technologies "without shame" in order to achieve popular appeal.[51] The music of the Jovem Guarda was based on British and American rock but was also rooted in the tradition of romantic ballads going back to Brazilian modinhas of the nineteenth century. Roberto Carlos's trajectory from rebel rocker in the mid-1960s to the leading stylist of música romântica in the 1970s can be situated within the tradition of Brazilian song. Nevertheless, the proponents of MPB denounced the Jovem Guarda as inauthentic and politically alienated. Some music fans and critics even perceived Roberto Carlos and his cohort as active agents of the military regime.[52] Between 1965 and 1967, the Brazilian rockers became targets of nationalist critique.

By the mid-1960s, television had become the principal site for cultural struggles in Brazilian popular music. Television stations in São Paulo and Rio de Janeiro competed to attract the viewing public with regular music programs and annual festivals. São Paulo's TV Record was the most popular station, and its ratings depended largely on the success of several musical showcases. Caetano Veloso first gained national attention on "Esta noite se improvisa" (Tonight we improvise), a show in which guests competed for prizes by performing Brazilian songs containing a randomly chosen word or phrase.[53] The MPB group coalesced around the TV Record program "O Fino da Bossa" (The best of bossa), which first aired in May 1965. Hosted by Elis Regina, the program featured invited guests backed by the Zimbo Trio or other jazz-bossa combos.[54] Regina's program, later renamed simply "O Fino," helped to launch several careers, including that of Gilberto Gil, who appeared on the show in June 1966 to perform "Eu vim da Bahia" (I came from Bahia), an affirmation of regional culture very much in the tradition of Dorival Caymmi.[55]

During the same period, Roberto Carlos commanded his own program on TV Record, "Jovem Guarda," which featured rising stars of Brazilian rock. The Jovem Guarda and MPB group competed for the top ratings of the Instituto Brasileira de Opinião Pública e Estatística (IBOPE, Brazilian Institute of Public Opinion and Statistics), which monitored television audiences and record sales. Much to the chagrin of MPB artists, the Jovem Guarda was a pop phenomenon, attracting an immense following among the urban working and middle classes. The image of youthful yet apolitical rebellion projected by the Jovem Guarda became extremely useful to record companies and other manufacturers of consumer items seeking to tap into a growing market for "youth culture." One publicity agency in São Paulo, Magaldi, Maia & Prosperi, marketed a full line of clothing based on the personalities of Jovem Guarda idols.[56]

The leading proponents of Brazilian rock came from working-class families, and few had attended university. In a perceptive analysis of class distinction in Brazilian popular music, Martha Carvalho has noted that Roberto Carlos turned to rock after failing as a bossa nova singer. He apparently lacked the "sophistication and education" of most bossa nova singers of Rio's South Zone.[57] The Jovem Guarda cohort also included young black singer-songwriters from Rio such as Tim Maia, who emerged as a proponent of rhythm and blues and soul after an extended period in the United States in the mid-1960s. Another Afro-Brazilian artist, Jorge Ben, who had achieved success and acclaim with his sui generis fusions of samba, bossa nova, and R & B, was initially embraced by the second generation of bossa nova and even performed on Elis Regina's musical showcase. After appearing on the Jovem Guarda program, however, he was barred from "O Fino" and estranged from the MPB camp.

Jovem Guarda songs tended to avoid political and social criticism, addressing instead the quotidian material and romantic desires of working- and middle-class urban youth.[58] Themes of male bravado, sexual liberation, fashionable clothes, fancy cars, and wild parties are most typical of Jovem Guarda songs. Although the rockers cultivated an image of rebellion against conservative social mores, they also saw their music as a palliative to political conflict and intergenerational strife. One singer declared: "In our songs we never speak of sadness, heartache, despair, hunger, drought, war. We always bring a message of joy to the people. . . . Iê-iê-iê has brought together parents and their children, making dialogue possible." [59] Robert Carlos's biggest hit during this period, "Quero que vá tudo pro inferno" (To hell with it all), is a good example of Jovem Guarda songs. Part of the song's appeal was in its expression of emotional dependence and pathos next to more familiar references to male bravado: "What is the worth of my good playboy life / if I get into my car and the solitude still hurts?" Driven by an electric guitar and organ, the song reveals a sensitive, vulnerable side to the masculine hero, which would become the hallmark of Roberto Carlos's romantic ballads in the next decade.[60]

Although popular musicians did not always fall neatly into bipolar categories, there was considerable conflict between those who embraced rock music and those who defended MPB. A cursory look at IBOPE music ratings from 1966 through 1968 shows that MPB musicians occasionally produced top-ten hits, usually following televised music festivals, but they were regularly outdone by foreign pop singers and Jovem Guarda stars.[61] There was a sense of urgency to televised MPB programs, considering the extraordinary success of the Jovem Guarda. In 1967, when "O Fino" began to falter, TV Record launched a new program, "Frente Única: Noite da Música Popular Brasileira," collectively hosted by several guests, including Elis Regina, Geraldo Vandré, Chico Buarque, and Gilberto Gil. This "united front" of MPB was inaugurated with a public demonstration in São Paulo against the influence of foreign pop music.[62] The event served as a striking example of how the terms of political resistance had been transferred to cultural struggle. But the high-minded anti-imperialist gesture also obscured more mundane and commercial motivations relating to competition in the televised entertainment market. The greatest beneficiary of the conflict was Paulo Machado de Carvalho, the owner of TV Record, who capitalized on the rivalry between both factions of his station.

Veloso's injunction to "return to the evolutionary line" in Brazilian popular music was in part a response to the emergence of a Brazilian rock movement with mass appeal. Although he identified with bossa nova and the MPB current, he was attracted to Jovem Guarda as a pop phenomenon. While many artists in the MPB camp regarded the Jovem Guarda as an aberration, a suspension of popular memory, and a betrayal of national culture, Veloso embraced it as an expression of urban modernity even though it lacked the musical and poetic sophistication of MPB. Just as the inventors of bossa nova had creatively appropriated jazz, young artists could absorb and transform rock. As a youth idol and national media phenomenon, Roberto Carlos was also a contemporary incarnation of the golden age radio singers who had so delighted Veloso as a child growing up in a small Bahian town. Developing the linha evolutiva meant revisiting Brazil's musical history but also coming to terms with a vital cultural manifestation with tremendous popular appeal.

<u>VIVA VAIA</u>: THE TELEVISED MUSIC FESTIVALS

In the struggle for media exposure, the MPB camp received an enormous boost from a series of televised music festivals that captivated mass audiences during the mid- to late-1960s. The Brazilian festivals were loosely modeled after the San Remo festival in Italy and the International Market of Records and Music Editors (MIDEM) record festival in France. Unlike the European festivals, which were conceived primarily as talent showcases for music industry professionals, the Brazilian festivals were structured as song competitions involving cash prizes for the best compositions, lyrics, interpretations, and musical arrangements.[63] In the contentious atmosphere of postcoup Brazil, the televised festivals became the most important venue for MPB musicians to promote their music and, in some cases, to register some form of protest. For the live audience, consisting primarily of middle-class students and urban professionals, the festivals also provided opportunities to vocally participate and express preferences, often with political overtones. Studio audiences organized themselves into torcidas (groups of fans) in support of their favorite artists. These audiences were generally united in opposition to the Jovem Guarda and the use of electric instruments. The festivals were interpreted as a venue for the mass-mediated promotion of "authentic" Brazilian music. Yet they were also extremely lucrative for the television stations, which consistently registered high IBOPE ratings during the festivals, and record companies (especially Philips, the Dutch multinational firm), which produced multivolume compilations of festival finalists. These events also had a significant influence on the genesis of MPB, leading to the consolidation of formulas for "festival music," which one journalist derisively characterized as "a structure in the form of an *aria* . . . supported by pompous orchestrations."[64]

The first televised festival was sponsored by TV Excelsior of Rio de Janeiro in 1965. It introduced a new generation of Brazilian performers to a viewing public beyond the university circuit, nightclubs, and theaters. Elis Regina was the great attraction of this festival, winning first prize for her interpretation of "Arrastão" (Dragnet) (Vinícius de Moraes–Edu Lobo), a song about the material and spiritual lives of fishermen on the Bahian coast, with references to Afro-Brazilian religion and popular Catholicism. After the success of the Excelsior contest, larger and more powerful stations organized televised festivals. The two most important contests from 1966 to 1969 were the Festival de Música Popular Brasileira of TV Record, which featured only Brazilian artists, and the Festival Internacional da Canção (FIC, International Song Festival), aired by TV Globo in Rio, which was divided into national and international competitions.

In 1966, TV Record sponsored the II Festival de Música Popular Brasileira, billing it as the successor to the Excelsior Festival.[65] This event established Chico Buarque as the premier singer-songwriter of the new generation and also propelled Geraldo Vandré, the leading proponent of protest music, onto the national stage. The two young singer-songwriters tied for first place, presenting, respectively, "A banda" (The band) and "Disparada" (Stampede), which were complementary examples of early MPB compositions. The festival was enormously successful and relatively free of controversy. Key proponents of MPB clearly benefited from the event, as evidenced by IBOPE ratings of October 1966.[66] Over 100,000 copies of the single "A banda" sold during the week following the festival, and Buarque became a national idol almost overnight.[67]

Buarque's composition was, as one critic noted, a "metasong" (a song about music as such) that commented on the role of popular music in the daily lives of ordinary people.[68] In Buarque's song, music becomes a ludic force to relieve the drudgery of existence: "My suffering people bid farewell to the pain / To see the band go by, singing songs of love." A simple Brazilian *marcha* (a traditional Luso-Brazilian form), "A banda" evoked the simplicity of a bucolic, premodern Brazilian town of the interior. The marching band creates a utopian space where people can momentarily experience collective pleasure. While "A banda" is not a protest song, it implicitly refers to an oppressive social order, which is disrupted by the ephemeral joy of popular song.

In an article written in 1968, Walnice Galvão identified a common rhetorical strategy in MPB in which artists evoked future political and social redemption in a "dia que virá" (coming day). She argued that the rhetoric of protest song frequently operated on a "mythological level" that thwarted human agency by constantly deferring action in the here and now for an imaginary day of redemption.[69] A prime example of this rhetoric was Gerald Vandré's "Disparada" (Vandré-Barros), a *moda-de-viola* performed at the festival by Jair Rodrigues and the Trio Novo. Using the first-person narrative voice of a poor cowherd, the song denounces injustice and exploitation in the rural *sertão*. The cowherd has been "keeping accounts" of grievances "so that together we can collect / in the day that is already coming." "Disparada" describes an epiphany of social and political consciousness: "I used to be part of the herd, but one day I mounted the steed." Spontaneous rebellion against unscrupulous ranchers was portrayed in Glauber Rocha's 1964 film *Deus e diabo na terra do sol* (Black god, white devil), perhaps the most influential Brazilian film of the decade. Vandré was likely inspired by an early scene in which the protagonist, a poor cowherd, kills his abusive boss and flees with his wife. In "Disparada," the cowherd's story of conversion and redemption is meant to serve as an example for others, so that individual rebellion could become a collective "stampede" and transform the social order. Yet the final stanza ("If you don't agree . . . I'll go sing elsewhere") conveys an ambiguous message, suggesting that the narrator's public is ultimately limited to those who already sympathize with his message.[70] Like the *Show Opinião* and other cultural events of the time, "Disparada" was addressed to an audience that was predisposed to rally around its discourse.

By 1967, the TV Record music festival had become a celebrated national media event. One journalist, writing for a national weekly magazine, summed up the festival's importance in the following terms: "In no soccer stadium does one see so much enthusiasm and passion, which suggests the immense importance attributed by Brazilians to music, its composers, and its singers."[71] After six months of preparation, three weeks of eliminatory rounds, and well over 3,000 entries, twelve songs were presented to the viewing public. TV Record awarded 52,000 cruzeiros novos (about $20,000) in prize money, with further contributions from the state and municipal governments.

At first sight, the 1967 festival merely confirmed the position of already consecrated artists. Edu Lobo and Marília Medalha, two popular exponents of MPB, received first prize for "Ponteio" (Strumming) (Lobo-Capinan), an uptempo *baião* structured around highly emotive crescendos. Like most protest songs, the lyrics of "Ponteio" claimed popular music as a vehicle for redemption in the face of intimidation and repression: "I won't leave behind my guitar / I'll see the times change / and a new place to sing." Chico Buarque received third place for his composition "Roda viva" (Wheel of life), which he performed with the vocal group MPB-4. TV Record's 1967 festival was an extraordinarily successful media event. According to IBOPE figures, 47.3 percent of the spectators of São Paulo viewed the finals broadcast from the Paramount Theater on October 21.[72] Success in the festivals translated into record sales as well. The three-volume set of festival songs, released by Philips during the final round, briefly supplanted the Beatles' *Sgt. Pepper's Lonely Hearts Club Band* as the best-selling LP in early November.[73]

The festival also witnessed a new level of live audience participation, as the *vaia* (jeer) became a central element in the event. Several artists suffered humiliation before the enthusiastic and intensely partisan audience. There were two distinct types of *vaia*—planned attacks directed at romantic balladeers and artists of the Jovem Guarda and spontaneous outbursts against compositions.[74] Most artists and critics were dismayed by these vocal assaults, but some observers also noted that these televised "happenings" attested to the vitality of the popular music scene. Augusto de Campos, for example, found poetic inspiration in these confrontations between the artist and the audience, producing a concrete poem entitled "VIVA VAIA" (1972), which he used as the title of his collected poems.

Sérgio Ricardo, a well-known singer-songwriter associated with protest music (he wrote the score to Glauber Rocha's *Deus e diabo na terra do sol*), suffered the second type of *vaia*. He was initially well received by the audience, but his song "Beto bom de bola" (a song about the travails of a soccer player) failed to satisfy its expectations. On the last evening of the festival, the audience vocally rebuked the jury's selection of his song for the final round and jeered Ricardo when he appeared on stage. Unable to perform his song over the din, he hurled condescending remarks to the audience: "I would ask those who applaud and those who jeer to demonstrate *lucidez* [lucidity] at this moment in order to understand what I'm going to sing." His appeal to *lucidez* (a popular term among leftist intellectuals denoting the most proper ideological perspective) to legitimize his song and shame critics, further provoked the ire of the audience. After a couple of false starts, he exclaimed: "You won. This is Brazil. This is an underdeveloped country! You're all a bunch of animals!" He proceeded to smash his guitar and hurl it at the audience, precipitating his disqualification from the festival.

Augusto de Campos sympathized with the beleaguered artist but barely concealed his satisfaction with the irony of this episode: "What most accentuates the drama of this unexpected *happening* on the last day of the festival was the painful confrontation based on mutual incomprehension between the public and the songwriter, an exponent of the nationalist-participant current of popular music, culminating in the symbolic *blow-up* of the broken guitar." [75] What did this "blow-up" signify? For Campos, this confrontation demonstrated that the artist could not overestimate the communicative power of popular themes like soccer at the expense of "formal elaboration." For Sérgio Ricardo, on the other hand, it demonstrated the alienation of the young audience, which he later characterized as a "gigantic mass of Brazilian atavism in a delirium of errors." [76] Perhaps it also suggested that there were no more "sacred cows" in Brazilian popular music. MPB had reached an impasse, and the time was ripe for new sounds.

O SOM UNIVERSAL

If, on one hand, the 1967 music festival of TV Record reaffirmed the popularity and prestige of MPB musicians such as Edu Lobo and Chico Buarque, it also revealed that "nationalist-participant" artists were not immune to audience disapproval. The Manichean divide between MPB and Jovem Guarda seemed to have lost some urgency and relevance. There was room for innovation in terms of musical form and lyrical content. At the same festival, Gilberto Gil and Caetano Veloso made their first intervention on the national music scene with what they called the *som universal* (universal sound). Gil and Veloso received second and fourth prizes, respectively, for "Domingo no parque" (Sunday in the park) and "Alegria, alegria" (Joy, joy). By December 1967, Veloso's song had climbed to the top of the IBOPE singles chart for record sales, while the winner of the festival, "Ponteio," hovered around tenth place.[77]

Veloso was jeered when he first performed during the eliminatory rounds with the Argentine rock band the Beat Boys. The audience reacted against the presence of a foreign rock group on stage with a young Bahian performer who had just released his first LP of bossa nova songs. At that time, the electric guitar was still regarded by many cultural nationalists as a sign of cultural "alienation." The very presence of a rock group suggested Veloso's affiliation with the Jovem Guarda. Yet he succeeded in winning over an initially hostile audience during the eliminatory round and was later received enthusiastically during the finals.

By using electronic instrumentation to perform a traditional *marcha*, Veloso departed from the dominant paradigms of MPB of that time. "Alegria, alegria" portrayed the confusing, fragmented reality of a modern Brazilian city, in this case, Rio de Janeiro, characterized by the ubiquitous presence of mass media and consumer products. As did previously cited festival hits such as "A banda," "Disparada," and "Ponteio," Veloso's song also used first-person narration, yet the subject was not cast as a valiant hero fighting for collective redemption through music. Like a tropical flaneur, the narrator merely enjoys a stroll through a Brazilian metropolis while casually absorbing a stream of disconnected images and sensations of his urban surroundings.[78]

The wandering narrator seems to be carefree, walking in the street "without a handkerchief, without documents, nothing in my pockets or hands." He has little concern for official ordinances, like carrying an identification card. Stopping at the newsstand to take notice of *O Sol*, a countercultural newspaper, he glances at images of Italian movie star Claudia Cardinale, local crime scenes, space exploration, and Ché Guevara's guerrilla campaign in Bolivia.[79] The media images of the newsstand become increasingly fragmented:

> Em caras de presidentes
> em grandes beijos de amor
> em dentes, pernas, bandeiras
> bomba e Brigitte Bardot

> Into faces of presidents
> into big loving kisses
> into teeth, legs, flags
> bombs and Brigitte Bardot

The narrator is overwhelmed by the array of visual and semantic information in which the erotic-ludic and the civic-political form pieces of a "kaleidoscopic verbal montage."[80] Images of national authority, patriotism, and political violence compete with film stars for his attention. Turning to existential questions, Veloso's self-styled narrator wanders on with a vague sense of joy and laziness in the summer sun of December. He exhibits little interest in ideological struggle and armed conflict, reflecting instead on an impending marriage and opportunities to sing on TV. He lives "without books and without guns / without hunger, without a phone / in the heart of Brazil." Individual desires and preoccupations obscure collective struggle, while music loses redemptive meaning, serving only to "console" him.[81] In this sense, Veloso's "Alegria, alegria" was similar to some Jovem Guarda rock songs yet was more attuned to the confusing and fragmented experience of urban life.

Gilberto Gil (center), Arnaldo Baptista of Os Mutantes (far right), and Dirceu (far left) perform "Domingo no parque" at the 1967 TV Record music festival. (T. Tavares Medeiros/Abril Imagens)

In musical terms, Gilberto Gil's "Domingo no parque" was the most innovative song of the festival. Rogério Duprat's arrangement featured a full orchestra, an experimental rock band, Os Mutantes, and a percussionist who played a berimbau, an instrument of Angolan origin typically used in capoeira. A call-and-response vocal pattern further reinforced the song's Afro-diasporic sensibility. Gil's lyrics form a rapidly changing montage of images from myriad perspectives, reminiscent of cinema.[82] The song attracted the attention of the concrete poets and emerging vanguardists who admired its defiance of lyrical convention. Antônio Carlos Cabral, a proponent of poesia-praxis, praised Gil's song because it "abandoned verbalism in order to adopt decidedly more dynamic arrangements, successions of word-scenes. It leaves behind the iron-clad logic of lyrics that blindly follow the model of versification."[83]

While the meandering narrative of Veloso's song constructs a subjective world of disconnected images and thoughts where nothing actually happens, Gil's lyrics, which are reported in the third person, compress a violent, public event into a brief moment. Set in Salvador, Bahia, where Gil spent much of his youth, "Domingo no parque" portrays a "crime of passion" involving two male rivals, José and João, and their mutual love interest, Juliana. Conflict arises when José arrives at the park and spies his friend romancing Juliana on the Ferris wheel. As the tempo of the song increases, call-and-response vocals introduce a series of verbal jump cuts that foreshadow the scene's bloody denouement. José fixates on the strawberry ice cream and a red rose in Juliana's hands: "the ice cream and the rose—ô José / the rose and the ice cream—ô José / spinning in his mind—ô José." The call-and-response crescendo builds with the jealous rage of José, who, in the final "scene," kills his friend with a knife. The working-class protagonists are not cast as heroic figures but rather as ordinary people caught up in tragic events.

Artists and critics of the nationalist left regarded the experiments of Gil and Veloso with suspicion, if not hostility. Their use of electric instruments, their open celebration of the mass media, and their highly subjective and fragmentary songs departed from the norms of MPB. Informed by experimental music, international popular music, and Brazilian musical forms, the "universal sound" of the Bahians testified to what García Canclini has called the "hybridization" of cultural spheres.[84] Veloso and Gil positioned themselves as leading proponents of a "pop" aesthetic just as the term was beginning to enter the critical and journalistic vocabulary in Brazil. In an article published on the day before the finals, Gil explained: "Pop music is music that is able to communicate—to say what it has to say—in a way which is as simple as a poster, a billboard, a stoplight, a cartoon. It's as if the author were seeking to sell a product or produce a journalistic account with text and photos. The song is presented in such an objective manner that, in a few verses, using musical resources and sound montages, it is able to say much more than it seems."[85] His use of the term "pop" was attuned to the English-language usage of "popular" to connote mass appeal and communicative efficacy, which implied a significant shift in the meaning of "popular" as it had been employed in Brazil up to that time. With the growth of urban populations and the expansion of mass media, it became increasingly difficult to reconcile the "popular" with traditional associations with rural folklore. Nor could the "popular" be defined solely by the imperatives of political consciousness-raising as the CPC had proposed. By invoking the concept of pop, Gil was not negating the oppositional potential of popular culture. Instead, he was suggesting that the emergence of a national market for cultural goods disrupted idealized definitions of the "popular" in Brazilian culture.

VANGUARDIAN ANGELS

Soon after the 1967 TV Record festival, Caetano Veloso stated in an interview: "I refuse to folklorize my underdevelopment in order to compensate for technical difficulties. Look, I'm Bahian, but Bahia is not just folkloric. And Salvador is a big city. There we don't just have *acarajé* but also fast-food joints and hot dogs, just like all big cities." [86] As other MPB musicians were using musical motifs and themes from the impoverished Northeast in order to denounce Brazil's underdevelopment, Veloso and Gil proposed a "universal sound" that claimed participation in an international modernity.

In refusing to "folklorize underdevelopment," Veloso implicitly embraced the cosmopolitan imperatives articulated by the concrete poets. It is important to note, however, that the concrete poets did not directly influence the initial work of Veloso and Gil, who had composed their festival songs before having had any contact with the São Paulo vanguard. After the Bahians moved to São Paulo, they established an intellectual relationship with the concrete poets, although this "convergence" of sensibilities was never articulated in a programmatic fashion.[87] In some of their songs, the Bahians adopted concretist strategies like nondiscursive syntax, poetic montage, and "verbivocovisuality" (simultaneity of verbal, vocal, and visual signification). Campos would speak of a "tropicalliance" based on a "community of interests" that advocated artistic experimentation and invention.[88]

Although it was only one facet of their work, the Bahians would continue to experiment with concrete poetics in subsequent decades.[89] Veloso later claimed that the concrete poets had "liberated our imagination for certain formal experiments that perhaps we wouldn't have otherwise risked. But we never lost sight of the fact that we were operating in different fields." [90] The concrete poets worked within the rarefied field of experimental poetry for a restricted audience of artists and critics, while the Bahians were working within a recording industry that targeted a mass market.

In terms of musical experimentation, the Bahians formed another alliance during the same period with several vanguard composers based in São Paulo associated with the Música Nova group. Like the Música Viva movement led by Hans Joachim Koellreutter, Música Nova was committed to international vanguardism and critiqued nationalist composers such as M. Camargo Guarnieri, the most accomplished heir to the mantle of Heitor Villa-Lobos. These young composers from São Paulo were not entirely disinterested in Brazilian musical sources but rather sought to reinterpret them in light of international vanguardist practices. In 1963, the group published a manifesto in *Invenção*, the second literary journal of the concrete poets. The manifesto defined Brazilian culture as a "tradition of internationalism . . . , in spite of economic underdevelopment, a retrograde agrarian structure, and a subordinate semi-colonial condition." Calling for a "total commitment to the contemporary world" and a "reevaluation of information media," the Música Nova manifesto echoed the cosmopolitan and urban-industrial concerns of the "Pilot Plan for Concrete Poetry." [91] The group's conception of national cultural affirmation followed the developmentalist spirit of the concrete poets with whom they collaborated. In the 1960s, a member of the Música Nova group, Gilberto Mendes, composed multiple-voice arrangements for several concrete poems, including Décio Pignatari's 1957 joco-serious antiadvertisement "Beba Coca-Cola" (Drink Coca-Cola).[92] Several Música Nova composers participated in summer workshops in Darmstadt, Germany, where they studied with Karlheinz Stockhausen and Pierre Boulez. In the mid-1960s, the Música Nova group was influenced by the antimusical "happenings" of American iconoclast John Cage. Around this time, the group began to elaborate a critique of vanguard music and gravitate toward the field of popular music.

In 1967, members of the Música Nova group (Rogério Duprat, Damiano Cozzela, Gilberto Mendes, and Willy Corrêia de Oliveira) participated in an irreverent group interview with maestro-arranger Júlio Medaglia in which they proclaimed the end of the musical vanguard and the beginning of a new era. In the words of Rogério Duprat, the composer would become a "sound designer" who would produce jingles, movie sound tracks, popular-music arrangements, and any other type of music for mass consumption.[93] With a nod to Pignatari's concept of *produssumo* (i.e., production + consumption), the composers heralded the simultaneous operation of musical production and consumption through channels of mass media. In a critique of the interview, Roberto Schwarz pointed out that their model of production-consumption ignored the problems of class society by camouflaging the mediation of capital.[94] The brash commercialism of the group was indeed striking, yet its collective position might be read as a logical response to the lack of public and private support for art music in Brazil. They argued that it was absurd and self-defeating to continue composing symphonies with the vain hope that one day they would be performed and appreciated by a restricted audience of critics and elite cognoscenti. Vanguardist experimentation had reached an impasse, making it necessary to abolish the distinction between art music and popular music. As Gilberto Mendes enthusiastically affirmed, this strategy was especially appropriate in Brazil, where popular music had a rich tradition: "It's difficult to interest the youth in some boring concert . . . when they have the best popular music ever made in the history of music at their disposal. It's necessary to turn art music into an object of mass communication."[95]

Several of these composers, most notably Rogério Duprat, initiated a close working relationship with the Bahian group during the tropicalist movement. Duprat's work elicited comparisons with that of the arranger George Martin, who was collaborating with the Beatles at that time. The tactical alliance between popular and erudite musicians was short-lived and ultimately proved untenable for the composers of the Música Nova group. In a memoir published in 1994, Gilberto Mendes lamented the "predatory influence of the media" in music, declaring that "great music should be heard as if it were part of an Oriental tea ceremony. In its proper place."[96] The relationship between vanguardist composers and the Bahian group came to an end in the 1970s, but this experiment would have a lasting impact on the production and arrangement of Brazilian popular music.

CONCLUSION

The artistic trajectory of the Bahian group between 1964, when they left Salvador, to 1967, when they gained national attention on the televised music festivals, touched upon some of the major debates in Brazilian culture during a period of conflict and crisis. They coalesced as a group in Salvador during a period of intense cultural effervescence generated by several initiatives at the local university. They were disciples of João Gilberto but initiated their careers at a time when emerging musicians were questioning the comfortable intimacy of early bossa nova and dedicating themselves to consciousness-raising efforts. The twin imperatives of anti-imperialism and social activism oriented the development of "national-participant" music, a project that became all the more urgent following the military coup of 1964.

Gil and Veloso responded somewhat differently to the conflict between the Jovem Guarda and the proponents of MPB, but both were ultimately dissatisfied with the terms of the debate. Their intervention at the 1967 TV Record festival relativized the conflict by demonstrating that electric instruments and rocklike arrangements need not be at odds with the tradition of Brazilian popular music. For Veloso, the elaboration of a "universal sound" in dialogue with bossa nova, iê-iê-iê, international rock, and vanguard music was a necessary phase in the "evolution" of this tradition. Gil acknowledged the role of mass communication and underscored connections between the "universal sound" and pop music. Their musical innovations coincided with watershed events in other areas of artistic production, converging under the name of Tropicália.

3
THE
TROPICALIST
MOMENT

ithin several months after Gilberto Gil and Caetano Veloso introduced the "universal sound" at the 1967 festival of TV Record, their music was dubbed "Tropicalismo" in the mainstream press. As noted in the introduction, the name of the movement referenced Veloso's composition "Tropicália," which in turn took its name from an installation by the visual artist Hélio Oiticica. The term was rich in connotations since it played on images of Brazil as a "tropical paradise" that date back to the letter written by Pero Vaz Caminha in 1500 to the king of Portugal relating the "discovery" of Brazil. Following Brazil's independence, mid-nineteenth-century Romantics celebrated their nation's tropical landscape as a symbol of Brazil's distinctiveness in relation to Europe. The designation also recalled "Luso-tropicalismo," a theory developed by Gilberto Freyre in the 1940s that exalted the Portuguese colonial enterprise in the tropics. For the tropicalists of the late 1960s, these official representations of Brazil provided ample material for ironic appropriation.

The tropicalists critiqued certain forms of cultural nationalism, including the conservative patriotism of the regime and the visceral anti-imperialism of the left-wing opposition. They satirized emblems of *brasilidade* and rejected prescriptive formulas for producing "authentic" national culture. It would be a mistake, however, to interpret the tropicalist movement as antinational or detached from Brazilian culture. Veloso has claimed that Tropicália promoted "aggressive nationalism" as opposed to the "defensive nationalism" of the anti-imperialist Left.[1] The work of modernist iconoclast Oswald de Andrade, which had been neglected since the 1920s, became central to the tropicalist project.[2] At the time, the concrete poets were engaged in producing several critical volumes of his work, which they imparted to Veloso and Gil. The tropicalists were particularly attracted to Oswald's notion of *antropofagia*, or cannibalism, as a strategy for critically devouring foreign cultural products and technologies in order to create art that was both locally inscribed and cosmopolitan. Veloso has stated that "the idea of cultural cannibalism fit us, the tropicalists, like a glove. We were 'eating' the Beatles and Jimi Hendrix."[3]

Oswald de Andrade seemed to hover like an irreverent specter over much of Brazilian cultural production, especially in popular music, theater, and film during the late 1960s. Renewed interest in the work of Oswald de Andrade was part of a more generalized revival of allegorical representation in the Brazilian arts. Like Oswald, the tropicalists revisited the question of national formation, but they also used allegory to represent and critique the regression to military authoritarianism in Brazil. The allegorical mode was not a constant in tropicalist song, but it surfaced intermittently in songs addressing the urban experience, political violence, and the geopolitical position of Brazil.

As hard-line forces within the military gained ascendancy in the regime, the redemptive power of art to change society seemed increasingly illusory and vain. There was a sense of skepticism regarding the notion that artists and intellectuals could serve as an enlightened vanguard leading the masses toward social revolution. The teleological march of history toward national liberation and revolution gave way to disenchantment and self-criticism. Artists began to gaze inward, exploring with caustic humor the social contradictions of middle-class urban intellectuals. The cultural manifestations associated with Tropicália were, as one critic has noted, an expression of crisis among artists and intellectuals.[4]

TROPICALIST CONVERGENCES

In the history of Brazilian popular music, Tropicália stands out as a movement that was particularly receptive to other artistic fields. Two events of 1967 were particularly influential: The release of Glauber Rocha's film *Terra em transe* (Land in anguish) and Teatro Oficina's production of *O rei da vela* (The candle king) under the direction of José Celso Martinez Corrêa. Both productions marked radical departures from both directors' previous work and signaled transformations within their respective artistic fields. In distinct ways, these events announced the political and existential crises of left-wing artists and intellectuals during the early period of military rule. They expressed a sense of disenchantment with the political and cultural populism of the Brazilian Communist Party, the CPC, and postcoup protest artists.

Glauber Rocha's films of the early 1960s conformed to the CPC's vision of a "revolutionary popular art." His 1964 film *Deus e diabo na terra do sol* (Black god, white devil) portrayed the violence and misery of the northeastern backlands perpetuated by the *latifúndio*, a monopolistic system of landownership that exploited disenfranchised workers. After killing an unscrupulous rancher, a poor cowherd and his wife join a radical millenarian religious movement that is eventually destroyed by federal authorities in concert with the Catholic Church. Following the massacre, the couple encounters a group of *cangaceiros* (rural bandits of the Brazilian Northeast), with whom they remain until tracked down by the same federal bounty hunters. The final shot shows them fleeing through the scrublands of the *sertão*, suggesting the possibility for popular redemption, despite the limitations of millenarian religious movements and banditry.[5]

First exhibited in April 1967, Glauber Rocha's *Terra em transe* signaled the artist's turn from redemptive utopianism to radical disillusionment. Set in an imaginary Latin American nation, Eldorado, the film critically portrays the position of artists and intellectuals in peripheral societies. The main protagonist is Paulo Martins, a poet and journalist with grandiose pretensions of working for radical transformation. He is a romantic revolutionary who believes that artists and intellectuals must serve as an enlightened vanguard and revolutionize the masses. Yet he ultimately despises and fears the dispossessed people for whom he claims to speak. Paulo goes to work for Felipe Vieira, a caricature of a populist politician who is running for governor. He is joined by Sara, a stalwart of the Communist Party who supports populist reformers as a gradualist strategy for a future proletarian revolution. The film represents populism as the carnivalization of politics in which a charismatic "man of the people" manipulates the popular classes through ostentatious displays of solidarity and promises for social reform. At Vieira's campaign rally, his followers hold up blank placards, suggesting a lack of substance in Vieira's electoral promises.[6] Like carnival, the populist political rally brings together people of all social classes for an exuberant celebration of popular will. Just as carnival ends on Ash Wednesday and order is restored, the populist leader typically perpetuates the status quo once he is in office.

Indeed, after the election, Paulo finds himself obliged to personally sup-

A still from Glauber Rocha's 1967 film *Terra em transe*. Vieira courts the masses
at a populist rally while supporters below hold blank placards and
musicians on the right play samba. (Photofest)

press and remove a group of landless peasants who have occupied the lands
of Colonel Morais, one of Vieira's propertied clients. Pre-election promises
to the peasants are ignored, and the security forces end up killing Felício, a
peasant leader. It is a stark moment in which theory is effaced by practice and
the left-wing utopian imagination is undercut by the cynical defense of class
interest.[7] The most startling scene of the film takes place at a mass rally to
protest a right-wing coup led by Porfirio Diaz (named after the Mexican dic-
tator of the early twentieth century), who represents conservative oligarchic
interests backed by foreign capital. As Diaz assumes the presidency of Eldorado, Governor Vieira and his political cronies join the masses to dance samba
in a useless gesture of popular resistance. Disgusted by the populist farce,
Sara exhorts a local union leader, Gerônimo, to speak on behalf of the people.
As the music fades, a paternalistic old senator approaches Gerônimo and
orders him to express his grievances: "Do not have fear my child, speak. You
are the *povo*. Speak!" After several moments of awkward silence, Gerônimo
stammers a few words about the class struggle and the present political crisis

but ends with the submissive recommendation that "the best route is to wait for the president's orders." He is immediately accosted and muzzled by Paulo. With his hand over Gerônimo's mouth, Paulo faces directly into the camera and sarcastically provokes the audience: "Do you see who the *povo* is? An imbecile! An illiterate! A de-politicized fool! Can you imagine Gerônimo in power?"

Rocha's film was a bitter self-critique aimed at left-wing artists who had embraced the Romantic notion that art could instigate and guide social revolution. At one point in the film, Sara consoles Paulo, telling him that "poetry and politics are too much for one man alone!" The actual relations of power, which structure class antagonism between peasants and landowners and between the proletariat and the bourgeoisie, expose the underlying contradictions of progressive intellectuals at the precise moment of conflict. Paulo and Sara attempt in vain to convince Felipe Vieira to resist the coup. When the populist governor refuses, Paulo quixotically strikes out on his own but is shot by security forces. He dies on the beach as Diaz is crowned, surrounded by Portuguese and Catholic symbols of colonial conquest. *Terra em transe* was an allegory of the collapse of populist politics and the ascension of an authoritarian regime in 1964. The film suggests that the nationalist and putatively "progressive" bourgeoisie ultimately share class interests with the conservative oligarchy and its multinational patrons. The poet, meanwhile, loses faith in the political efficacy of his art and dies while resisting the coup.

Glauber Rocha's *Terra em transe* had an immediate and profound impact on artists in other fields. Caetano Veloso later claimed that "all of that Tropicália thing was formulated inside me on the day that I saw *Terra em transe*." [8] Another artist who claimed Glauber Rocha's film as inspiration was José Celso Martinez Corrêa (a.k.a. José Celso), who directed the Teatro Oficina's production of Oswald de Andrade's *O rei da vela* in the fall of 1967. After seeing the film, José Celso felt that Brazilian theater had fallen behind cinema in terms of audacity and aesthetic innovation. Oswald wrote the play in 1933, but it was not published until 1937, the same year that Getúlio Vargas established the authoritarian Estado Novo. It was censored by the Vargas regime and then later ignored by directors and critics during the 1940s and 1950s when Brazilian theater companies such as the Teatro Brasileiro de Comédia (TBC) aspired to present elaborate productions modeled after Broadway.

Oswald wrote *O rei da vela* around the same time that the French dramatist Antonin Artaud published a series of manifestos and articles outlining his theory of a "theater of cruelty." For Artaud, mainstream theater had become a sterile, overly psychological exercise that restricted itself "to probing of a few puppets, thereby transforming the audience into Peeping Toms." He sought to "bring back the idea of total theater, where theater will recapture from cinema, music-hall, the circus, and life itself, those things that always belonged to it." Theater was for Artaud a kind of collective ritual involving direct contact between actors and the audience.[9] Some of the techniques and theories of Artaud were incorporated into Oficina's staging of O rei da vela, although never in an orthodox or programmatic fashion. Oficina cannibalized Artaud to create its own theatrical practice grounded in the Brazilian context. José Celso stated at the time that he no longer believed in the efficacy of rational theater; the only possibility left was "theater of Brazilian cruelty, of Brazilian absurdity, anarchic theater."[10]

Within the field of theatrical production itself, Teatro Oficina positioned itself against "bourgeois" theater such as the TBC, as well as nationalist-participant theater of Teatro de Arena and Grupo Opinião. José Celso argued that Brazilian theater and its public were blinded by certain "mystifications" regarding the efficacy of protest theater: "Today it is necessary for the theater to demystify, to place this public in its original state, face to face with its misery, the misery of its small privileges gained at the expense of so many concessions, so much opportunism, and so much castration and repression, and of so much misery of a people. . . . Theater cannot be an instrument of popular education, of transformation of mentalities through do-gooderism. The only possibility is precisely through diseducation, the provocation of the spectator." If the productions of Teatro de Arena attempted to establish common ground between the stage and the audience, the "guerrilla theater" of Teatro Oficina sought, above all, to provoke the audience into confronting its own complicity with forces of repression.

David George has noted that Oficina's production of O rei da vela represented the first attempt to apply Oswald de Andrade's concept of cannibalism to Brazilian theater. The text itself "cannibalized" Ubu Roi by French playwright Alfred Jarry.[11] The play focuses primarily on forms of "low cannibalism" described in Oswald's "Cannibalist Manifesto" as "the sins of catechism—envy, usury, calumny, murder." Economic dependency, foreign imperialism, and the cynical preservation of class interest during times of economic crisis are the central themes of the text.

The play revolves around the "candle king," a prosperous and brutal loan shark, Abelardo, who takes advantage of the international financial crisis of the early 1930s to exploit the disenfranchised. On the side, he also runs a brisk business selling candles, symbolically multivalent objects referring to death (i.e., objects used in funeral rites), underdevelopment (i.e., sources of light in the absence of electricity), and sexual dominance (i.e., phallic objects). His equally unsavory partner, Abelardo II, proclaims himself to be "the first socialist to appear in Brazilian Theater" and states his intentions to eventually take over the business:

> Abelardo I: From what I see, socialism in backward countries starts off like this . . . Striking a deal with property . . .
> Abelardo II: Indeed . . . We're in a semicolonial country . . .
> Abelardo I: Where we can have ideas, but they're not made of iron.
> Abelardo II: Yes. Without breaking tradition.[12]

The "socialist" might harbor radical ideas, but these are flexible enough so as not to threaten the "tradition" of class privilege.

The central plot involves a ruined coffee planter aristocrat, Coronel Belarmino, who arranges for his daughter, Heloísa de Lesbos, to marry the upstart bourgeois candle king in order to save his family from financial ruin. The second act, set in Rio de Janeiro, features a cast of bizarre and deceitful characters of the Belarmino family, who are all vying for the attention of Abelardo. Heloísa's aunt, Dona Poloquinha, openly flirts with Abelardo while proclaiming her virtue and aristocratic pedigree. Her fascist brother, Perdigoto (apparently a member of the Integralist Party), attempts to secure Abelardo's financial support to organize a "patriotic militia" to suppress the labor movement. Abelardo himself is completely subservient to Mr. Jones, the American investor who ultimately claims his "right" to have Heloísa.

Oficina's staging of *O rei da vela* was a phantasmagoric farce that satirized official pomp, openly derided "good taste," and reveled in the grotesque. The scenographer, Hélio Eichbauer, borrowed techniques from German Expressionism to create outlandish scenes. A revolving stage produced a delirious, merry-go-round ambiance in which the actors and the set were in perpetual motion. In the first act, Abelardo II is dressed as an animal tamer as he subjugates a group of caged debtors with a whip, suggesting a circuslike atmosphere of their brutal enterprise. The second act, which is set on an island beach near Rio de Janeiro, features the cast on vacation. Eichbauer's garish backdrop portrays Abelardo dressed as a tropical dandy and holding dollar bills. Banana leaves and coconuts frame a panorama of Guanabara Bay with popular tourist destinations, Sugar Loaf Mountain and Corcovado, in the distance (plate 11). For this scene, José Celso incorporated the low-class, semipornographic style of the Brazilian Teatro de Revista, as well as elements from the B-grade popular and musical comedy films, or *chanchadas*.[13] An inscription over the set ironically quotes Olavo Bilac, the fin de siècle Parnas-

A scene from the second act of Oswald de Andrade's *O rei da vela*, produced by
Teatro Oficina, 1967 (Fredi Kleeman/Multimeios-PMSP)

sian poet noted for his gushing patriotism: "Criança, nunca, jamais, verás
um país como este!" (Child, never, ever, will you see a country such as this
one). The third act treats the tragicomic death of Abelardo, the ascendance
of Abelardo II, and the intervention of Mr. Jones as ultimate arbiter of power.
José Celso opted for operatic melodrama by punctuating the scene with music
from Carlos Gomes's opera *Lo schiavo* (The slave) (1889), thereby alluding to
the vassal-like dependency of Brazil.[14] José Celso's use of opera during the
final act was most likely inspired by Glauber Rocha's *Terra em transe*, which featured operatic excerpts from Gomes's *Il Guarani* and Verdi's *Otello*.[15] In both
productions, opera was used to create an aura of phony artifice and deceit.

José Celso later claimed that his staging of Oswald's play was partially inspired by foreign stereotypes of Brazil: "When I was studying *O rei da vela*, the
cover of *Time* magazine featured a color photo of President Costa e Silva with
a green and yellow banner in the background. Inside, a story with photos, for
the foreigner to see, of 'our people' and 'our riches.' This shocked me: the
other side of the story reverberated in my ears."[16] On one level, this state-

ment suggests that Oficina's staging represented a capitulation to "banana republic" stereotypes that its contemporaries sought to combat. But it also suggests a reading of Brazilian culture that was attuned to the "other side of the story," which had been obscured by the regime's efforts to project an idyllic image at home and abroad. Teatro Oficina sought to ironically appropriate stereotypes about Brazilian culture and society in order to make a statement about dependency and exploitation under military rule.

Teatro Oficina's production of O rei da vela was a milestone event in the Brazilian stage. In 1968, the troupe performed the play in international festivals in Italy and France and produced several revivals of it after returning to Brazil.[17] In the early 1970s, José Celso initiated production of an experimental film of O rei da vela that was completed in 1984 but never distributed. In the cinematic version, the sequence of the play was substantially altered, producing an extended, nonlinear film featuring a mixture of stage scenes, archival footage, and improvised "happenings" shot in public.

Like all of the arts in Brazil during the 1960s, theater productions were increasingly scrutinized by state and federal censors. By 1968, government intervention had become so intense that the theater community in São Paulo declared a general strike to protest censorship.[18] Even more sinister forms of interference and repression subsequently threatened the theater community. Following O rei da vela, José Celso directed Roda viva (Wheel of life), a play written by Chico Buarque about the cynical manufacturing of pop stars for mass consumption. José Celso's experiments with theater of cruelty were further radicalized in Roda viva, in which the stage and the audience became almost indistinguishable. In one scene, the pop star protagonist, Ben Silver, is ritually crucified and pieces of raw liver are distributed among spectators, who thereby become implicated in the cannibalistic consumption of the pop idol. Another scene features the Virgin Mary in a bikini, gyrating in front of the phallic lens of a TV camera. One character merely circulates throughout the theater shouting obscenities at the audience. The staging of Roda viva would eventually provoke the ire of right-wing elements in Brazilian society. During one performance, a right-wing paramilitary organization, the Comando de Caça aos Comunistas (CCC, Command for Hunting Communists), invaded the theater, destroyed the props, and beat up the actors, alleging that the play was "immoral" and "subversive." When Roda viva toured to Porto Alegre, the CCC kidnapped the lead actor and actress and threatened to execute them.[19]

Teatro Oficina's O rei da vela was well received by theater critics and had a significant impact on the elaboration of the tropicalist project. Although Caetano Veloso had composed his song-manifesto "Tropicália" before seeing the play, he acknowledged its influence in an interview in late 1967: "I am the 'Candle King' of Oswald de Andrade produced by the Teatro Oficina."[20] Seeing the play, Veloso realized that there was a convergence of sensibilities in several areas of cultural production that suggested the outlines of a formal "movement."[21]

Not all critics and artists were so enthusiastic about *O rei da vela*. Roberto Schwarz argued, for example, that Oficina's aggressive theater, which often involved the physical and verbal taunting of audience members, played with "the cynicism of bourgeois culture faced with its own image." Oficina's tactics ultimately amounted to "psychological manipulation" that closed off all avenues for political action.[22] While Schwarz remained skeptical of the redemptive and communitarian spirit of the Opinião and Arena productions, he was particularly disturbed by the nihilism of Oficina, which seemed only to demoralize the Left.

Augusto Boal, the director of Teatro de Arena, wrote the most severe critique of Teatro Oficina's "guerrilla theater." It is useful to examine his attack because it echoed more general denunciations of the tropicalist movement. In late 1968, Boal organized the Primeira Feira Paulista de Opinião, a festival that brought together artists, mostly theater directors and popular musicians, including Edu Lobo, Sérgio Ricardo, Caetano Veloso, and Gilberto Gil. In the festival program, Boal published the essay "O que você pensa do teatro brasileiro?" (What do you think about Brazilian theater?), in which he analyzed the main currents of leftist theater in Brazil. In this essay, Boal explained that the intention of the event was to foster unity among a divided left-wing artistic community. Yet his essay turned out to be a broadside attack on the Teatro Oficina and the tropicalist movement in general. He critiqued the tropicalist movement on several grounds, claiming that it was "neo-Romantic," because it only attacked the appearances of society, and "homeopathic," in that it was only capable of criticizing through ironic affirmation of *cafonice* (bad taste). He asserted that tropicalist satire was "inarticulate" since it ultimately provided entertainment for privileged audiences, instead of shocking them: "[I]t intends to *épater*, but it only succeeds in *enchanter les bourgeois*." Finally, he argued that the tropicalist phenomena was "imported" since the musicians imitated the Beatles and the theater directors emulated the Living Theater (an experimental theater troupe from the United States). Other critics echoed Boal's allegation that the tropicalists were imitative. One journalist writing for *Última Hora* derided tropicalist musicians for "copying" foreign pop: "It's necessary to establish a parallel between the work of the young tropicalists and the English original. The Beatles demonstrate more clearly their creative impulses. It's basically a difference of cultural evolution."[23] In other words, for these critics, Tropicália was no more than a second-rate imitation of metropolitan models.

Boal concluded that Tropicália was misguided and potentially dangerous for left-wing artists because of its "absence of lucidity." He seemed to be most disturbed by the iconoclastic and ambiguous attitude of the tropicalists, and he vigorously defended his own camp, the *sempre de pé*, or "always standing," faction, which included the Teatro de Arena. He defended a binary, or "Manichaean," view of culture and politics that had no patience for ambiguity: "Let this be clear: the 'always standing' faction, its specific techniques, Manichaeanism and exhortation—all of this is valid, activating, and functional, politically correct, forward looking, etc., etc., etc. Nobody should be shy about exalting the people, which is what seems to have happened to the shamefaced left. . . . The dictatorship is Manichaean. Against it and against its methods left-wing art must rise up Manichaeistically."[24] The "politically correct" stance of Augusto Boal, rooted in the populist experience of the CPC, found little common ground with the anarchic and ironic attitude of the tropicalists.

The tropicalist musicians also maintained a dialogue with the visual arts, especially with Neorealismo Carioca and Nova Objetividade, two distinct currents based in Rio de Janeiro. Neorealismo shared many of the same characteristics found in Anglo-American pop art—a rejection of modernist "high" art; an interest in popular media such as graphic design, comics, and newspaper photos; experimentation with mass production; and a focus on quotidian urban life. In comparison with metropolitan pop art, however, the neorealists were more engaged in social and political critique.

Rubens Gerchman, for example, produced a series of paintings, *Os Desaparecidos* (The disappeared) (1965), based on stark black-and-white photographs of missing people, presumably the victims of military repression after the coup. Other Gerchman paintings from this period appropriated kitsch iconography of urban popular culture. *Concurso de Miss* (Beauty pageant) (1965) features a line of somewhat awkward-looking women in bathing suits with plastic smiles before a group of photographers and onlookers. Unlike Andy Warhol's Marilyn Monroe series, the female contestants representing various Brazilian states utterly lack glamour and fame.[25] Gerchman's *O rei do mau gosto* (The king of bad taste) (1966) is a multimedia piece incorporating the insignia from a local soccer team, a heart containing the words "Amo-te" (I love you) surrounded by ornate beveled glass, and a lacquered serving tray featuring two parrots, a palm tree, and the Sugar Loaf Mountain at sunset (plate 8).

The use of these items suggested that the "popular" could be found among the seemingly mediocre objects and emblems of the urban masses. His most famous piece from the 1960s, Lindonéia, was the inspiration for a tropicalist song by Caetano Veloso that will be discussed below.

The most radical innovator and theorist of Brazilian visual arts during the 1960s was Hélio Oiticica.[26] Much in the spirit of vanguard movements such as Dada, Oiticica was concerned with abolishing the separation between art and life. In other words, the question for Oiticica was not how reality was represented in art but how experiments in art could be applied to life. His conceptualization of vanguardist practice was not based on aesthetic innovation but rather on the creation of what Brazilian critic Mário Pedrosa called "ambient antiart" that would create sites and contexts for collective behavioral experiments. Art was to be an "experimental exercise in liberty" capable of transforming individuals through sensory experience.[27]

For Oiticica, the artist should be a "proposer of practices" and not a creator of artistic objects for passive contemplation.[28] In the early 1960s, he first experimented with ambient antiart that required the active involvement of spectator/participants. During this time, he developed a close relationship with members of the Mangueira samba school, who inspired him to explore the performative dimensions of visual art. His first experiment along these lines was the creation of parangolés, a series of multicolored and multilayered capes to be worn by active participants who become the work of art itself. The designation parangolé was a slang expression used in Rio de Janeiro to describe a spontaneous and sudden "happening" that produces joy. According to Oiticica's annotations, the use of parangolés requires "direct corporal participation," since "it beckons the body to move, to ultimately dance." [29] The first public exhibit of the parangolés in 1964 at the Museum of Modern Art featured samba dancers from Mangueira.

Oiticica further radicalized his experimentation with ambient antiart in 1967 when he presented the installation Tropicália at the collective show Nova Objetividade Brasileira at the Museum of Modern Art in Rio de Janeiro (plate 9). He conceived the project as a critique of international pop art and its Brazilian manifestations, seeking to create a "new language with Brazilian elements" by creating a three-dimensional ambient space inspired by the favela of Mangueira. The installation referenced the "organic architecture" of the favelas, the unfinished constructions, the vacant lots, and other material forms of an urban space in the process of formation. Oiticica described Tropicália as the "very first conscious, objective attempt to impose an obviously Brazilian image upon the current context of the avant-garde and national art manifestations in general." The work consists of two structures, called *penetráveis* (penetrables), made of wood and brightly colored printed fabric, which are reminiscent of *favela* shanties. Sand and pebble paths and tropical plants circle the structures, and live parrots flutter about in a large cage. The main *penetrável* invites the participant into a dark, labyrinthine passage at the end of which is a functioning television. The structure "devours" the participant in the incandescent glow of the televised image. Mindful of Oswaldian poetics, Oiticica called it the "most cannibalistic work of Brazilian art." [30] The use of such a ubiquitous symbol of modern communication placed within a shanty-like structure surrounded by parrots and flowered cloth underlined the disjunctions of modernity in a developing country, where gaps between the technological and the tropical, the modern and the archaic, the rich and the poor create stark contrasts. This sort of juxtaposition, which suggested that underdevelopment was inscribed in the process of conservative modernization in Brazil, would become a hallmark of tropicalist cultural production. The secondary *penetrável* is an open structure containing the inscription "Pureza é um mito" (Purity is a myth), a tropicalist maxim that suggests the impossibility of native authenticity.

There is some debate as to whether these manifestations in film, theater, and visual arts should be regarded as tropicalist. Antônio Risério has argued that "Tropicália was essentially dreamed up by Caetano" and in no way constituted a general artistic movement.[31] In fact, Tropicália only coalesced as a self-conscious movement in the field of popular music. Glauber Rocha's *Terra em transe*, Teatro Oficina's *O rei da vela*, and Oiticica's installation *Tropicália* were identified as tropicalist only after the emergence of the musical movement. In 1967, when these works were shown, they were not necessarily understood as part of the same cultural logic that cut across artistic fields. They were interpreted within the specific fields of film, theater, and visual arts, respectively. This being said, it is nevertheless important to recognize the profoundly dialogic nature of late-1960s cultural production in Brazil. Veloso himself has consistently affirmed that *Terra em transe* and *O rei da vela* were crucial events that revealed to him a "movement that transcended the sphere of popular music." [32]

Even within the more restricted realm of popular music, Risério's "Caetanocentric" appraisal underestimates the contributions of his Bahian cohorts and their allies, which are registered on tropicalist solo albums from 1968–69 by Gilberto Gil, Tom Zé, Os Mutantes, Rogério Duprat, Nara Leão, and Gal Costa. Even Veloso's sister, Maria Bethânia, who did not formally participate in the tropicalist movement, recorded a live album in 1968 featuring tropicalist songs. Veloso was the leading voice of Tropicália, especially after it coalesced as a formal movement, but he worked collectively with the Bahian group and in dialogue with artists in other areas who were articulating similar ideas.

THE RELICS OF BRAZIL: TROPICÁLIA AND ALLEGORY

The watershed cultural events of 1967, especially Glauber Rocha's *Terra em transe*, Teatro Oficina's *O rei da vela*, and Hélio Oiticica's *Tropicália*, signaled a revival of the modern allegory. In its classical Greek definition, allegory denotes any verbal or visual representation that "speaks otherwise" (*allos-agoreuein*), often generating meaning obliquely through figural abstractions. In Greco-Roman mythology and in biblical exegeses of the medieval and baroque periods, allegory was a mode of representation that evoked correspondences between material reality and the spiritual world. In the nineteenth century, Romantic poets rejected allegorical conventions as mechanical and arbitrary allusions. In opposition to the allegory, the Romantics privileged the symbol as a mode of representation that crystallized eternal and universal truths. Whereas the allegory merely alluded to a concept, the symbol was the very incarnation of the idea.

Modern formulations of allegory are particularly indebted to Walter Benjamin's critique of the Romantics in his study of the *trauerspiel*, the melancholic "sorrow play" of the German Baroque. Benjamin detected similarities between the baroque period and post–World War I Europe, which were both marked by decadence, and defended allegorical expression as particularly relevant to the dilemmas of modernity. The use of allegory is often identified with artistic expressions of political defeat or disillusionment.[33] Whereas the symbol constructed images of organic totality, Benjamin asserted, the allegory represented history as a heterogeneous ensemble of fragments: "Allegories are, in the realm of thought, what ruins are in the realm of things."[34] Glauber Rocha's *Terra em transe* and Teatro Oficina's staging of *O rei da vela* might be read as modern Brazilian *trauerspiel* in which the colonial past and the neocolonial present were rendered as spectacles of political defeat and decadence.

Not all tropicalist allegories of Brazilian history and culture were as caustic and despairing as *Terra em transe* and *O rei da vela*. One of the most striking national allegories of this period was Glauco Rodrigues's painting *Primeira missa no Brasil* (First mass in Brazil) (1971), produced after the height of the tropicalist movement but clearly inspired by its allegorical insights (plate 12). Rodrigues's painting was a tropicalist parody of a celebrated painting of the same name produced in 1861 by Vitor Meirelles, an academic artist of the late Romantic period in Brazil. Meirelles's painting represents the first mass celebrated by Portuguese explorers following the arrival of the fleet led by Pedro Alvares Cabral in 1500. In the painting, a priest and a retinue of clerics and soldiers, who seem to ascend toward the heavens, consecrate the newly discovered tropical lands in the name of Portuguese Christendom. Native Brazilians hang from trees and kneel reverentially on the ground to witness the event with great awe and curiosity. Meirelles's naturalist painting enacts two dominant themes of nineteenth-century Euro-American Romanticism: the epic encounter between Civilization and Nature and the catechism and domestication of the "noble savage."

Rodrigues maintained Meirelles's basic schemata with prelates and conquistadors ascending upward toward the left corner of the frame. Several Portuguese celebrants almost seem to have been lifted directly from the original painting. Yet Rodrigues's painting also features a host of anachronistic and displaced figures of diverse historical temporalities, social classes, and cultures. A white middle-class beach bum saunters by, observing the ceremony with casual interest. He is adorned with an indigenous feather headdress, a tooth necklace, and body paint, yet he also wears the sunglasses, yellow swim trunks, rubber sandals, and blue towel of a modern habitué of a Copacabana beach. Behind him to the right stand a *porta-estandarte* (flag bearer) and a *passista* (dancer) of a samba school from Rio de Janeiro. In the foreground, an *iawô* (initiate) of the Afro-Brazilian religion, Candomblé, sits in trance. In Meirelles's painting, the Indians are rendered as objects of nature or as reverent converts to the colonialist faith. In Rodrigues's painting, by contrast, two native Brazilians with their backs to the ceremony directly confront the viewer as if to question our perception of this foundational moment of the colonial enterprise. Aside from two cartoonish parrots and some tropical plants, there is no evidence of nature. There is only a white background, as if to suggest that the nation, past and present, cannot be apprehended as a coherent totality but only as an incomplete tableau of "so many irreconcilable Brazils," as one critic noted.[35] The religious solemnity of the first mass is humorously satirized in Rodrigues's carnivalesque allegory of Brazilian history and culture.

Veloso's song-manifesto "Tropicália," the opening track on his first solo album of 1968 (plate 3), is the most outstanding example of allegorical representation in Brazilian song. As a national allegory, the song evidences both the bitter despair of Rocha's film and the carnivalesque exuberance of Rodrigues's painting. The lyrics of "Tropicália" form a fragmentary montage of events, emblems, popular sayings, and musical and literary citations. Although unnamed, the most immediate referent in the song is Brasília, the monument to high modernist architecture and developmental modernization that became the political and administrative center of the military regime after 1964. "Tropicália" alludes to the trajectory of Brasília from a utopian symbol of national progress to a dystopian allegory of the failure of a democratic modernity in Brazil. Veloso has explained: "It was an image of great irony, a more or less unconscious expression of what it was like to be in Brazil and be Brazilian at that time: you'd think of Brasília, of the *planalto central* [central high plains] and you'd expect to derive a certain feeling of pride from the architecture, and yet it was not at all like that. The feeling was more like 'What a monstrosity!' And this is because Brasília was built, and then the dictatorship came, and so Brasília remained there as a center of this dictatorship."[36] In the song, Brasília is presented as a "monument" made of "papier-mâché and silver," suggesting that the brilliant grandeur of the exterior conceals a fragile structure, just as the triumphant completion of the futuristic capital obscured a larger context of underdevelopment and social inequality.

Veloso's "Tropicália" is also an ironic monument to Brazilian literature and culture that includes textual references to Romantic writer José de Alencar, Parnassian poet Olavo Bilac, composer Catulo da Paixão Cearense, and pop icons Carmen Miranda and Roberto Carlos. The song opens with a declamation that cleverly parodies a foundational text of national literature. As the sound engineer, Rogério Gauss, was testing the microphones for the recording, the drummer Dirceu extemporaneously parodied the *Carta de Pero Vaz Caminha*, a letter to the king of Portugal written after the Cabral fleet had landed on the South American coast in 1500. "When Pero Vaz Caminha discovered that the Brazilian land was fertile and lush, he wrote a letter to the king saying that all that is planted grows and flourishes. And the Gauss of that time recorded it." Attuned to aleatoric and comic gestures in vanguard music of the 1960s, the conductor-arranger of the session, Júlio Medaglia, decided to incorporate the anachronistic parody over the "primitive" sounds of drumbeats, bells, and high-pitched, birdlike whistles. Following the witty anachronism, the sound of a brass and string orchestra enters, creating an atmosphere of epic suspense and drama.

The song is narrated in the first person, as if Veloso himself were the main protagonist of this surreal journey through the heartland of Brazil. In the first stanza, the narrator positions himself as a leader surveying Brasília: "I organize the movement / I orient the carnival / I inaugurate the monument / in the central high plains of the country." The first refrain introduces a binary opposition between the modern and the archaic that structures the discourse of the entire song: "viva a bossa-sa-sa / viva a palhoça-ça-ça-ça." Bossa nova, the sophisticated "finished product" associated with modernity is coupled with palhoça, a type of mud hut common in the Brazilian interior. Subsequent refrains rhyme mata (forest) and mulata, Maria and Bahia, Iracema (the female protagonist of José de Alencar's Indianist novel), and Ipanema (the upscale beachfront neighborhood of Rio). Veloso's "Tropicália" updates the Oswaldian binary metaphor of the "forest and the school." Augusto de Campos would later note the song's affinities with Oswald de Andrade's modernist poetics, calling it "our first Pau-Brasil song."[37]

As the narrator approaches the entrance to the futuristic monument in the second stanza, spatial and temporal contexts collapse into the archaic realm: "the monument has no door / the entrance to an old, narrow, winding street." Inside the monument, we find "a smiling, ugly, dead child extending his hand" as if to plea for alms. More than any other, this passage resonates with the Benjaminian allegory: "Everything about history that, from the very beginning, has been untimely, sorrowful, unsuccessful, is expressed in a face—or rather in a death's head."[38] The specter of the dead child allegorizes the defeat of redistributive modernization and the maintenance of abject poverty.

Celso Favaretto has noted the ways in which "Tropicália" specifically allegorizes the Brazilian political context of the 1960s through references to right and left hands.[39] In the third stanza, for example, Veloso parodies a traditional samba–de roda, replacing the second phrase of the line "a mão direita tem uma roseira / que dá flor na primavera" (the right hand holds a rose bush / which flowers in the spring) with "autenticando a eterna primavera" (authenticating eternal spring), a phrase that suggests the willful manipulation of nature to project an image of eternal paradise. The subsequent phrase, however, undermines the idyllic scene with a pointed reference to scavenger birds, a sign of impending death when the Northeast backlands are afflicted by drought: "in the gardens the vultures circle over the sunflowers all afternoon." The left, meanwhile, is rendered as an armed bandit who incongruously tries to wield a gun using his wrist. His failure to act is compensated by an appeal to popular culture, suggested by the phrase "his heart jumps to a samba on the tambourine."

The final stanza alludes directly to the popular music scene of the 1960s. Unlike the metasongs of Chico Buarque and Edu Lobo, which reflect on the redemptive value of music, "Tropicália" satirizes the central conflict of post-1964 popular music between the second generation of bossa nova and the rock stars of the Jovem Guarda:

domingo é o fino da bossa
segunda-feira está na fossa
terça-feira vai à roça, porém
o monumento é bem moderno
não disse nada do modelo do meu terno
que tudo mais vá pro inferno meu bem

Sunday "O fino da bossa" is on
Monday is the pits
Tuesday on the farm, however
the monument is quite modern
you said nothing about the style of my suit
to hell with everything else my love

Elis Regina's popular television program "O Fino da Bossa," broadcast on Sunday afternoons, the *fossa*, a popular idiom denoting angst and depression used to describe a melodramatic vocal style from the 1950s, and the farm, a reference to rural Brazil, suggest a regression from the modern to the archaic. He also cites Roberto Carlos's hit song from 1965 and his personalized line of clothing. The song erupts euphorically in the final refrain—"viva a banda-da-da, Carmen Miranda-da-da-da"—which couples Chico Buarque's 1966 festival hit, "A banda," with Brazil's first international star for export.

With the repetition of the final syllable of "Miranda," Veloso also invoked Dada, an avant-garde project that sought to expose, and ultimately undermine, the social, cultural, and institutional mechanisms involved in producing and consuming an object recognized as "art." In the 1960s, pop artists enacted a similar attack on high modernism, epitomized by abstract expressionism, by generating representations of banal objects and icons of mass society such as the Campbell's soup can and Marilyn Monroe. Veloso once remarked that citing Carmen Miranda in this song "was like Andy Warhol putting the soup can in his painting."[40]

Several critics have interpreted tropicalist recycling of dated or banal material as a form of parody involving ironic ridicule akin to modernist practices oriented toward an aesthetic of rupture with past styles and cultural discourses.[41] Yet Veloso's "Tropicália" seems more attuned with pastiche, which maintains a neutral stance in relation to the past. According to Fredric

Caetano Veloso (right) and Gilberto Gil relax backstage in 1968. (Abril Imagens)

Jameson, pastiche is "devoid of any of parody's ulterior motives, amputated of the satiric impulse, devoid of laughter and of any conviction." It is a "blank parody" involving the "random cannibalization of all styles of the past," a characteristic of much postmodern cultural production.[42] Although tropicalist songs often convey a sense of ironic distance in relation to literary texts and cultural discourses that shaped Brazilian national identity, there are several instances in which they express a more "neutral" attitude proper to pastiche aesthetics.

Veloso's own reading of "Tropicália," especially his provocative reference to Carmen Miranda at the end of the song, suggests an aesthetics akin to pastiche. The song itself was not a musical pastiche of Carmen Miranda, since it made no mimetic reference to her unique vocal style. Instead, its relationship to pastiche aesthetics may be detected in the "neutral" way, free from sarcasm, in which her name is invoked as a cultural icon. Noting that his first exposure to American pop art at the XIX São Paulo Biennial in 1967 had "confirmed a trend we were exploring in tropicalismo," Veloso describes his relationship with Carmen Miranda, a figure who had become a "culturally repulsive object" for his generation:

> [Y]ou want to bring in an object that's culturally repulsive, so you go embrace it and then you dislocate it. Then you start to realize why you

chose that particular object, you begin to understand it, and you realize the beauty in the object, and the tragedy involved in its relationship with humanity . . . and finally you begin to love it. . . . But before that, there's a moment when you arrive at that neutral point, when you become uncritical in relation to that object. This was the case with Andy Warhol, who I think stayed at that point right to the end of his life: you cannot think that he is saying: "Look how this is tacky, kitsch, horrible, we should transcend it." Not at all; he's at that neutral point when the object is just the object: Bang! It's in your face and it has nothing to say about itself. So Carmen Miranda, at the time that I wrote "Tropicália," had reached that point of neutrality for me. . . . She had been recovered: a kind of salvation.[43]

Although not articulated explicitly as such, Veloso's commentary suggests that he was reading the past (i.e., Carmen Miranda) through the "neutral," although not necessarily dispassionate, lens of pastiche. He was not proposing a rupture with Carmen Miranda and all that she represented as a samba stylist and international emissary of Brazilian popular culture. By citing Miranda at the end of "Tropicália" and reflecting on the "tragedy" of her vexed relationship with the post–bossa nova canon, he was reading her as an allegory of Brazilian culture and its reception abroad.

The allegorical impulse in Tropicália was further developed on the group album Tropicália, ou panis et circencis, which featured the core members of the tropicalist group: Veloso, Gil, Tom Zé, Gal Costa, Os Mutantes, Rogério Duprat, and poets Torquato Neto and José Carlos Capinan. Nara Leão, the erstwhile "muse" of bossa nova and protest song, also participated after adhering to the tropicalist project. Favaretto has aptly described the album as the "tropicalist summa" that "integrates and updates the tropicalist aesthetic project and language experiments."[44] It was recorded in May 1968 and was released in late July. By October the album had already sold twenty thousand copies, which were strong sales for that time.[45]

Tropicália, ou panis et circencis was Brazil's first concept album integrating song lyrics, musical arrangements, visual material, and a text in the form of a discontinuous movie script on the backside of the album cover. Authored by Veloso, the movie script played with the idea of Tropicália as a media phenomenon. In the opening scene, a chorus of international celebrities sings "Brazil is the country of the future" as Veloso quips "this genre is out of fashion," an acerbic reference to patriotic samba-exaltação (samba-exaltation). Subsequent scenes featured various members of the tropicalist group discussing their musical project: Torquato Neto and Gal Costa ponder the meaning of references contained in several tropicalist songs, while Nara Leão and Os Mutantes argue about the merits of Brazilian music in relation to international pop. Tom Zé reads the concrete poetry journal *Noigandres* and takes notes. In the last scene, João Gilberto sits in his house in New Jersey (where he was living at the time), telling Augusto de Campos to inform the tropicalists that he is "looking at them from here." Veloso's homage to João Gilberto in the film script/liner notes reaffirmed the tropicalists' affinity with bossa nova and their position in the "evolution" of Brazilian popular music.

The album cover of *Tropicália, ou panis et circencis* was a parody of a bourgeois family photo (plate 1). Costa and Neto appear as a conventional, well-mannered couple; Gil sits on the floor in a bathrobe printed with tropical motifs holding a graduation portrait of Capinan; Duprat daintily holds a chamber pot as if it were a tea cup; Tom Zé plays the northeastern migrant, holding a leather satchel; Os Mutantes ostentatiously show off their guitars; and Veloso is seated in the middle holding a large portrait of Nara Leão wearing a floppy beach hat. The cover photo was a visual allusion to the title track of the album, "Panis et circenses" (Bread and circus) (Gil-Veloso), which satirized the conventions of a traditional bourgeois family. The title of the song and the album refers to the famous statement by the classical poet Juvenal, who expressed his disdain for ancient Roman citizens who were placated by the calculated use of "bread and circus." [46] In the song, a first-person poetic voice unsuccessfully attempts to rouse the family from its state of immobility and mediocrity: "I tried to sing / my illuminated song / I unfurled the sails over the masts in the air / I set free the lions and the tigers in the backyard / but the people in the dining room are busy being born and dying." Recorded by Os Mutantes with arrangements and sound effects by Rogério Duprat, "Panis et circenses" is reminiscent of several Beatles recordings of the time, which was no coincidence. [47]

When the tropicalist album appeared, it was heralded as a Brazilian response to The Beatles' *Sgt. Pepper's Lonely Hearts Club Band*. [48] The Beatles' famous concept album of 1967 was a major innovation in modern rock that was qualitatively different from their previous albums. A purposeful mix of various styles, it was a commentary on the history of popular music that self-consciously played with clichés of the British music hall tradition. In a comparable fashion, *Tropicália, ou panis et circencis* incorporated a broad array of old and new styles of national and international provenance such as rock, bossa nova, mambo, bolero, and liturgical hymns. Veloso has explained the concept behind the album: "Instead of working as a group in order to develop a homogeneous sound that would define a new style, we preferred to utilize several recognizable sounds from commercial music, making the arrangements an independent element that would clarify the song, but also clash with it. In a way, we sought to 'sample' musical scraps and we used the arrangements as ready-mades."[49] With arranger Rogério Duprat, the tropicalists were beginning to experiment with concepts and techniques that were current among vanguard composers and cutting-edge pop artists.

Their appropriations of dated material on the concept album oscillated between parody and pastiche. More parodic tracks included a slapstick rendition of the Cuban mambo "Três caravelas" (Three caravels) (Algueró-Moreu), a jocular pseudotribute to Christopher Columbus sung in a mixture of Spanish and Portuguese. Other songs were recorded in a manner that was remarkably "straight" and lacking in ironic distance. Veloso's rendition of "Coração materno" (Maternal heart), a melodramatic paean to motherly love and dedication, was strikingly genuine; any residual parodic effect depended solely on his position as a young pop star. The song was composed and recorded by Vicente Celestino, a pre–bossa nova radio singer who starred in several popular *chanchada* films. Within the context of the concept album, with its panoply of past styles, Veloso's rendition comes off more like a pastiche rather than a parody of Celestino's sentimental ballad. The album closed with a rendition of "Hino ao Senhor do Bonfim," the official hymn of the Bonfim Church in Salvador. The tropicalists recorded an upbeat version of the hymn, mixing traditional brass band processional music with bossa nova stylizations.

Tropicália, ou panis et circencis featured the other principle song-manifesto of the tropicalist movement, "Geléia geral" (General jelly), written by Gilberto Gil and Torquato Neto. The concept of *geléia geral* was first advanced by concrete poet and critic Décio Pignatari following an argument with modernist writer Cassiano Ricardo, who had suggested that the concrete poets would eventually have to relax their inflexible position regarding formal experimentation. Pignatari retorted that "in the Brazilian *geléia geral* someone has to exercise the function of spine and bone!"[50] In other words, vanguardist rigor was needed to provide form to the protean mélange of Brazilian culture as it was broadcast in fragments through the mass media. Torquato Neto appropriated the trope in a highly ambiguous fashion that simultaneously expresses critique and complicity with the *geléia geral*. Of all the songs on the concept album, "Geléia geral" was most closely aligned with the ironic stance of parody.

Gilberto Vasconcellos called attention to the juxtaposition of the "tropical universe and the urban-industrial universe" that occurs throughout "Geléia geral."[51] As discussed in Chapter 1, this binary structured Oswald de Andrade's "Brazilwood Manifesto," which attempted to reconcile the "forest and the school." Unlike Veloso's "Tropicália," which poses the opposition between the archaic and the modern as an aberration, "Geléia geral" is a buoyant song that proposed a synthesis. In the refrain, for example, the traditional folkloric dance *bumba-meu-boi* (buck my bull) and Brazilian *iê-iê-iê* merge into one dance: "É bumba-iê-iê-iê / É a mesma dança meu boi" (It's bumba-iê-iê-iê / It's the same dance my bull). By suggesting the possibilities of new cultural hybrids based on traditional dances and rock, the song challenged prevailing notions of cultural authenticity in Brazil. In a scene from the pseudoscript on the *Tropicália* album cover, Torquato Neto preempts criticism by expressing disingenuous anxiety over how a renowned Brazilian folklorist will interpret the song: "Do you think that Câmara Cascudo will think that we mean that *bumba-meu-boi* and *iê-iê-iê* are the same dance?"

Like Oswald's manifesto, "Geléia geral" also appropriates the symbolic repertoire of the Brazilian literary tradition in an effort to satirize the pomposity of "high" culture. This irreverent gesture was brilliantly enacted on the cover of Gil's 1968 tropicalist solo album (plate 4). Created by Rogério Duarte, Antônio Dias, and David Zingg, the album cover featured a photo of Gil dressed in the official attire of the Brazilian Academy of Letters, a group of forty peer-elected "immortals" consisting at that time entirely of white males. He is wearing bifocals similar to those used by Machado de Assis, the first president of the academy from 1897 until his death in 1908. Machado de Assis was of partial African descent, but his position as the most consecrated literary figure in Brazil gained him access to white elite social circles. The image of a black popular musician dressed as an "immortal" ridiculed the academy's elitism by making a subtle allusion to the ambiguous position of Machado de Assis and by implicitly questioning the academy's refusal to acknowledge the literary value of popular song.

"Geléia geral" is the most self-consciously "literary" composition of the tropicalist songbook in that it parodies ornamental language and conventional verse while also using montage techniques similar to those used by Oswald de Andrade. The first stanza invokes the figure of the official poet who praises Brazil's natural beauty.[52] Using a barrage of rhyming clichés that are reminiscent of the fin de siècle poetry, the song satirizes patriotic discourse and belles lettres pomposity:

> o poeta desfolha a bandeira
> e a manhã tropical se inicia
> resplandente, cadente, fagueira

num calor girassol com alegria
na geléia geral brasileira
que o *Jornal do Brasil* anuncia

the poet unfurls the flag
and the tropical morning commences
resplendent, refulgent, radiant
in joyous sunflower heat
in the general jelly of Brazil
that the *Jornal do Brasil* announces

Gil's flamboyant vocal delivery establishes ironic distance in relation to the patriotic celebration of tropical exuberance. Famous literary passages of consecrated writers are parodied throughout the text, including Gonçalves Dias's "Canção do Exílio" (Song of exile) (1843) and Olavo Bilac's "Hino da Bandeira" (Hymn to the flag) (1906). Rogério Duprat added musical citations of Carlos Gomes's opera *Il Gaurani* (1870) and Frank Sinatra's "All the Way." Even Oswald de Andrade, the literary and spiritual godfather of Tropicália, does not escape tropicalist parody in this song. His maxim from the "Cannibalist Manifesto," "a alegria é a prova dos nove" (happiness is the proof of nines), is followed by the line "e a tristeza é teu porto seguro" (and sadness is your safe harbor). Oswald's utopian "matriarchy of Pindorama" outlined in the 1928 manifesto is ironically heralded as the "country of the future," an allusion to flag-waving patriotism.

Shifting from Parnassian verse to modernist verbal montage, the middle of the song features a declamatory interlude in which Gil recites an inventory of quotidian sayings, clichés, and references to popular culture, forming an allegorical panorama of everyday life in Brazil. In this section, Torquato Neto's lyric recalls the *poemas piadas* (joke poems) of Oswald de Andrade's *Poesia Pau-Brasil* that stitch together fragments of verbal "ready-mades" devoid of poetic language.[53] The elliptical references describe public and private spheres of national life ironically exalted as the "relics of Brazil":

doce mulata malvada
um elepê de Sinatra
maracujá mês de abril
santo barroco baiano
superpoder de paisano
formiplac e céu de anil
três destaques da Portela

carne seca na janela
alguém que chora por mim
um carnaval de verdade
hospitaleira amizade
brutalidade jardim

sweet wicked *mulata*
an LP of Sinatra
passion fruit in April
baroque Bahian saint
superpower of the peasant
formica and blue skies
three highlights of Portela
dried meat in the window
someone who cries for me
a true carnival
hospitable friendship
brutality garden

These heterogeneous emblems of *brasilidade* recall García Canclini's description of popular culture as the product of "complex hybrid processes using as signs of identification elements originating from diverse classes and nations." [54] The modernist stereotype of the "sweet wicked *mulata*" — so reminiscent of the characters of Jorge Amado novels — is juxtaposed with an "LP of Sinatra," a foreign cultural icon adored by the Brazilian middle class. Further down, a grandiose stock phrase of patriotic poetry used to describe Brazil's blue skies, *céu de anil*, is coupled with a mundane industrial product, *formiplac* (formica). Images of a bucolic and folkloric Brazil are juxtaposed with banal items from an urban-industrial Brazil.

The critique of *brasilidade* turns mordant in the final two lines, which juxtapose "hospitaleira amizade" (hospitable friendship), a reference to Brazilian cordiality, and "brutalidade jardim" (brutality garden), a line from Oswald de Andrade's 1924 novel *Memórias Sentimentais de João Miramar*.[55] Oswald's phrase is particularly striking because it does not follow Portuguese syntax (i.e., "jardim da brutalidade") in which the garden would necessarily be the site of brutality. Instead, the phrase constitutes a cubist montage in which the two halves contaminate each other but never cohere. The garden and brutality coexist in contradictory juxtaposition. Oswald's phrase captures the ambivalent stance of the tropicalists, who were fascinated with the Edenic national mythology yet also cognizant of its ideological premises and insidious uses.

The military regime sought to represent Brazil as a peaceful "garden" even as it brutally suppressed its opposition. Oswald's paradoxical phrase, alluding to violence within a tropical arcadia, telegraphically encapsulates the drama of Brazil in the late 1960s as seen through the tropicalist lens.

Roberto Schwarz was the first to note the use of allegory in Tropicália.[56] According to him, the military coup had created the conditions for the revival of archaic social forces and retrograde cultural values. Yet the military regime was also committed to capitalist modernization by intensifying Brazil's integration into the international economy. The coup signaled a victory for the traditional landowning elite and for modernizing urban technocrats, such that, according to Schwarz, the "archaic world" became an "intentional instrument" of conservative modernization. By subjecting archaic or anachronistic emblems to the "white light of ultramodernity," the tropicalists generated an allegory of Brazil. The tropicalist allegory was painfully revealing — "like a family secret dragged out into the middle of the street, like treachery to one's own class." The private dramas of the bourgeoisie were conflated with the public life of the nation, a typical feature of allegorical representation, as Jameson has noted.[57] Schwarz conceded that, in its most caustic and ironic manifestations, Tropicália could "capture the hardest and most difficult contradictions of present intellectual production." Ultimately, however, he argued that the tropicalist allegory was an "absurdity" because it posited the simultaneous existence of the modern and the archaic, or, in economic terms, the developed and the underdeveloped, as an aberration and not as a contradiction to be resolved dialectically through social transformation.

Schwarz argued that the "anachronistic conjunction" of the archaic and the modern in tropicalist productions lacked critical value since "the 'ready-made' images of the patriarchal world and imbecilic consumerism start signifying on their own, in a shameless, unaestheticized fashion." In other words, the recycled images — generated by the conjunction of a traditional, patrimonial society and its attendant conservative, antimodern social values, on the one hand, and a modernized facade of consumer society, on the other — effectively lose their critical impact when they take on a life of their own. Once stripped of ironic intention, these images may be appropriated, reproduced, and acritically consumed within capitalist society. In short, they become affirmative and celebratory, instead of negative and ironic.

For Schwarz, the tropicalists posited an "atemporal idea of Brazil" in which these contradictions were fatalistically rendered as timeless "emblems" of national identity. As several critics subsequently noted, Schwarz's critique of the tropicalist allegory was informed by the work of Hungarian philosopher György Lukács.[58] In contrast to Benjamin, Lukács was highly critical of allegorical representation, arguing that it produced a phantasmagoric view of history that could not be grasped as a coherent, socially determined totality. According to this position, a politically efficacious work of art ought to propose or insinuate a dialectical resolution of historical contradictions. As a counterpoint to Tropicália, Schwarz referenced the work of Paulo Freire, the radical educator from Recife who directed a massive literacy campaign in the early 1960s under the auspices of the Movimento de Cultura Popular and with support from the progressive governor of Pernambuco, Miguel Arraes. Unlike Tropicália, Freire's literacy method was founded on a dialectical concept of history: illiteracy, poverty, and "the archaic nature of rural consciousness" could be overcome by popular education and redistributive modernization. In Schwarz's view, the tropicalist allegory reified historical contradictions (i.e., the coexistence of the archaic and the modern) by obscuring their basis in class society and pushing them into the realm of aesthetics.

Schwarz's analysis raises important questions about the roles of artists and intellectuals in Brazilian society and elsewhere. Comparing Paulo Freire to the tropicalists was somewhat analogous to comparing Martin Luther King Jr. to James Brown, or Noam Chomsky to Frank Zappa in the North American context. The comparison seems to overlook the considerable differences between the work of an activist engaged in popular education and artists elaborating a project of aesthetic renovation and cultural critique within the realm of mass media. Sartre made a useful distinction between intellectuals, who pursue theoretical and practical research, education, and political activism, and writers engaged in artistic production. For Sartre, the "true intellectual" is one who resists the universalist claims to bourgeois humanism, recognizes his or her own class position, and resolves to serve exploited classes by helping them obtain practical "knowledge of the world in order to change it." [59] Freire's literacy method, which has clear affinities with Sartre's principles, draws upon the everyday experience of learners so that they may attain literacy and "situate" themselves in class society. Sartre claims a separate, but related, role for the writer, which applies to artists in general: "The writer can testify only to his being-in-the-world, by producing an ambiguous object that suggests allusively." Veloso's own self-fashioning as an artist was informed by Sartre's notion of "being-in-the-world." [60] For a middle-class artist in urban Brazil at the end of the 1960s, this meant an encounter not only with military repression, student activism, and incipient guerrilla activity but also with domestic and foreign mass culture. The tropicalists produced an "ambiguous object" that shed light on the contradictions of Brazilian modernity but did not advance any concrete program for collective action.

The tropicalist allegory simply did not fit into Schwarz's dialectical view of history in which the simultaneous coexistence of the archaic and the modern only could be perceived as a series of absurd "anachronisms" or "a real historical abyss" produced by "a juncture of different stages of capitalist development." There is a curious parenthesis in Schwarz's essay that is particularly revealing in this regard: "For the purposes of this argument, we are not interested in the celebrated cultural variety of Brazil in which it is true that one finds African religions, indigenous tribes, workers sometimes sold as slaves, share-cropping and industrial complexes." What is crucial for him is the "systematic character of this coexistence." Schwarz brackets this "cultural variety" because for him it merely represents different *stages* of capitalist development. While it may be true that slavery, sharecropping, and industrial production represent different stages of capitalism, it is less clear that African religions and indigenous tribes may be located, presumably as premodern residues, within the same temporal scheme. His analysis presupposes the progressive development not only of productive forces but also of culture itself toward an ideal model of Western modernity.

Schwarz's text became a key point of reference for subsequent analyses of the movement but also drew criticism for its dialectical rigidity. Silviano Santiago, for example, argued that the absurd was a category of "traditional Western thought" used to discredit anything that did not conform to its logical premises. He criticized Schwarz for not paying adequate attention to the specificity of Brazilian culture: "It's essential to perceive that certain radical stances sometimes contain a dose of Eurocentrism that when confronted with the revolutionary 'Brazilian' object, belittles it to the point of destroying its combative potential simply because it doesn't follow the *model*."[61] Whereas Schwarz analyzes the coexistence of the archaic and the modern in Brazil as a symptom of its economic dependency in a global capitalist system, Santiago flags it as a mark of Brazil's constitutive difference in relation to metropolitan centers.

Instead of focusing on the contradictions of class society, Santiago understood Brazilian society in relation to its history of colonial domination that set up a hierarchy of cultural values in which Europe became the universal model. Colonialism set up a relationship of dependence in which Brazil was exploited for its raw materials and its cultural life was reduced to a pale imitation of metropolitan thought. Santiago interprets colonization as a "narcissistic operation" in which "the Other is assimilated as the reflected image of the conqueror." Despite its emancipative ends, the Hegelian-Marxist model of dialectical progress was not innocent of European ethnocentrism. According to Santiago, historical materialism was capable of understanding "minorities" (i.e., blacks and Indians) only in terms of "their total and definitive integration into the process of westernization." [62] Recognizing the agency of the Other within a global system of colonialism (and various forms of neo-colonialism), Santiago proposes the notion of "differentiated universality" to describe the way in which dependent cultures subvert Eurocentric hierarchies. Universality exists either as a "colonizing process" leading toward total westernization or as a "differential process" in which dependent cultures disrupt the colonial relationship by asserting their alterity in relation to metropolitan cultures.[63]

Several years later, Veloso himself responded to Schwarz in the song "Love, love, love" from the LP *Muito* (1978). He did not take issue with Schwarz's reading of Tropicália as an "absurdity," acknowledging with wry humor that Brazil may be *absurdo*, but it is not *surdo* (deaf):

> absurdo o Brasil pode ser um absurdo
> até aí tudo bem nada mal
> pode ser um absurdo mas ele nõ é surdo
> o Brasil tem ouvido musical que não é normal

> absurd Brazil may be absurd
> nothing wrong with that
> perhaps it is absurd but it can hear
> Brazil is extraordinary for its musical ear

At first glance, Veloso's punch line seems to confirm Schwarz's suspicions about the tropicalists' "fatalist" view of Brazil, but it also delineates a space of national difference premised on a specific form of cultural competence that frequently combines the pleasurable with the political.

MADE IN BRAZIL: TROPICÁLIA, MASS CULTURE, AND THE URBAN EXPERIENCE

As described in Chapter 2, most tropicalist singers and songwriters came from small towns in Bahia before moving to Salvador for schooling. In the mid-1960s, they moved to Rio de Janeiro and eventually to São Paulo, where they began to elaborate their musical project. São Paulo was the ideal site for the tropicalist movement. It was home to the concrete poets, the vanguardist composers and arrangers of the Música Nova group, and Os Mutantes, Brazil's first truly original rock band. The city also served as the base of operation for Brazil's largest television networks, TV Tupí and TV Record, although these two stations would soon be eclipsed by TV Globo in Rio de Janeiro. Perhaps more importantly, São Paulo was a city that was outside of prevailing standards of "good taste" defined largely by the cultural elite of Rio de Janeiro. Most tropicalist songs depict some aspect of urban life, from the disparities of uneven modernization to the shifting perceptions of technology, space, and affective experience. The tropicalists expressed fascination with the urban ambiance of São Paulo, with its large billboards, media networks, and heavy industries.

Veloso would later compose a famous tribute to São Paulo titled "Sampa" (the city's nickname) in which he reflected on his first impressions of the city during the tropicalist period. The song, featured on his 1978 LP *Muito*, conveys a sense of detached wonder in relation to this immense and unattractive industrial city that was so far removed from the glamour and style of Rio or the baroque charm of Salvador:

> é que quando cheguei por aqui
> eu nada entendia
> da dura poesia concreta de tuas esquinas
> a deselegância descreta de tuas meninas
>
> when I arrived here
> I understood nothing
> about the hard concrete poetry of your street corners
> the discrete inelegance of your girls

Above all, "Sampa" pays tribute to artists who "translated" the city for him, including the concrete poets Augusto and Haroldo de Campos, Rita Lee of Os Mutantes, José Agrippino de Paula (author of *Panamérica*), and the members of Teatro Oficina. The tropicalist movement was to some degree a product of the creative tension between the Bahians and the cosmopolitan cultural milieu they encountered in São Paulo.

Several tropicalist songs dramatized the experience of northeastern migrants who were forced to leave the impoverished rural Northeast to try to make a living in the large industrial capitals of center-south Brazil. Gilberto Gil's "Coragem para suportar" (Courage to persevere), for example, is reminiscent of *Show Opinião* songs in depicting the dire social conditions in the *sertão* that force people to migrate. Veloso's song "No dia que eu vim-me em-bora" (The day I left home) describes the sad farewell of a young man who, after leaving behind his family, realizes to his chagrin that his leather satchel, although cured, emits an awful stench as he travels "all alone to the capi-tal." In contrast, "Mamãe Coragem" (Mother courage) (Veloso-Neto), which was featured on the tropicalist concept album, describes an imaginary letter from a migrant who, after declaring he'll never return, consoles his mother by telling her to read a popular romance to keep from crying. The city offers him excitement, a chance to "play in carnival," and an opportunity to live independently and anonymously in a city "with no end."

In marked contrast to bossa nova songs, tropicalist compositions tend to eschew the convergence of nature and affective experience. One of Veloso's first tropicalist songs, which he composed while he was living in Rio de Janeiro, explicitly subverted the poetics of "ecological rationality" in bossa nova. In "Paisagem útil" (Useful landscape), from his first solo album (1968), technology becomes a surrogate for nature. The song's title is a parody of Tom Jobim's "Inútil paisagem" (Useless landscape), a bossa nova standard that declares with melancholy and pathos that the natural landscape (i.e., sky, sea, waves, wind, flowers) of Rio de Janeiro is "useless" in the absence of a lover. Veloso's song, in contrast, effaces nature altogether in favor of the luminous beauty of the Rio cityscape at night, with its "lights of a new dawn-ing" and its speeding cars that "appear to fly." The song suggests affinities with the avant-garde poetics of futurism in its celebration of the city lights, machines of velocity, and modern urban-industrial life. In the final stanza, Veloso conjures the moon, a celestial body often associated with romance in popular songs:

> mas já se acende e flutua
> no alto do céu uma lua
> oval vermelha e azul
> no alto do céu do Rio
> uma lua oval da Esso
> comove ilumina o beijo
> dos pobres tristes felizes
> corações amantes
> do nosso Brasil

> suddenly it lights up and hovers
> high in the sky a moon
> a red and blue oval

high in the sky over Rio
an oval moon of Esso
inspires and illuminates the kiss
of the poor sad happy
loving hearts
of our Brazil

At this point, Veloso's voice waxes melodramatic in the style of Orlando Silva, a great romantic crooner from the 1940s and 1950s.[64] The moon in "Paisagem útil" is most inauthentic: "the oval moon of Esso." Instead of the eternal, symbolic moon of nature, Veloso invokes a historically determined, allegorical moon produced by a multinational company. An incandescent logo of a North American oil company hovers above as a simulacrum of nature, yet the lovers find romance anyway under the sign of foreign capital.

As elsewhere in the developing world, the mass-mediated, larger-than-life icons of the American culture industry, including Hollywood stars and comic book heroes, have been ubiquitous in Brazilian cities at least since World War II. Several tropicalist songs evoke these figures much in the manner of American pop art such as Warhol's assembly-line screenprints of Marilyn Monroe and Roy Lichtenstein's dramatic cartoon paintings. As an "impure genre" that combines iconic and literary cultures and has mass appeal across class lines, comic strips epitomize the sort of hybrid cultural practices that emerged with modernization and urbanization.[65] One song from Veloso's 1968 album, "Superbacana" (Supergroovy), invokes the hyperbolic, pyrotechnic world of cartoon superheroes in command of an arsenal of technology used to defeat the forces of evil. Set to a fast-paced *frevo*, an up-tempo carnival rhythm, the song adopts the condensed, discontinuous narrative structure of comics, citing in rapid-fire succession a series of fragmented images and characters. Veloso introduces an imaginary Brazilian comic strip hero, "Superbacana," who flies around Copacabana and does battle with Uncle Scrooge (known in Brazil as "Tio Patinhas"), the miserly character in Donald Duck cartoons who controls economic power. Resistance to U.S. imperialism is humorously rendered as the epic struggle of a Brazilian cartoon superhero against the forces of evil represented by Uncle Scrooge and a battalion of cowboys. As one critic has observed, Veloso's "Superbacana" is reminiscent of José Agrippino de Paula's "pop-tropicalist" novel, *Panamérica*, in its portrayal of international confrontation between developed and underdeveloped societies.[66]

Another song based in part on the world of superheroes was "Batmacumba" (Gil-Veloso), featured on the tropicalist concept album and on Os Mutantes' first recording. The musical arrangement foregrounds the conga drums, combining a heavy rock beat with Afro-Brazilian rhythmic sensibilities. Along with several other tropicalist compositions, the formal structure of "Batmacumba" was indebted to concrete poetry in its use of verbal montage and nondiscursive syntax.[67] The song is based on one poetic fragment ("batmacumbaiêiê batmacumbaobá") containing a series of semantic units pertaining to popular comics (Batman), Brazilian rock (iê-iê-iê), and Afro-Brazilian religion, sometimes referred to as macumba (bá, obá). With each line of the song, a morpheme is dropped until only "bá" remains and then gradually expands to the original phrase. Augusto de Campos later transcribed "Batmacumba" as a visual poem with two triangular "wings" meant to suggest a bat in flight.[68] "Batmacumba" is perhaps the most hybrid song in the entire tropicalist repertoire. Its formal structure is based on concrete poetry, while its semantic elements make reference to sacred and secular cultural domains. Campos related to the song the literary conflicts of the 1920s: "Instead of the nationalist 'macumba for tourists' that Oswald [de Andrade] condemned, it seems that the Bahians decided to create a 'bat-macumba' for futurists."[69] By intentionally fusing these diverse elements, "Batmacumba" suggests that products of the multinational culture industry like Batman and rock have been "Brazilianized" and, conversely, that Afro-Brazilian religion is central to Brazilian modernity and not to a folkloric vestige of a premodern past.

As suggested by the songs discussed above, Gil and Veloso generally embraced São Paulo's mass-mediated commercial culture with palpable enthusiasm. Tom Zé, on the other hand, observed his new urban environment, which offered a dazzling array of commodities and media attractions, with irony and skepticism. His first solo album of 1968 may be read as a satiric chronicle of his first impressions of São Paulo, especially its aggressive capitalist culture. Recorded with two Jovem Guarda bands, Os Versáteis and Os Brazões, and arranged by vanguard composers of the Música Nova group, Damiano Cozzela and Sandino Hohagen, the album featured startling combinations of organ- and guitar-driven iê-iê-iê, rural sertanejo music, jinglelike ditties, experimental music, and the aleatoric noises of everyday urban life. It was originally released on Rozenblit, an independent label from Recife that went out of business in the 1970s. When the album was finally released on CD over thirty years later, critics heralded it as a lost treasure of Brazilian popular music, or, in the words of one critic, as the unjustly overlooked "side B of Tropicália."[70] The album cover (plate 2), somewhat reminiscent of Ruben

Gerchman's pop aesthetic, features a cartoon facade of a São Paulo street with neonlike signs and billboards advertising sales, discounts, bingo, toothpaste, gasoline, movies, free newspapers, raffles, striptease shows, and even blatant rip-offs like "Take 2, Pay for 3." A photo of the artist framed within a television screen appears under the advertisement "Grande Liquidação: Tom Zé" (Big sale: Tom Zé), an ironic acknowledgment that as a pop artist he too was a commodity for sale.

The album was conceived as a satiric critique of the culture industry with its false promises of bliss and plenitude for urban consumers. In some ways Tom Zé's perspective echoed the famous critique outlined by Theodor Adorno and Max Horkheimer, two leading Marxist theorists of the Frankfurt School who argued that the culture industry was a standardized system of "mass deception" that stifled individual creativity and critical thought. They argued that the culture industry "perpetually cheats its consumers" with promises of material abundance, freedom, and happiness but ultimately blinds them to the drudgery and exploitation of everyday life under capitalism.[71] Tom Zé advanced a similar critique in the liner notes to the album, which open with the wry observation: "We are an unhappy people, bombarded by happiness." He goes on to describe a world completely saturated by cheerful media images, in which "television proves on a daily basis that nobody can be unhappy anymore."

The song lyrics evoke an urban milieu replete with hurried businessmen honking in traffic, unscrupulous loan sharks offering easy credit, and models with glorious smiles selling products to the masses. One song, "Catecismo, creme dental e eu" (Catechism, toothpaste, and me), suggests that consumer capitalism has become the new bourgeois religion that indoctrinates the public to buy personal hygiene products:

> um anjo do cinema
> já revelou que o futuro
> da família brasileira
> será um halito puro, ah!

> an angel of the cinema
> has revealed that the future
> of the Brazilian family
> will be fresh breath, ah!

In another song, Tom Zé lampoons the social conventions that discriminate against the poor, who obviously do not have the means to fully participate in the culture of consumer capitalism. "Curso intensivo de boas maneiras" (Intensive course in good manners) parodied the elitist discourse of a well-known social columnist of the time, Marcelino Dias de Carvalho, who dispensed advice for gaining acceptance in "respectable" social circles: "First lesson: stop being poor / because it's quite unsightly."

In several compositions, he employed the musical form of hard-sell capitalism, the jingle, to great parodic effect. The song "Sem entrada, sem mais nada" (No down payment, nothing more), opens with the lament:

> entrei na liquidação
> saí quase liquidado
> vinte vezes, vinte meses
> eu vendi meu ordenado

> I went for the sale
> and was sold down the river
> twenty payments, twenty months
> I sold my salary

This warning against the dangers of easy credit is then ironically effaced by a celebratory jingle that serves as the refrain to the song:

> sem entrada, sem mais nada
> sem dor e sem fiador
> crediário dando sopa
> pro samba já tenho roupa
> oba, oba, oba

> no down payment, nothing more
> no pain, no guarantor
> credit is easy
> for the samba party I now have clothes
> oba, oba, oba

A parody of the classic samba by Noel Rosa, "Com que roupa?" (With which clothes?) (1933), about a poor man with no clothes to wear to a samba party, Tom Zé's song pokes fun at the hoopla, or "oba oba," surrounding credit-driven consumerism.

Tom Zé's "Parque industrial" (Industrial park), featured both on his solo album and on the tropicalist concept album, lampooned the civic pride generated by the inauguration of a new industrial complex. In the recording, a brass band and crowd ambiance evoke the official pomp of a military parade. The lyrics, sung by Gil, Veloso, Tom Zé, and Gal Costa, address the crowd using the *vós* imperative typically associated with liturgical rites and lofty patriotic discourse, which further reinforces the satiric effect of the song:

> retocai o céu de anil
> bandeirolas no cordão
> grande festa em toda nação
> despertai com orações
> o avanço industrial
> vem trazer nossa redenção

> touch up the blue sky
> streamers on a string
> a great national festival
> rise and hear the orations
> industrial progress
> has brought our redemption

As with "Geléia geral," the stock phrase of Parnassian poetry, *céu de anil*, announces the parodic gesture. If in Veloso's "Paisagem útil" nature is effaced by multinational capital, in "Parque industrial" it is subjugated to the state ideology of industrial progress. The sky has fallen, so to speak, into mundane immanence; it no longer evokes celestial transcendence. The fabled blue sky, symbolizing natural splendor, is subtly reduced to a polluted artifice that needs "touching up" for the grand occasion. The following stanzas satirize an array of consumer products vying for attention in the urban space: the billboards featuring tender airline stewardesses, the "bottled smile" that can be reheated for use, the working-class newspaper, and the tabloid magazine relating the "sins of a movie star."

As several critics have noted, "Parque industrial" satirizes developmentalist zeal, as suggested in the ironic claim that "industrial progress has brought our redemption."[72] Industrial development certainly had not brought "redemption" for millions of urban workers whose bargaining powers had been severely curtailed by the military regime. Furthermore, by 1968, the environmental effects of irresponsible development had begun to have horrendous consequences for many poor communities, most notoriously in Cubatão, an industrial city between São Paulo and the port of Santos.[73] Although the excessively sanguine language suggests satire, there is also a measure of pride in the modernization of Brazil. Tom Zé has claimed that the tropicalists "had a passion for the industrial park" since it was so important for the nation's development.[74] The finale ends with the resounding refrain in English that exalts, with a mixture of sarcasm and affirmation, export products that are "made, made, made / made in Brazil." As in most tropicalist songs, there is a mixture of critique and complicity in relation to the satirized object.

Veloso's exquisite pop song "Baby" may be understood as a companion piece to "Parque industrial." While Tom Zé ridicules blind faith in the redeeming powers of industrial production, Veloso satirizes unbridled consumption among the urban middle class. Using up-to-date youth lingo, the lyric parodies hard-sell advertisements, creating an inventory of all the items one "needs" to be happy and successful in consumer society: swimming pools, margarine, gasoline, ice cream, songs by Roberto Carlos and Chico Buarque ("Carolina"), and finally, English lessons, the key to success and a rite of passage for Brazilian middle-class youth. An anonymous voice of commercial publicity interpellates middle-class youth and creates needs for the consumer. It is not clear whether the song is critically questioning or affirming the value of these products. Gal Costa's demure and sensitive vocal interpretation suggests a degree of blissful satisfaction. The last stanza affirms: "I don't know, all is cool with me / all is peaceful with you / we live in the best city / of South America." Veloso has claimed that he was referring to Rio de Janeiro, where he had lived for a while before moving to São Paulo.[75] Given the climate of political conflict in Rio de Janeiro, the blithe celebration of the city is ambiguous. "Baby" can certainly be read as a song that was "alienated" from the harsh reality of urban Brazil under a dictatorship, but it can also be interpreted as an ironic critique of complacency and consumerism. All of these tropicalist songs are marked by similar ambivalence in relation to the mass media and consumerism.

ATENÇÃO! TROPICÁLIA AND POLITICAL VIOLENCE

Although most tropicalist songs were musically upbeat and jubilant, quite often they conveyed, both subtly and overtly, an atmosphere of violence and official repression in Brazilian cities during the late 1960s. In March 1967, hard-liners within the military assumed control of the government under the leadership of a new president, Artur da Costa e Silva. The tenuous alliance between conservative civilian politicians and the military leadership unraveled, while more radical sectors of the opposition intensified their campaign against the regime. In early 1968, middle-class university and high school students staged a series of protests in Rio de Janeiro over rising fees,

Art and commerce. Caetano Veloso exhibits a toy stove in 1968.
(J. Ferreira da Silva/Abril Imagens)

poor facilities, and budgetary cuts for education. During one demonstration in March, a young student was shot and killed by the military police, provoking another round of antigovernment rallies that were violently suppressed. Around the same time, metalworkers staged strikes in Contagem, a town in Minas Gerais, and in Osasco, an industrial suburb of São Paulo.

In late June 1968, broad sectors of civil society, including students, professors, artists, clergy, workers, and liberal professionals participated in a massive demonstration known as the *Passeata dos cem mil* (March of one hundred thousand) in downtown Rio de Janeiro. Several key figures of MPB appeared at the event, including Gil, Veloso, Chico Buarque, Edu Lobo, Paulinho da Viola, Milton Nascimento, and Nana Caymmi, along with José Celso, Ítala Nandi, Renato Borghi of the Teatro Oficina, Cinema Novo actor Paulo Autran, and writer Clarice Lispector. The march took place without incident, but the government reacted immediately by prohibiting further public demonstrations. Violent confrontation in the streets was not limited solely to police repression. In September 1968, students of the conservative Mackenzie University attacked the School of Philosophy of the University of São Paulo, which was noted for its left-wing sympathies. Members of the CCC, the anticommunist paramilitary organization responsible for attacks on the Teatro Oficina, participated in the siege, injuring several students and destroying the school's main building. A month later, police arrested nearly a thousand members of the UNE, who were meeting clandestinely in Ibiúna, a small town in the interior of São Paulo.

As opportunities for nonviolent opposition in civil society diminished, greater numbers of antiregime militants joined clandestine guerrilla organizations. The earliest acts of armed resistance to military power took place soon after the coup of 1964 but only really began to have an impact in 1968. Dissidents of the Brazilian Communist Party, which generally eschewed armed struggle, formed several of the most important groups. The most celebrated novel of the period, Antônio Callado's *Quarup* (1967), portrayed the political and existential dilemmas of a left-wing priest who leaves the Catholic Church to join a rural guerrilla movement. Of the nearly three dozen armed organizations, however, most were based in the urban areas and involved few artists and intellectuals. The emergence of an armed opposition movement marked a turn away from symbolic activism associated with the CPC and postcoup cultural protest in which artists and intellectuals sought to fashion themselves as a revolutionary vanguard that would "raise consciousness" among the masses. Alex Polari, a member the Vanguarda Popular Revolucio-

Brazilian artists participate in the March of One Hundred Thousand in June 1968. In the front row, from left to right: Edu Lobo, Ítala Nandi, Chico Buarque, Aruíno Colassanti, Renato Borghi, José Celso Martinez Corrêa, an unidentified student, Caetano Veloso, Nana Caymmi, Gilberto Gil, and Paulo Autran. Placards express solidarity with the student movement and denounce censorship and repression. (Hamilton Corrêa/Agência JB, *Jornal do Brazil*)

nária (VPR), claimed that the guerrilla movement emerged "without artists, poets, critics, novelists, dramatists, dancers, therapists, writers." Corroborating this view, Ridenti has shown that left-wing artists constituted less than 1 percent of the guerrilla movement.[76]

The most prominent guerrilla leader, Carlos Marighella, a member of the Ação Libertadora Nacional (ALN), argued that the guerrilla movement was the vanguard of revolutionary transformation. To this end, guerrilla organizations robbed banks to fund their operations, raided arsenals for guns and munitions, and bombed army barracks and U.S. military installations. The most notorious operation involved the ALN and the Movimento Revolucionário 8 (MR-8), which kidnapped the ambassador of the United States, Charles Elbrick, in September 1969. In exchange for the ambassador, the government was forced to broadcast the group's revolutionary manifesto on all

1. *Tropicália, ou panis et circencis* (1968)
(Courtesy of Universal Records)

2. *Tom Zé*, 1968 (Courtesy of Tom Zé)

3. *Caetano Veloso* (1968)
(Courtesy of Universal Records)

4. *Gilberto Gil* (1968)
(Courtesy of Universal Records)

5. *Gal Costa* (1969)
(Courtesy of Universal Records)

6. *Jorge Ben* (1969)
(Courtesy of Universal Records)

7. Rubens Gerchman's *Lindonéia, a Gioconda dos subúrbios* (1966)
(Gilberto Chateaubriand Collection. Photo courtesy of Rubens Gerchman)

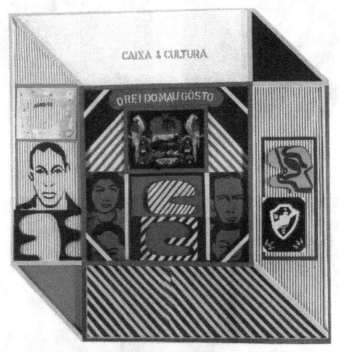

8. Rubens Gerchman's *O rei do mau gosto* (1966)
(Luis Buarque de Hollanda Collection. Photo courtesy of Rubens Gerchman)

9. Hélio Oiticica's *Tropicália* (1967) (Photo by César Oiticica Filho/Projeto Hélio Oiticica)

10. Hélio Oiticica's *Seja marginal, seja herói* (1968) (Projeto Hélio Oiticica)

11. Hélio Eichbauer's scenography for act 2 of *O rei da vela*, produced by the Teatro Oficina (1967). (Photo courtesy of Hélio Eichbauer)

12. Glauco Rodrigues's *A primeira missa no Brasil*, 1971.
(Gilberto Chateaubriand Collection. Photo courtesy of Glauco Rodrigues)

Brazilian radio stations and to free fifteen imprisoned guerrillas, allowing them to go into exile in sympathetic nations. With the success of this guerrilla operation, the VPR carried out kidnappings of Japanese and West German diplomats in 1970. With each operation, the government intensified efforts to liquidate the guerrilla movement. Clandestine organizations were brutally suppressed, and their members were invariably tortured and often murdered once apprehended by military agents.

Caetano Veloso has claimed that the tropicalists secretly admired Marighella and other guerrilla leaders, which was evident in their tribute to Ché Guevara in "Soy loco por tí, América" (discussed below). Fernando Gabeira, a former member of the MR-8 who participated in the Elbrick kidnapping, recalls listening to a song while he was hiding from his eventual captors in which Gilberto Gil makes a veiled reference to Marighella, who had been assassinated in São Paulo by police agents that same year.[77] He was likely referring to Gil's song "Alfômega," featured on Caetano Veloso's second solo album (1969), in which Gil exclaims "iê-ma-ma-Marighella" at one point in the song. Polari has asserted that the tropicalists were "in tune" with his sensibility: "[T]ropicalismo and its diverse manifestations were without doubt the perfect cultural expression for that which we incipiently represented in politics."[78] More conventional protest singers, notably Geraldo Vandré, paid homage to the guerrilla struggle in several songs from his 1968 album *Canto Geral*, but Polari was more interested in the countercultural attitude of Tropicália, which seemed to promise new ways of integrating politics, individual behavior, and artistic practice.

Several songs on the concept album, *Tropicália, ou panis et circencis*, alluded to a general context of political violence in the urban areas. The opening track, "Miserere Nobis" (Gil-Capinan), critiques the ideological and coercive mechanisms that maintain structures of inequality in Brazil. The song begins with solemn chords of a church organ, abruptly interrupted by the ring of a bicycle bell, followed by the upbeat strumming of an acoustic guitar. Gil intones the liturgical Latin phrase of the title, which venerates the nobility of poverty, but then subverts it by questioning the promise of future redemption: "[I]t's in the always will be, oh, mamma." Expressing impatience with the fatalistic acceptance of poverty, the song calls for equality in the here and now. Given the church's historic complicity in maintaining the status quo in Brazil, it was vulnerable to critique by the antiregime opposition. But the song should not be read as an indiscriminate attack on the Catholic Church, which was at the time politically divided among progressive, conservative, and moderate wings. Its ranks included several important opposition leaders, notably

Dom Helder Camara, the archbishop of Olinda and Recife, and Dom Paulo Evaristo Arns, the archbishop of São Paulo, who would later organize a scathing report on the use of torture by successive military regimes in Brazil.[79]

"Miserere Nobis" might be interpreted instead as a denunciation of complacency, whether spiritual or political, in the face of injustice. The tone of irreverence and defiance intensifies in the final stanza: "Let us spill wine on the tablecloth, soaked in wine and stained with blood." The line ironically alludes to transubstantiation, in which wine symbolically becomes the blood of Christ, but also insinuates a climate of violence. Toward the end of the song, Gil spells out, letter by letter, the words "Brasil-fuzil-canhão" (Brazil, rifle, cannon), a message that was perceptible to attentive listeners but subtle enough to avoid censorship.

In another song from the tropicalist concept album, "Enquanto seu lobo não vem" (While Mr. Wolf is away), Caetano Veloso creates a frightening, surrealistic view of Rio de Janeiro based on the "Little Red Riding Hood" fable. Beginning as an amorous invitation to "take a walk in the forest," the song proceeds to make subtle references to street demonstrations and rural guerrilla movements: "Let's travel through the United States / of Brazil / Let's travel clandestinely." This invitation may be read as an allusion to the exodus of student leaders and urban guerrillas from the cities to avoid arrest and to organize rural *focos*, moving pockets of revolutionary resistance in the hinterland.[80] In the final passage, references to the political context are no longer oblique: "let's go underneath the streets / underneath the bombs, the flags / underneath the boots." The presence of bombs, flags, and boots clearly suggests guerrilla activity and official repression. As Veloso sings these words, Gal Costa repeatedly intones in a high distant voice "os clarins da banda militar" (the clarions of the military band) that reinforce the presence of official order.

The foregrounding of political and cultural conflicts is most pronounced in "Divino maravilhoso" (Divine marvelous), a rock song written by Veloso and Gil. Gal Costa performed this song at the TV Record music festival of 1968 and then later featured it on her first solo album from 1969 (plate 5). In this song, Costa employs the sort of rock histrionics that were typical of American female vocalists like Janis Joplin or Grace Slick of Jefferson Airplane. Toward the end of 1968, the tropicalists adopted the title as the name of their television program on TV Tupi. "Divino maravilhoso" dramatically expressed the mood of the late 1960s, which was simultaneously an exciting period of countercultural experimentation and severe political repression. Nearly every line begins with the warning "atenção!" (attention) leading up to the repeating refrain, "everything is dangerous, everything is divine marvelous." The second stanza urges the listener to "pay attention to the stanza, to the refrain" of the song while suggesting that it is necessary to reflect critically on their meaning. In this sense, it is another metasong on the position of the artist, the role of reception, and the primacy of open interpretation. The song also calls attention to the *palavra de ordem* (political slogan) and *samba-exaltação*, suggesting a critique of left-wing orthodoxy, on one hand, and conservative patriotism, on the other.

The final stanza alludes to the very real dangers of armed conflict between military agents and opposition groups:

> atenção para janelas do alto
> atenção ao pisar no asfalto o mangue
> atenção para o sangue sobre o chão
>
> pay attention to the windows up high
> pay attention while stepping on asphalt the swamp
> pay attention to the blood on the ground

The reference to "windows up high" is oblique, but one might speculate that it is an allusion to police agents who took positions in the high-rise buildings of the downtown area during protest marches. Political conflicts are situated within a social context in the next line, which hints at the distance between the ideals of modernization and the reality of precarious infrastructure, contained in the opposition asphalt/swamp (i.e., urbanized center vs. underdeveloped periphery). The aftermath of political violence—blood on the ground—bears witness to military repression.

Other tropicalist songs addressed the violence of everyday life in Brazilian cities and how it affected those not directly involved in contesting the regime. Veloso's "Lindonéia," performed by Nara Leão on the tropicalist concept album, narrates the story of a young woman from the working-class suburbs of Rio who mysteriously "disappears" in the bustle of the city. The song was directly inspired by Ruben Gerchman's print *Lindonéia, a Gioconda dos subúrbios*, a rendering of Leonardo da Vinci's "La Gioconda" (plate 7). Gerchman's portrait depicts a young female victim of domestic violence with a swollen lip and a black eye. A glass frame engraved with kitsch flowerlike designs surrounds the battered image of Lindonéia (i.e., *linda/feia*, or beautiful/ugly). Over the frame an inscription recalls the headlines of the crime page in the popular press: AN IMPOSSIBLE LOVE—THE BEAUTIFUL LINDONÉIA—DIED INSTANTLY AT AGE 18. Veloso's musical rendering of Gerchman's Lin-

donéia imagines her life before she disappears "behind the mirror" and re-appears "in a photograph on the other side of life."

Veloso's "Lindonéia" is a bolero, a Cuban genre of love song noted for its sentimentality and melodrama that was popular in Brazil in the 1940s and 1950s. The urban Brazilian sophisticates who created and consumed bossa nova regarded the bolero as the epitome of Latin American kitsch associated with working-class taste, which is precisely why Veloso used this form for a song about a poor suburban woman. The song describes Lindonéia's quotidian life as a single woman of color in the city, referencing the ubiquitous presence of the mass media, urban violence, and police surveillance. Favaretto has speculated that Lindonéia is a domestic servant from the working-class periphery who escapes from her tedious existence by consuming radio and television *novelas* (soap operas).[81] That she "disappeared in indolence, in progress, in the hit parade" may suggest that she drifted into the fantasy world of mass culture. Yet the legalistic terms that describe her in the song—*solteira* (single), *cor parda* (brown-skinned)—are denominations used in the census and police reports, which suggest that Veloso may have also read Gerchman's painting more literally. In either case, Veloso's song portrayed the experience of a marginalized urban woman, focusing on her solitary existence and lack of options in life.[82]

"Lindonéia" also alludes to the violence and repression of quotidian life in the city under military rule:

> despedaçados, atropelados
> cachorros mortos nas ruas
> os policiais vigiando
> o sol batendo nas frutas, sangrando
> ai, meu amor
> a solidão vai me matar de dor

> ripped to pieces, run over
> dead dogs in the street police
> surveilling the scene
> the sun hitting the fruit, bleeding
> ay, my love
> the pain of solitude will kill me

Within the context of late-1960s Brazil, the trampled dogs recall the victims of state violence. The reference to fruit in the sun suggests tropical abundance, but even this cheery image is undermined by the gerund "bleeding."

This image is followed by the repeating refrain "ai, meu amor / a solidão vai me matar de dor" (ay, my love / the pain of solitude will kill me), an obvious cliché that, unlike the rest of the song, conforms to the poetic conventions of the bolero form. Veloso's songs oscillated constantly between personal and public registers, suggesting how official repression circumscribed the everyday life of urban citizens, even those who were not directly engaged in opposition struggles.

FIM DO MUNDO: TROPICÁLIA ON THE MARGINS

In an interview from 1968, Caetano Veloso remarked: "I cannot deny where I live, nor can I forget what I have read."[83] For artists and intellectuals situated on the periphery of global political and economic power, the dialectic between sense of place and cosmopolitan affinities is often simultaneously a source of anxiety and inspiration. Veloso was, of course, living under a military dictatorship in an unevenly developed nation. He was "reading" the Beatles, Bob Dylan, and Jimi Hendrix, as well as Jean-Paul Sartre, Jean-Luc Godard, the concrete poets, and Oswald de Andrade.

Since the early 1920s, samba composers and musicians had assimilated musical information from abroad, including tangos from Argentina, especially jazz and fox-trot from the United States, and boleros from Cuba. The first generation of bossa nova dialogued with West Coast jazz, and the Jovem Guarda embraced American rock 'n' roll. Even the "nationalist-participant" artists were influenced by Latin American *nueva canción* (new song) and, perhaps to a lesser extent, American antiwar protest singers. The tropicalists, of course, drew freely from British and American rock, Latin American rhythms, and international vanguard music. The lyrical content of most Brazilian popular music of the 1960s, however, focused primarily on local or national contexts. In general, tropicalist songs were no different in this regard, yet there were notable exceptions that situated Brazil within Latin American and/or global contexts.

Tom Zé occasionally advanced anti-imperialist critiques that were similar to agitprop songs of the CPC in the early 1960s. One song from his first album, "Profissão ladrão" (Profession thief), described a poor northeastern migrant with "many professions" in the informal economy who is arrested for petty theft. In long convoluted verses reminiscent of rapid-fire *embolada* singing from the northeastern *sertão*, the arrested man protests to the police officer, reminding him that theft and corruption is rampant among all classes.

Only the poor are stigmatized for their transgressions while the wealthy and powerful are often rewarded, as suggested in the proverb of the fourth stanza:

> Sei que quem rouba um é moleque
> aos dez, promovido a ladrão
> se rouba cem, já passou de doutor
> e dez mil, é figura nacional
> e se rouba oitenta milhões . . .

> I know that he who robs another is a waif
> after ten, he's promoted to thief
> if he robs a hundred, he becomes a respected expert
> and ten thousand, he's a national celebrity
> and if he robs eighty million . . .

At this point, Tom Zé inserted a pop instrumental interlude driven by a brass section that contrasts sharply with the colloquial discourse and vocal delivery of the northeastern protagonist. This ironic juxtaposition of musical styles sets the stage for the punch line to the unfinished verse:

> é a diplomacia internacional
> a "Boa Vizinhança" e outras transas

> it's international diplomacy
> the "Good Neighbor" and other schemes

When the entire nation (at the time Brazil's population was around 80 million) is exploited, it is called "international diplomacy," exemplified here by the "Good Neighbor" arrangement between Brazil and the United States during the 1940s. Tom Zé's use of proverbial knowledge to critique global power in this song is comparable to strategies later employed by postcolonial artists such as Bob Marley and Fela Kuti.

Another key tropicalist song, "Soy loco por tí, América" (I'm crazy for you, America) (Gil-Capinan), positioned Brazil within the context of anti-imperialist struggle in the hemisphere. First recorded by Caetano Veloso on his solo album of 1968, the song made an appeal to Latin American solidarity, which suggested that the tropicalists were aware that their movement had continental implications.[84] The appeal to *latinoamericanidad* operated on a musical level as well. The song mixed several different Latin American rhythms, such as Colombian *cumbia* and Cuban mambo, and its lyrics were in *portunhol*, a mixture of Portuguese and Spanish. For Augusto de Campos, the song represented "anti-Monroe Tropicalismo," since it implicitly denounced

North American dominance in the hemisphere as sanctioned by the Monroe Doctrine.[85] Like Eldorado, the fictive nation depicted in Glauber Rocha's *Terra em transe*, the song is meant to transcend nationality. In Capinan's lyrics, all national symbols are elided; only the "sky serves as the flag" for this "country without a name." The central though unnamed icon of the song is Ché Guevara, the Argentine-born Cuban revolutionary who was hunted down and killed by the Bolivian army in 1967. The Brazilian regime prohibited the circulation of his name in the mass media. In "Soy loco por ti, América," he is simply referred to as "el hombre muerto" (the dead man). The song shares affinities with protest music in its expression of redemptive hope that Guevara's vision might be consummated "before the definitive night falls over Latin America."

On his second solo album (1968), Gilberto Gil recorded "Marginália II" (Gil–Torquato Neto), a song that explicitly situates Brazil within the context of Third World struggles. Although the lyrics are somewhat melancholic, invoking an image of Brazil as the *tristes tropiques*, the music is upbeat and affirmative, based loosely on the northeastern *baião* rhythm with brass arrangements. Beginning with the dramatic lines "I, Brazilian, confess," Torquato Neto's lyrics offer the revelation of guilt, affliction, degradation, secrets, and dreams to an imagined audience of compatriots. The entire song oscillates between a tone of dramatic seriousness and blithe sarcasm. One line, for example, quips, "[T]his is the Third World, ask for your blessing and go to sleep," which may be read as an ironic critique of religious fatalism.

In the final stanza, Neto parodies "Canção do Exílio" (Song of exile), by Romantic poet Antônio Gonçalves Dias, which begins with the lines: "Minha terra tem palmeiras / onde canta o sabiá" (My land has palm trees / where the song-thrush warbles). In sharp contrast, Neto's lyric made explicit reference to political violence and economic dependency:

> minha terra tem palmeiras
> onde sopra o vento forte
> da fome do medo muito
> principalmente da morte . . .
> a bomba explode lá fora
> agora vou temer
> oh yes nós temos banana
> até pra dar e vender
>
> my land has palm trees
> where strong winds blow

of hunger and great fear
mostly of death . . .
the bomb explodes outside
now I have fear
oh yes we have bananas
even to give away and sell

"Canção de Exílio," probably the most parodied work of the Brazilian literary canon, expressed a longing for an Edenic tropical homeland of natural beauty that modernist writers such as Oswald de Andrade, Murilo Mendes, Cassiano Ricardo, and Carlos Drummond de Andrade found so useful for ironic appropriation.[86] In his poem "Canto do regresso à pátria" (Song of the return to the fatherland) (1925), for example, Oswald de Andrade substituted "palmeiras" (palm trees) with "Palmares" (the largest and most famous runaway slave community in Brazilian history), a reference to a history of oppression and resistance. In parallel fashion, Torquato Neto replaced Gonçalves Dias's images of bucolic tranquillity with allusions to political upheaval and fear under military rule. The last two lines cited the title of an old samba, "Yes, nós temos bananas" (1938), which satirized Brazil's status as a producer of raw materials for export. By the 1960s, of course, Brazil was no longer only a producer of raw materials and certainly did not conform to the "banana republic" stereotype, yet Torquato Neto's citation served as a reminder of its subaltern position in the global economy.

The refrain of the song, "aqui é o fim do mundo" (the end of the world is here), which is repeated several times, further reinforces a position of marginality. An idiomatic expression, the phrase expresses something like "we're in the middle of nowhere" while maintaining residues of more apocalyptic connotations. In subverting the ideal of Brazil as a serene tropical paradise, "Marginália II" stakes out a political and ethical position in global terms. In this sense, marginality connotes not only a political and economic reality but also a critical position vis-à-vis dominant nations. More than any other tropicalist song, "Marginália II" presaged the more overtly third worldist stance of Gil's work in the 1970s.

CONCLUSION

Tropicália was a cultural movement articulated primarily in popular music but with significant manifestations in other artistic fields. Inspired by the radical iconoclasm of Oswald de Andrade, Tropicália proposed a rereading of Brazilian culture that critiqued the nationalist and populist assumptions that oriented much of the protest culture being produced at the time. The vehicle of this critique often involved the cultural products originating from, or mediated by, the United States and Europe, which elicited charges of political alienation and inauthenticity. José Ramos Tinhorão, for example, suggested that there was an organic link between the international orientation of Tropicália and the economic program of the military regime with its heavy emphasis on multinational capital investment. In his estimation, the tropicalists "served as a vanguard for the government of 1964 in the realm of popular music." [87] Among other limitations, this homology does not encompass the ways in which Tropicália foregrounded the glaring social contradictions and the repressive mechanisms of modernization under military rule. The tropicalists elaborated their own critique of the conservative Right, participated in public manifestations against authoritarianism, and recorded songs that alluded to a context of violence in urban Brazil.

As hopes for political redemption began to fade, the tropicalists made use of allegorical representations to reflect on some of the contradictions of modernity in Brazil. At the same time, they embraced the urban experience, with its plethora of mass-mediated images and sounds, and sought engagement with a cultural industry increasingly subjected to the interests of the regime. Although tropicalist recordings provoked controversy among artists, critics, and fans, the censors largely ignored them. As the tropicalists gained visibility and notoriety in 1968, however, their irreverent performances would prove vexing for the military regime.

4
IN THE ADVERSE HOUR
TROPICÁLIA PERFORMED
AND PROSCRIBED

To fully appreciate the controversy generated by Tropicália, it is necessary to remember that many MPB artists, particularly the protest singers, maintained an ambivalent, if not antagonistic, relationship with the mass media. Sérgio Ricardo, the artist who was booed off stage at the 1967 TV Record festival, has provided insights into the tension between committed artists and media professionals. Moments before his disastrous performance, Ricardo remembers a backstage encounter with Paulo Machado de Carvalho, the station's owner:

> In that dressing room corridor of the Paramount Theater, two antagonistic universes whose alliance had led to stagnation confronted each other. One universe presented its artistic product, and the other facilitated its sale with one motivation in mind: profit. One side was interested in prestige and consecration; the other in money. Both sides depended on each other. Business is based on hard mathematics, in which some products are replaced by others when sales decline. Art is dynamic and free by nature and so when it becomes dependent on anything, it stagnates and only the worst products survive.[1]

Although not intentional, Ricardo's denunciation of the "universe" of mass media resonates with Frankfurt School analyses of the "culture industry" as a total system that degrades art by reducing it to a mere commodity. He seems to embrace a typically modernist position that art is essentially autonomous ("free and dynamic by nature") and only "stagnates" when co-opted by the media.

The tropicalists began with the assumption that cultural production in the age of mass media was not an autonomous or "free" domain. By publicly advocating "pop" following the 1967 TV Record festival, Gil and Veloso implicitly acknowledged that art was ultimately a commodity for mass consumption even if it expressed opposition to dominant political and cultural institutions. Veloso stated as much in the fake movie script written for the back side of the album cover of *Tropicália, ou panis et circencis*. In the script composer-arranger Rogério Duprat argues that music must be understood as a commercial product for sale. He challenges the young Bahian musicians: "How will you react to the news that an album is made to sell? . . . Do you understand the risk you're taking? Do you know you can make a lot of money with this?" Duprat's provocation goes unanswered, but it suggests that the tropicalists were aware of the implications of engaging with the culture industry. This understanding informed their compositions, which often appropriated the formal techniques of mass media oriented toward rapid communication.[2]

This view of art and commerce would have particularly dramatic effects as the tropicalists fashioned a public image for mass consumption. Under the direction of André Midani, their record company, Philips (later Polygram), sought to capture a youth audience, and Tropicália was readily marketable as a transgressive novelty.[3] Veloso would later claim that Tropicália "was a way to create a public image while critiquing this image and knowing what was involved in the creation of a public image. In a way, we made explicit the mechanisms of marketing and exposed the commodification of popular musicians."[4] It was not always clear, however, whether they were critiquing these mechanisms or simply using them for a competitive advantage.

Another set of ambiguities were generated by the tropicalists' ironic recycling of dated, stereotypical, or "low-brow" material from Brazilian culture of the archaic past and the mass-mediated present. In contrast with the seriousness and "good taste" of their post–bossa nova colleagues of MPB, the tropicalists consciously embraced cultural emblems considered vulgar and kitsch. The earliest press commentaries about Tropicália fixated on this dimension and interpreted the movement as a playful and ironic parody of dated styles and retrograde values. With the revival of conservative social values under military rule, these gestures served to critique the law-and-order patriotism of the regime. Yet, as I will discuss below, the tropicalists' use of dated material was not always parodic and scornful. In particular, their relationship to the tradition of Brazilian song was curiously devoid of ironic distance, suggesting more "neutral" pastiches of past styles.

Throughout 1968, these ambiguities would be dramatized in numerous live performances, some of them televised, which consistently drew substantial media attention. Indeed, the tropicalists' musical innovations generated less controversy than their flamboyant performances of this new aesthetic. Whereas the 1967 TV Record festival provided a venue for formal musico-poetic innovation, one festival performance of 1968 occasioned a disruptive polemic with the audience. At this event, Veloso and Gil were more concerned with performative effect than with song quality. Their objective was not to win the festival and garner critical acclaim, as it was the year before, but rather to question the status of the festivals as a platform for defending Brazilian traditions. The 1968 music festivals, club dates, and televised shows became venues for staging tropicalist "happenings." These events attracted media attention, exacerbated tensions with Gil's and Veloso's detractors in the MPB camp, and helped them to sell records. Yet these performances also aroused the suspicion of military authorities, who feared that tropicalist interventions in the cultural realm were potentially subversive.

TROPICAL KITSCH

One of the central aesthetic operations of Tropicália was the irreverent citation and celebration of all that was cafona (denoting "bad taste") or kitsch in Brazilian culture. The kitsch object bears the mark of a temporal disjuncture, often appearing as anachronistic, inauthentic, or crudely imitative. The tropicalists' calculated use of kitsch material was highly ambiguous and multivalent. First, it served to contest the prevailing standards of "good taste" and seriousness of mid-1960s MPB. In this sense, it was a gesture of aesthetic populism because it acknowledged that the general public consumed and found meaning in cultural products that many critics dismissed as dated, stereotypical, and even alienated. Second, the tropicalists incorporated kitsch material as a way to satirize the retrograde social and political values that returned with military rule.[5]

By the summer of 1968 (January–March), Tropicália had become something of a fashion in Rio de Janeiro and São Paulo. Young journalists such as Ruy Castro and Luiz Carlos Maciel of Correio da Manhã and Nelson Motta of Última Hora (Rio) produced a continuous stream of articles and reviews in support of the tropicalists, focusing primarily on their tongue-in-cheek recycling of hackneyed stereotypes of life in the Brazilian tropics. Motta initiated a "tropicalist crusade" on behalf of the incipient movement, proposing to "embrace everything that life in the tropics can give without aesthetic prejudices, without rejecting kitsch and bad taste, merely living tropicality." [6] He imagined an inaugural party at the Copacabana Palace with tropical decorations, palm trees, and *Vitoria Regia* (Royal water lilies) covering the swimming pool. Guests would be served bologna and cheese sandwiches, *vatapá*, and instead of liqueurs, Bromil syrup. Motta's ideas for tropicalist sartorial fashion recycled stereotypes of Brazilian cultural styles from previous decades. He recommended that the men slick back their hair with gobs of brilliantine and wear white linen suits, rayon shirts, brightly colored ties, Panama hats, two-tone shoes of crocodile or snake skin, and zodiac rings. Combining elements of the traditional *malandro* (hustler) and a mod tropical dandy, Motta's fashion proposal was simultaneously old-fashioned and ultramodern. For the women, the colors orange, turquoise, and aquamarine were fashionable, along with hoop skirts, petticoats, and hair set with "liters of hair spray." In the realm of music, he recommended sentimental pre–bossa nova *samba-canção* and the hits of Carmen Miranda.

Motta also outlined a "tropicalist philosophy," which consisted of popular sayings like "I brought up my children and married off my daughters and now I can rest in peace," "Modern art is for tricking the fools," and "In my time there was none of this!" Ruy Castro later added more aphorisms under the title "Why I am proud of my country," a reference to Afonso Celso's famous grade school primer, *Por que me ufano do meu país*, a patriotic tract published in 1901.[7] Satirizing the reactionary slogans of the military regime and its supporters, he wrote: "In Brazil there is no racism, here blacks know their place" and "The Armed forces are unified and perfect calm reigns through the land." These retrograde values and beliefs were carted out as a grotesque spectacle of conservative modernization.

During this time, the tropicalists publicly embraced mass-mediated figures of low-brow culture, which was scandalous for artists originally identified with MPB. Throughout 1968, Gil and Veloso made appearances on popular televised music and variety shows, such as the TV Globo program "Discoteca do Chacrinha," hosted by Abelardo "Chacrinha" Barbosa, a corpulent clown who was widely regarded by the national intelligentsia as a reactionary lout.[8] In one interview, for example, Chacrinha proclaimed: "I think that the people should be given what they ask for. The day my public is more literate, I'll change my program. . . . If the government paid less attention to these people who make money criticizing things they don't even under-

Caetano Veloso makes an appearance on the popular variety show hosted by
Chacrinha in January 1968. Chacrinha wears a sign proclaiming, "Here I am ladies."
(Agência JB, *Jornal do Brasil*)

stand, there would be a lot of protest singers dying of hunger."[9] Chacrinha
fancied himself the spiritual father of the movement he helped to launch on
his television show. In the same interview, he declared: "I've been psychedelic for twenty years and I can consider myself the first active tropicalist."
His program was enormously popular among the working classes precisely
for its aggressive and carnivalesque humor. He promoted an "antistyle" that
celebrated *mau-gosto* (bad taste), which offended the sensibilities of those
who sought to affirm more dignified representations of Brazilian culture. The
tropicalists found Chacrinha interesting because he recreated the grotesque
excess and irreverence of carnival on his programs.[10]

After Veloso participated in a special program hosted by Chacrinha called
"Noite da banana" (Night of the banana), one journalist worried that the
singer was getting involved with "commercial machinery that is leading him
to begin his career where everyone else generally ends up: the circus. . . .
The desire to transform Chacrinha into a symbol of tropicalismo will demoralize the movement. It's too much for someone who came from Bahia

with good intentions."[11] In other words, Veloso would lose cultural prestige and be reduced to self-parody. Veloso's appearance on the Chacrinha program probably helped to increase his popularity outside of the middle-class university-educated milieu of MPB consumers. One survey conducted in October 1968 suggested that Veloso's approval rating was highest among the working class.[12] Beyond market considerations, these appearances on Chacrinha's program also figured into the tropicalists' aim to undermine cultural hierarchies that defined what was tasteful and what was vulgar.

The tropicalist group further developed their ironic critiques of Brazilian society in a television special for TV Globo, "Vida, paixão e banana do tropicalismo" (Life, passion, and banana of tropicalismo). José Carlos Capinan and Torquato Neto wrote a script for the production, which called for a huge cast, featuring the tropicalist musicians, filmmaker Glauber Rocha, film star Othon Bastos, theater director José Celso, and stage actors Renato Borghi, Ítala Nandi, and Etty Fraser. The program was also to include several radio stars from the pre–bossa nova era such as Linda Batista, Araci de Almeida, Emilhinha Borba, Vicente Celestino, and Luiz Gonzaga. Capinan and Neto imagined a chorus of invited guests that featured American tourists, Peace Corps volunteers, national politicians, and members of the prestigious Brazilian Academy of Letters. Of course, such an elaborate production would have been impossible; the cast list itself was obviously a joke. The script was rejected, but a more modest production, featuring members of the original cast and hosted by Chacrinha and black comedic actor Grande Otelo, eventually aired in September 1968.[13]

Although much of the script was never aired, it merits discussion as a tropicalist text subsequently published in the collected works of Torquato Neto.[14] The script proposed a collagelike variety show allowing for spontaneous "happenings" involving the cast and the audience. Its sound track featured well-known tropicalist songs, such as "Tropicália," "Marginália II," "Soy loco por tí, América," "Lindonéia," and "Parque industrial," as well as patriotic sambas, such as "Aquarela do Brasil" and "Hino do carnaval brasileiro," and national classics, such as Carlos Gomes's opera Il Guarani and Villa-Lobos's "Bachianas Brasileiras." Placards placed around the stage referenced one-liners from Pero Vaz Caminha's discovery letter to the Portuguese crown ("All That Is Planted Will Grow"), positivist maxims ("Order and Progress"), Oswald de Andrade's "Cannibalist Manifesto" ("Tupi or Not Tupi, That Is the Question"), Vargas era populist slogans ("The Oil Is Ours"), and authoritarian proclamations of the military regime ("The Most Perfect

Order Reigns in the Country"). As previously described, the tropicalist critique juxtaposed these seemingly disconnected and contradictory inventories of historical references.

Most of the script is in the ironic and sarcastic vein of Motta's "tropicalist crusade." One cast member, for example, rejoices that "[o]ur political regime is one of the most perfect in history. Here perfect democracy reigns. In the area of folklore, we find a people that have no complexes, whose days are filled with sambas and macumbas. It's their great fortune for residing in such a beautiful land. Our Indians are the best, marvelous tarzans of the great José de Alencar, and they live in an earthly paradise." [15] During the most patriotic numbers, cast members were to hold up placards featuring boosterish slogans of the military regime such as "I Love with Faith and Pride" and "Without Order, there is no Progress." The caustic humor of this script, as well as its truncated production for television, depended on the use of parody to ridicule conservative nationalist discourse.

Although it was not always explicit, the tropicalists also parodied "Luso-tropicalism," a theory developed by Gilberto Freyre, the modernist architect of the "racial democracy" thesis. First articulated in the 1940s, Freyre's theory asserted that the "Portuguese world," including the European metropolis, Brazil, and colonies in Africa and Asia, should be understood as a "Luso-tropical totality" in which differences between colonizer and colonized were transcended and racial antagonisms were largely absent.[16] The long history of Moorish presence in Iberia, Freyre theorized, made the Portuguese colonizers uniquely disposed toward harmonious and procreative interaction with non-Europeans. Portuguese men would have a particularly important role in the colonial enterprise since they sired large numbers of mixed-race offspring with women of color, both free and enslaved, generating a new mestiço civilization in the tropics. Freyre heralded Brazil as a pioneer in the development of more democratic and humane societies. In light of the racially motivated holocaust in Nazi Germany and postwar struggles for desegregation and racial equality in the United States, Brazil's "experiment in miscegenation" could serve as a model for other multiracial societies.[17] Despite its egalitarian pretensions, Freyre's Luso-tropicalism projected an overly sanguine and somewhat static view of Brazilian culture and society. A champion of Portuguese colonialism in Africa and a staunch defender of military rule at home, Freyre was anathema to progressive artists and intellectuals in the 1960s.[18]

Freyre was cast in the original script of "Vida, paixão, e banana do tropicalismo," which suggests that Neto and Capinan regarded Luso-tropicalism as a target for parodic citation. At one point in the program, the announcer was to interview Freyre, asking him if his "tropicalist science is not being corrupted by these young composers, dramatists, and filmmakers." As Freyre's participation in the cast was only imaginary, we have no way of knowing how he would have responded. Although Freyre's intellectual project was far removed from the mass-mediated circus of Tropicália, the relationship between these two distinct "tropicalisms" did elicit commentary among critics who were versed in Brazilian intellectual history.

The poet and theorist Mário Chamie was perhaps the first critic to argue for a radical distinction between "tropicalism" (with its Freyrean resonances) and the emergent movement "Tropicália." He contrasted the timeless and harmonious character of Freyre's model, based on social relations of the colonial plantation, to the ever-changing and contradictory view of Brazil advanced by the young Bahians. Chamie argued that Freyre's tropicalism maintains "the diachronic immutability of our personality," while Tropicália "only admits the synchronic contingency" of a world in constant flux because of the incessant barrage of information disseminated through the mass media.[19] With calculated hyperbole, the concrete poet Décio Pignatari summed up the differences between Freyre's model and the emergent cultural movement in a polemical debate with students at the University of São Paulo in 1968: "Gilberto Freyre sees the tropics from the point of view of the big house. We see things from the slave quarters." [20] Although it is doubtful that these young middle-class artists perceived Brazilian society "from the slave quarters," they certainly articulated a more dynamic and conflictual view of national culture.

IT'S FORBIDDEN TO FORBID: FIC 1968

During the later part of 1968, the focus of tropicalist performance shifted gradually from ironic satire toward a more aggressive engagement with international countercultures. The most polemical moments of the tropicalist movement occurred during the festival season (September–November) in the second half of 1968. As described in Chapter 2, Veloso and Gil had achieved national recognition with their "universal sound" at São Paulo's Festival de Música Popular Brasileira aired by TV Record. In 1968, they gained notoriety at the Festival Internacional de Canção (International Song Festival), also known as FIC, sponsored by TV Globo in Rio de Janeiro.

Initiated in 1966 as a Brazilian analogue to the San Remo music festival in Italy, FIC was composed of a national contest to select one Brazilian song to compete in an international competition with invited pop singers from abroad. During its first two years, FIC was upstaged by the festival of TV Record, although it did provide a venue for emerging artists such as Milton Nascimento. In 1968, FIC came of age, attracting top performers and garnering significant media attention. A series of eliminatory rounds in São Paulo and Rio de Janeiro preceded the finals of FIC III. Veloso and Gil participated in two eliminatory rounds held at the Teatro da Universidade Católica (TUCA) in São Paulo.

At that event, Gilberto Gil presented a song called "Questão de Ordem" (Question of order), which introduced stylistic elements of rock and African American soul music. At the FIC eliminatory rounds, Gil was jeered by the collegiate audience and his song was disqualified from the contest. Even critics who had praised Gil's earlier work were critical of Gil's new tendency. The erstwhile tropicalist crusader Nelson Motta complained that

> Gil has slipped into a more African current, more identified with modern international black music, but he isn't understood by the public, nor by me. . . . Now with his crazy howling, even while seeking liberty and disorder, he does not offend anyone, he does not enchant anyone, he does not move anyone, he does not overturn anything. . . . He only irritates. . . . In compensation, when Gil sings his admirable "A falência do café" in which he "oswaldandradianly" ridicules the Paulista coffee aristocracy conquered by industry . . . everyone likes it, he crystallizes a very relevant form of expression.[21]

Motta refers here to a satiric composition "A falência do café, ou a luta da lata" (The coffee collapse, or the struggle of the tin can), released as the flip side of the "Questão de ordem" single in 1968.[22] Much in the spirit of Oswald de Andrade's *O rei da vela*, the song lampoons the decadence of São Paulo's coffee barons, which was exacerbated by the introduction of instant coffee in tin cans. Motta appreciated Gil's light-hearted satire of the landed aristocracy but was perplexed by his stylistic turn to international black music. In a memoir written more than thirty years later, Motta reiterated his assessment of Gil's song, claiming that "nobody liked that stuff, screaming guitars, a band member beating the hubcap of a car, Gil sporting a beard, a moustache, and an afro, shouting confused words, there was no music, no rhythm, it was all noise."[23] Other artists and critics defended Gil's performance for opening up new creative avenues in universal pop. In a long article published in the *Correio da manhã*, the conceptual artist Hélio Oiticica argued that Gil's music created "new structures" in popular music: "Gil seems to sing and compose with his whole body . . . using strong vocals similar to the incisive and direct style of northeastern singers: his presentation was a moment of glory. He was sure of what he was doing while the fascistic jeering devoured him.[24]

Gil has claimed that during the tropicalist phase he began to identify with "the whole liberationist attitude of America, the New Left, American university life, new experimental literature and theater, the Black Power experience in the United States, drug experimentation . . . with the iconoclastic attitude of internationalist youth."[25] In the United States, this was the year in which opposition to the Vietnam War intensified in response to the Tet Offensive, university students rebelled, Martin Luther King Jr. was assassinated, and James Brown recorded his hit of collective identity, "I'm Black and I'm Proud." Gil was also attracted to the musical experiments of Jimi Hendrix, whose influence can be heard on "Questão de ordem." The lyrics critique the concept of "order" as used by the regime and by the orthodox Left: "I'm preparing slogans / for my companions / who wait in the streets / throughout the world / in the name of love." Clearly influenced by First World countercultural slogans (e.g., "make love, not war"), the song advocates an international politics of anarchy. Gil cast himself as the "commander" who addresses the people "in the name of love."

More significant was Gil's performance of the song at TUCA during the eliminatory round at FIC. He wore a West African–style tunic, which he began wearing on stage regularly toward the end of 1968. He later explained the meaning of his outfit in an interview: "These clothes are my nudity. Since I can't walk around naked, just as any person would like, I disguise nudity. I am certain that if I seek beauty in my negritude, clothes cease to be an abstraction. . . . On the stage, my outfit is part of the spectacle. This is important: spectacle. It's a contradiction: in this festival, many accepted my music but jeered at my outfit. Why? I don't want to be judged according to my lyrics, my music, much less my clothes. The arrangement is like the outfit, the presentation is an integral part of the spectacle, the spectacle is the spectacle."[26] Like many American and British rock stars of their generation, the tropicalists understood that unique or outlandish performance styles, clothes, and scenography were key elements in the production and consumption of popular music. Gil's insistence on the centrality of the "spectacle" also suggests an affinity with earlier performers such as Carmen Miranda, whose flamboyant style had become passé with the advent of bossa nova.

Until the advent of Tropicália, performative gestures among MPB artists were limited to arm swinging, discrete dance steps, and suggestive facial expressions. Even the TV Record festival of 1967 seemed extraordinarily tame

Gilberto Gil performs "Questão de ordem" at the eliminatory rounds of the 1968 International Song Festival. (Cristiano Mascaro/Abril Imagens)

and well behaved compared with subsequent festivals and shows. Veloso and Gil had broken ranks and wore sport coats and turtleneck sweaters instead of the usual tuxedos. By 1968, Gil was wearing brightly colored tunics and Black Panther–style leather jackets, while Veloso sported lime green futuristic plastic suits together with stereotypically "primitive" necklaces made with alligator teeth. Tom Zé and Gal Costa wore clothing reminiscent of San Francisco hippies. Their personal manager, Guilherme Araújo, was largely responsible for the creation of the tropicalists' sartorial style and public image.[27] The theatrical dimensions of musical performances were developed most extensively by Os Mutantes, who wore special thematic outfits for festival appearances. When they presented "Dom Quixote" (based on Cervantes' Spanish epic) at the 1968 TV Record festival, the Baptista brothers dressed as Don Quixote and Sancho Panza and Rita Lee dressed as Dulcinea.

It was also significant that Gil publicly introduced a discourse on negritude in relation to his music. The poet and critic Affonso Romano de Sant'anna had suggested a similar connection in an article written for the *Jornal do Brasil*. He had speculated that "tropicalismo has possibilities for embracing some of the ideals of negritude insofar as it considers tropical miscegenation as a positive factor."[28] His use of negritude specifically referred to the literary and cultural movement of Francophone Africa and the Caribbean. It is therefore rather curious that he associated "negritude" with "tropical miscegenation" given that the term, although contested, generally affirmed a distinctly "black" collective identity.[29] Sant'anna's reading of negritude falls within the modernist discourse of *mestiçagem* and the related ideology of "racial democracy" explained in Chapter 1. Insofar as the tropicalists were articulating a critique of overly sanguine interpretations of Brazilian culture and national identity, they maintained an ironic relationship with this discursive tradition. Gil used the term simply to denote "blackness" without any explicit connection to the Francophone movement. He was more likely thinking of identity politics typically associated with African American Black Power. In this performance, Gil introduced a black aesthetic as a component of the tropicalist movement. According to Gil, the audience rejected this aesthetic, which was signified primarily by his stylized African attire.

At the same event, Caetano Veloso presented "É proibido proibir" (It's forbidden to forbid), which took as its title a popular slogan of the May 1968 student uprising in France. In the studio recording of the song and during the first performance at TUCA, Veloso recited the poem "D. Sebastião" (1934), by Portuguese modernist writer Fernando Pessoa.[30] The poem is narrated in the first-person voice of Dom Sebastião, the adolescent king of Portugal who perished in 1578 while fighting the Moors in the deserts of North Africa: "Sperai! Caí no areal e na hora adversa" (Wait! I have fallen in the sand dunes in the adverse hour). After falling in the "adverse hour," the king makes a mystical proclamation of return and redemption, which generated the foundational myth of Sebastianism, a messianic movement predicated on the restoration of the Portuguese Empire. The mixture of rock music, French radical politics, and Pessoa's epic poem suggests the transhistorical and international scope of the song.

Like Gil's "Questão de ordem," Veloso's song also expressed an anarchic attitude toward culture and politics. The song is divided into two parts. In the first part, Veloso alludes to various mechanisms of social control such as traditional family values, mass media, and formal educational institutions.[31] In the second part, he calls for the subversion of these rules and restrictions, beginning with the image of a burning car:

> me dê um beijo meu amor
> eles estão nos esperando
> os automóveis ardem em chamas
> derrubar as prateleiras, as estantes
> as estátuas, as vidraças, louças, livros, sim

> give me a kiss my love
> they are waiting for us
> the automobiles are in flames
> demolish the shelves, the bookcases,
> the statues, window panes, dishes, books, yes

The "relics" of the traditional Brazilian home, ironized in earlier tropicalist songs (i.e., "Geléia geral," "Misere Nobis," "Panis et circencis"), are smashed in a carnivalesque and cathartic gesture. Even books, those prized objects of culture, civilization, and education, are discarded with the family china.

During the first round of the TUCA eliminatory, Veloso had invited an American friend, John Danduran, to join him on stage and provoke the audience with loud screaming. In press reports, Danduran was described as a "hippie" from San Francisco who had come to Rio with his rock band, The Sounds, and decided to remain in Brazil. As a musician who was involved with the American and Brazilian countercultures in the late 1960s, Danduran provided an interesting comparative analysis of the two cultural contexts: "A lot of people are offended by us, but what is happening with Caetano happened in the United States with Bob Dylan. When Bob Dylan broke with musical tra-

Caetano Veloso, Os Mutantes, and the *hippie americano* Johnny Danduran provoke a "happening" during their performance of "É proibido proibir" at the eliminatory rounds of the 1968 International Song Festival. (Abril Imagens)

ditions—including protest music—there was a big uproar." [32] Just as Dylan had provoked the ire of folk purists when he performed with an electric guitar at the 1965 Newport Folk Festival, Veloso created a stir with his noisy and atonal rock song backed by Os Mutantes.

Approved for the second eliminatory, Veloso's final performance of "É proibido proibir" at TUCA on September 15 turned into a chaotic happening. Earlier in the evening, a riot in the auditorium had ensued after a tropicalist devotee held up a placard reading "Folclore é Reação!" (Folklore is reaction) while Geraldo Vandré presented his protest song, "Caminhando." After this incident, the partisans of nationalist-participant music, mostly university students, targeted Veloso for revenge, which became a watershed "happening" in the history of Brazilian popular music. Veloso has related the scene: "The song opened with more than a minute of atonal music composed by Os Mutantes. This caused complete hysteria among the students. They already hated us. To tell you the truth, I deliberately provoked them. It was a *happening.* . . . So I sang the song, and I was moving my hips back and forth, dressed in that shiny black and green plastic outfit, with my long hair and a lot of electrical cords around my neck."[33] It was obviously a planned strategy that was designed to provoke the audience even more. In the middle of the song, with the crowd of students screaming in rage and throwing garbage at the stage, Veloso made a famous rambling speech on culture and politics in Brazil, which was recorded and quickly released as a single:

This is the youth that says it wants to take power? . . . You're the same youth that will always, always kill the old enemy who died yesterday. You understand nothing, nothing, absolutely nothing! . . . Today I came here to say that Gilberto Gil and I had the courage to confront the structure of the festival . . . and explode it. . . . The problem is the following: you want to police Brazilian music. . . . I want to say to the jury: disqualify me. I have nothing to do with this. . . . Gilberto Gil is here with me to put an end to the festival and the imbecility that reigns in Brazil. . . . We only entered the festival for this reason. . . . We, he and I, had the courage to enter all of the structures and leave them. And you? If you are the same in politics as you are in aesthetics we're done for! Disqualify me with Gil. The jury is very nice, but incompetent. God has been set free.[34]

In affirming participation in all of the "structures" of the mass media, Veloso was recognizing that there was no "pure space" for artists who participated in the mass-mediated music industry. At best, artists could critique the system from within while remaining cognizant of their status as professionals within this industry.

In the end, both Veloso and Gil were absent from the final round of FIC in 1968. Of the tropicalist group, only Os Mutantes participated with their song "Caminhante Noturno" (Night walker), which was awarded a prize for the best interpretation and placed sixth in the overall competition. Even without the participation of Veloso and Gil, the final round of FIC at Maracanã-zinho stadium was marked by heated controversy. Most of the 20,000 spectators supported Geraldo Vandré's antiregime anthem, "Caminhando (Pra não dizer que não falei das flores)" (Walking [so they don't say that I didn't speak of flowers]), but the contest was won by Chico Buarque and Tom Jobim with the song "Sabiá." Like several tropicalist songs, "Sabiá" alluded to Gonçalves Dias's Romantic poem "Canção de exílio" but without the element of corrosive parody. When Chico Buarque performed the song with the vocal duo Cibele and Cinara, he was roundly jeered by the audience.

Vandré's song was musically less complex, but its lyrics were extremely poignant in light of the political context, and he was warmly received by the audience. A live recording registered Vandré's attempts to calm his fans before starting the song, telling them that "Chico and Tom deserve our respect" and reminding them that "festivals are not everything in life." [35] His magnanimous gesture served to further intensify audience support. "Caminhando" expressed a new level of militancy in Brazilian protest song. Absent from the song were the familiar appeals to a "coming day" of future redemption; the verbs were largely in the present tense and the tone was urgent. The song exhorted the audience to join a collective march while "following the song." Vandré was calling for armed resistance: "come, let's go away / waiting around we'll never know / those who know make history / they don't wait for it to happen." Declaring that "throughout the country there is hunger on the plantations," the song derided those who participated in "indecisive" protest marches, believing that "flowers will defeat cannons." Symbolic protest marches and "flower power" were useless in the face of armed forces. The last stanza denounced the young soldiers used to repress demonstrations who are "taught old lessons / to die for the patria and live without reason."

When "Sabiá" was awarded first prize, the audience erupted in protest, rightly perceiving that the jury had succumbed to political pressure. The jury included Donatelo Griecco, the chief of the Cultural Division of Itamaraty (the Brazilian foreign relations department), who later remarked to the press that "Caminhando" was a dangerous left-wing song.[36] Vandré's critique of military discipline was particularly troubling for military officials, who interpreted it as an affront to their authority. One high-ranking officer declared: "This song is an attack on the dignity of the nation. As a general and secretary of security, if I had been part of the jury, I wouldn't have allowed the song to enter and win second prize." [37] It was clear that local authorities had intervened to ensure that it was not awarded first prize. Following the festival, police agents confiscated the single of "Caminhando" and radio stations were prohibited from airing it. Vandré's song subsequently became a popular anthem for the democratic opposition to military rule.[38]

Soon after the national finals of FIC III, an unsigned article appeared in the *Jornal do Brasil* that praised the secretary of tourism of Guanabara. Denouncing "the immaturity of a vocal sector of the public which insists on viewing artistic manifestations as political acts of ideological value," the article noted that the festival was important "not only for its cultural content and what it represents for the state and for the country but also for the opportunity which it offers the Carioca people to congregate at a high-quality festival, unified by authentic values coming from the most diverse social classes, in a fraternization which rejects all prejudice." [39] The article accurately describes the way in which the local authorities perceived the music festival. FIC III was, above all, an international showcase of Brazilian culture. Like Brazil's World Cup soccer victory in 1970, it served to obscure the fact that the country was entering the most repressive and violent phase of military rule.

A TROPICALIST MUSIC FESTIVAL

While tropicalists were largely absent from FIC III, they dominated the 1968 music festival of TV Record even without the participation of Veloso and Gil. This televised event witnessed the emergence of Gal Costa and Tom Zé as tropicalist media personalities in their own right. It also revealed the extent of the tropicalist intervention in national culture. In Pierre Bourdieu's terms, the tropicalists had transformed the "field of cultural production," specifically the field of Brazilian popular music.[40] Tropicalist influence was particularly evident among younger artists, such as Suely e os Kantikus, who won a local university music festival in São Paulo with the iê-iê-iê song "Que Bacana" (How cool), with the gushing lyric "I come home and put on a record by Caetano Veloso—how delicious!" Critics of the TV Record festival complained that the overwhelming majority of the contestants were attempting to imitate the tropicalists. Several critics lamented the widespread use of operatic performance styles, electric instruments, special effects, and outlandish multicolored costumes based on the tropicalist aesthetic.[41]

The TV Record event also generated the first public misunderstanding between the tropicalist group and Chico Buarque. It was reported that during the final round, Gilberto Gil had jeered Buarque's song "Bem-vinda" (Welcome) for being passé. Although Gil denied the episode, Buarque responded with a discrete essay criticizing Gil and remarking that "not all madness is ingenious, not all lucidity is old."[42] The tropicalists downplayed the incident with ambiguous praise for Buarque. Tom Zé, for example, ironically quipped: "I respect Chico. I mean, I have to respect him. After all, he's my grandfather."[43] For his part, Veloso denied that there was any conflict between himself and Buarque but noted that "while he speaks of super-nostalgia, I speak of super-reality."[44]

The 1968 TV Record festival was something of a coming out event for Gal Costa, who gave an electrifying performance of the rock song "Divino maravilhoso" (discussed in Chapter 3). Before the festival, she was known primarily for her collaboration with Caetano Veloso on the recording *Domingo* and her sublime rendition of "Baby" on the tropicalist concept album. She

The studio audience cheers for Gal Costa as she performs "Divino maravilhoso" at the 1968 TV Record music festival. (Paulo Salmão/Abril Imagens)

was an orthodox devotee of João Gilberto's bossa nova, but by the time of the festival in late 1968, she had also become an avid fan of Janis Joplin and Aretha Franklin.[45] At the TV Record festival, she adopted the stage persona of an audacious American rock star. Dressed in an elaborate psychedelic tunic embroidered with mirrors, she strutted about the stage, playing to the audience, and punctuating each refrain with full-throated shouts. The studio audience at the Teatro Paramount responded with wild applause, grasping at her tunic and covering her with carnival streamers as she shimmied around the orchestra pit where the jury was seated. Although her performance of "Divino maravilhoso" only received third place, Gal Costa emerged from the festival as the diva of Tropicália and a model for young female vocalists.

Accompanied by a local rock group, Os Brazões, and a vocal quartet, Canta Quatro, Tom Zé won first prize at the 1968 TV Record festival with "São São Paulo," featured on his first solo album of 1968. The song was an ambivalent homage to Brazil's largest city from the point of view of a northeastern migrant. In the refrain, Tom Zé articulated the contradictory feelings so often inspired by the city: "São São Paulo, quanta dor / São São Paulo, meu amor" (so much pain/my love). It begins with a series of paradoxes about urban inhabitants who "hassle each other courteously" and "hate each other with love" in the "agglomerated solitude" of the city:

são oito milhões de habitantes
aglomerado solidão
por mil chaminés e carros
gaseados a prestação
porém, com todo defeito
te carrego no meu peito

there are eight million inhabitants
agglomerated solitude
in a thousand smokestacks and cars
gassed up on credit
however, despite your faults
I carry you in my heart

He portrays São Paulo as an ultramodern dystopia where "concrete flowers grow / clear skies are never seen." Attuned to the omnipresence of mass media sensationalism, one stanza adopts the tone of a tabloid headline reporting on the dramatic increase in prostitution in downtown São Paulo: "sinners have invaded / the city's center / armed with rouge and lipstick." Parts of the song were censored, including the line "Brasília is on vacation / in São Paulo there's only work," which was read as a gibe at the incompetence of the federal authorities in Brasília. That this innocuous line was censored while the much more critical "Divino maravilhoso" was approved for the festival, suggests the arbitrary or incompetent nature of censorship under the regime.

Tom Zé's other success of the TV Record festival of 1968 was "2001," which evokes Stanley Kubrick's science fiction movie *2001: A Space Odyssey*, released earlier that year. This futuristic fantasy was set to a *moda-de-viola*, a traditional musical form of rural São Paulo, with interludes of hard rock. Os Mutantes presented the song together with Gilberto Gil on accordion and Liminha (Arnolpho Lima Filho) on the *viola caipira* to evoke a rural feel. Rita Lee used a homemade theremin (an early electronic instrument) to produce eerie sound effects like those heard in classic science fiction films.[46] Unlike Kubrick's film about an omniscient and vindictive spaceship supercomputer that turns against the astronauts in outer space, Tom Zé's "2001" celebrates the powers of science and technology to resolve human problems:

a cor do céu me compõe
o mar azul me dissolve
a equação me propõe
computador me ressolve

Rita Lee of Os Mutantes, Tom Zé (center), and composer-arranger Júlio Medaglia at the 1968 TV Record music festival (Paulo Salomão/Abril Imagens)

> the color of the sky composes me
> the blue sea dissolves me
> the equation proposes me
> the computer resolves me

In the last stanza, Tom Zé quotes directly from Caetano Veloso, who once remarked in an interview that he was simultaneously Bahian and foreign: "nearing the year 2000 / I was born ageless / I'm married, I'm single / I'm Bahian and a foreigner."[47]

Like the astronaut in Kubrick's film who is transported to another dimension where he simultaneously experiences his own death and birth in an endless cycle, Tom Zé claims to be young and old, on the edge of death and constantly reborn. This circular conception of time also relates to his complex identity, which is both Bahian and foreign. If it seems that the song was a delirious, futuristic trip, it is worth noting that similar paradoxes of space, time, and identity exist in northeastern popular culture, which has always informed his work.[48] Tom Zé integrated space-age fantasy into his own circular conception of time and his own complex identity.

The 1968 TV Record event reconfirmed tropicalist hegemony in the televised festivals following the debacle of FIC III. Yet this festival also marked the beginning of the end of the televised music festivals, which had been so central to the development and promotion of MPB during the latter half of the 1960s. Unlike earlier festivals, the TV Record event of 1968 was subject to interference by state censors.[49] Because of the repressive atmosphere, many of the musicians who had achieved mass acclaim in these televised events left the country and the music festivals entered a period of decline. The structure of the song competition, in which composers would submit their entries to be performed and judged by a jury of specialists, seemed increasingly outdated to some artists and critics. Hélio Oiticica drew a comparison with the world of visual arts, noting that the music "festivals are like the salons of modern art and the biennials: old structures that have become increasingly academic and suffocate innovation." [50] The manager of the tropicalists, Guilherme Araújo, stated what was perhaps more to the point: "The festivals are in decline. First, because they were not seen for what they really are: TV programs. They were regarded as competitions when in fact artists were there to make some money." [51] Gilberto Gil, for his part, remarked, "I don't like festivals. I would prefer something more open in Brazil, a grand music fair . . . open air, everyone singing what they want, like the jazz festival of Newport in the United States. Lots of sandwiches and Coca-Cola." [52] The Woodstock and the Isle of Wight festivals of 1969 might have provided models for such a festival, but by that time the military dictatorship had entered its most repressive phase and would have never allowed a massive open-air gathering of youth. TV Globo's Festival Internacional da Canção continued into the early 1970s along with the amateur Festival Universitário aired by TV Tupi, but the golden age of music festivals was effectively over.[53]

TROPICALIST HAPPENINGS OF 1968

By this time, Gil and Veloso were becoming more invested in the spectacle of performance than in music-making as such. The concept of the "happening," which was central to cultural production in the United States at that time, was appropriated by Brazilian artists to describe their own experiments. The tropicalists were early advocates of spontaneous happenings involving polemical interaction with the audience. Veloso's provocative performance of "É proibido proibir" and the audience's enraged reaction to it constituted perhaps the first happening involving MPB. By late 1968, the happening became the modus operandi of the tropicalist group.

As TV Globo and the official agencies were producing FIC III, the tropicalists staged an alternative event at the Sucata, an upscale nightclub in Rio de Janeiro. The Sucata shows, which took place during the first two weeks of October 1968, marked the tropicalists' first open confrontation with official authorities. Until then, their ironic critiques of Brazilian culture and society had largely gone unnoticed by censors. According to press reports, the Sucata shows were chaotic spectacles every night and involved a high degree of audience participation. During one show, while Gil was performing "Batmacumba" with Os Mutantes, an inebriated woman stood up and started calling him a *bicha* ("queer"). Soon Gil and the other vocalists started to chant "bi-cha-cha, bi-bi-cha-cha" to the rhythm of the song, thereby defusing her aggressive behavior and incorporating it into the performance.[54] As Gil sang "Batmacumba" on another night, he was joined on stage by Jimmy Cliff, who had come to Rio de Janeiro representing Jamaica in the finals of FIC III.[55] This was a significant diasporic moment that prefigured Gil's exploration of reggae in the 1970s and Cliff's ongoing involvement with Brazilian music.

During the later stages of the movement, there was a tendency in tropicalist art to affirm social marginality as a possible response to an unequal and militarized society. Sympathetic representations of the outsider who refuses to conform to normative social behavior constitute a long tradition in Brazilian song. The figure of the wily *malandro* (hustler) who beats the system (or at least attempts to work around it) has been a stock character in samba compositions since at least the 1930s. Subsequent post-tropicalist works from 1969, such as Rogério Sganzerla's film *O bandido d luz vermelha* (The red light bandit) and Jorge Ben's soul-samba "Charles anjo 45," paid homage to outlaws living on the margins of society.

The affirmation of marginality was particularly central to the work of Hélio Oiticica, who had lived for a time in the Mangueira *favela* and worked closely with its famous samba school. He was a personal friend of Cara-de-Cavalo (Horseface), a famous bandit who is often cited as the first victim of the notorious *esquadrão da morte* (death squad), a group of off-duty policemen who hunted down and murdered suspected criminals and other "marginals" with impunity. In 1968 Oiticica created a red banner that featured the silk-screened image of Cara-de-Cavalo's bullet-ridden corpse with the inscription *Seja marginal, seja herói* (Be marginal, be a hero) (plate 10). At the time of the Sucata shows, Oiticica explained that the banner was a "protest against the Brazilian mentality that has its faithful representatives in the death squads which treat the marginal like an object." [56]

The Sucata shows came to an end in late October following an incident involving an agent for the Department of Political and Social Order (DOPS), who took issue with Oiticica's banner. The DOPS agent, Carlos Mello, denounced the banner, remarking that it should read instead "be studious, be a hero." His authoritarian and censorious objections to Oiticica's work were ridiculous since the same banner had just been displayed in a public exhibition sponsored by the state government. Guilherme Araújo was probably right when he later remarked to the press that the agent and his colleagues denounced the banner in order to "impress the ladies who accompanied them." [57] Male bravado aside, the agent's behavior should also be understood within the context of the intensifying of state repression.

The tropicalists ceded to the agent's demand to remove the banner, but Veloso denounced the censor during the show and was immediately charged with "disrespecting authority." Veloso later refused to sign a document promising not to make improvised speeches during the performance, and the Sucata engagement was abruptly canceled. Later, a radio announcer from São Paulo, Randal Juliano, contacted the authorities, claiming that the tropicalists had parodied the national anthem at Sucata in a rendition using electric guitars. Although Veloso has denied that such a parody ever occurred, the military authorities seemed to have taken the allegations seriously and began monitoring tropicalist events. Secret documents of one state agency that were uncovered in 1997 reveal that military agents did not always distinguish Tropicália from other currents in popular music. The tropicalists were identified variously as proponents of "protest music," "bossa nova," and even "folklore music." [58] The documents suggest that most agents of military repression did not perceive or understand the specific nature of the tropicalist critique and simply associated the movement with a broad range of artistic activities identified broadly as "subversive" or "communist."

Following the Sucata fiasco, the tropicalists initiated their own television program on the now-defunct TV Tupi in São Paulo. The station had contracted Veloso, Gil, Gal Costa, Tom Zé, Os Mutantes, and Jorge Ben for a program called "Divino Maravilhoso." The program was their most radical experiment to date and also signaled a departure from their earlier tropicalist work. It featured invited guests, including musicians from the pre–bossa nova era like Luiz Gonzaga, the "king of the baião," and the radio singer Silvio Caldas, who performed his old hit "Chão de Estrelas" (Floor of stars). TV Tupi took all precautions to avoid problems with censors. The program was recorded on video tape and then edited before being aired. Unlike other televised music shows at the time, it was completely open to spontaneous invention.

When it was first aired on October 28, 1968, Caetano Veloso surprised the

Tropicalists perform on their TV Tupi program "Divino Maravilhoso" in late 1968. (Paulo Salomão/Abril Imagens)

audience by appearing on stage wearing a coat and tie with his hair combed and slicked back. He performed "Saudosismo," an affectionate parody of early bossa nova that cites standards such as "A felicidade," "Lobo bobo," "Desafinado," and "Chega de saudade." The song reflected the profound political and cultural changes that had occurred since 1958, when João Gilberto recorded "Chega de saudade" and initiated the bossa nova movement. It alluded to bossa nova's dual association with national optimism and musical innovation that was "out of tune" in relation to conventional song. It invoked the era of bossa nova as a joyous carnival for the nation that ended with the military coup of 1964, marking the beginning of a prolonged "Ash Wednesday":

> eu você depois
> quarta-feira de cinzas no país
> e as notas dissonantes
> se integraram ao som dos imbecis

me you afterwards
Ash Wednesday in the country
and the dissonant notes
blended with the sounds of imbeciles

At the end of the song, Veloso repeatedly intoned "Chega de saudade," which literally means "enough of this longing." In the bossa nova standard by Tom Jobim and Vinícius de Moraes, the phrase refers to the separation of two lovers. In Veloso's song, the expression functioned as a literal renunciation of melancholic nostalgia and a call for new creative directions. When Veloso performed it on "Divino Maravilhoso," he exclaimed, "chega de saudade!" at the end of the song and announced to the audience: "We're going to show our new work. An attempt to create a free sound [som livre] in Brazil." [59] In Gal Costa's 1969 recording of "Saudosismo," the final exhortation "chega de saudade" is repeated several times to the sound of a distorted electric guitar, an arrangement that negates the bossa nova aesthetic. For the tropicalists, the only way to follow the radical innovations of bossa nova was to create an aesthetic that was diametrically opposed to it.

In one of the final episodes of "Divino Maravilhoso," the tropicalists staged a televised "funeral" in which they solemnly ended their movement. It was a vanguardist gesture of closure, in which they displayed a placard reading "Here lies Tropicalismo." By this time, Tropicália had run its course as a collective musical project. During the last program in late December, Veloso sang the Christmas samba "Boas Festas" by Assis Valente, a Bahian samba composer of the forties and fifties while pointing a revolver at his head. Television audiences, mostly from the interior of São Paulo, subsequently began to write letters of protest to TV Tupi, and the show was canceled.

THE DEMISE OF TROPICÁLIA

On the morning of December 27, 1968, Caetano Veloso and Gilberto Gil were arrested by military police in their apartments in São Paulo. At the time, the motive for their arrest was not clear. After all, they were not generally perceived as overtly oppositional artists. In fact, left-wing artists and intellectuals had been very critical of their music, their involvement with the culture industry, and their popular success. Most of the protest musicians escaped imprisonment, while the leaders of the tropicalist movement were arrested and exiled to London for two and half years. As noted above, censorship and repression, especially of cultural production, was largely arbitrary and misinformed. What else could explain the censorship of "São São Paulo" and not "Divino maravilhoso"? Or "Dom Quixote" by Os Mutantes and not Vandré's "Caminhando," which was censored only after it had been performed, recorded, and distributed?

There are a few possible explanations for the somewhat capricious action of the authorities. The tropicalists encountered problems with the military regime as their irreverent critique of official order and good taste became more obvious. The fact that they were doing this on television, and not just in theaters and clubs, seemed particularly dangerous to a regime that used the vehicles of mass media to project their own harmonious view of Brazil. Ramon Casas Vilarino has uncovered several DOPS files pertaining to Veloso's arrest that describe him as a "drug-addicted *marginado* [sic]," a description that was false but likely conformed to official perceptions of his "hippie" image. These documents also indicate that DOPS agents believed that Veloso had planned to incorporate the Communist International Hymn in the song "Tropicália" for the televised program "Vida, paixão e banana do tropicalismo." [60] Like Randal Juliano's denunciation of the Sucata show, many of these allegations were based on rumor, but they provide compelling evidence that the military *perceived* the tropicalists as potentially dangerous subversives. This suspicion was likely exacerbated by Veloso's public denunciation of the DOPS agent at the Sucata club—an event that was widely reported in the Carioca press. Veloso's and Gil's visibility and notoriety had become threatening to military authorities, who, until then, had either ignored Brazilian popular musicians or exalted them as international representatives of Brazilian culture. Caetano Veloso has provided some insights into the mentality of the Brazilian military government: "Tropicalismo lasted for a year only, and the military didn't know what to make of it—they didn't know whether it was a political movement or not—but they saw it as anarchic, and they feared it. There were some intellectuals in the military who had some understanding of what we were doing—they were the ones who recommended that we be imprisoned." [61] Veloso has described an interrogation session that took place while he was in prison in which the military officer claimed that tropicalist song was more subversive than protest music because it "undermined the structures" of Brazilian culture and society.[62] It was clear that the irreverent performances of the tropicalist group had been alarming to the military authorities, even if the artists' critique of modern Brazil in song lyrics passed largely undetected.

FROM KITSCH TO COUNTERCULTURE

In December 1968, nearly a year after his ironic "tropicalist crusade," Nelson Motta published a curious piece based on Norman Mailer's famous list of what was "hip" and "square" in the United States. By this time, the attitudes and practices of an emerging Brazilian counterculture had largely supplanted the playful celebration of tropical kitsch. Below is an abbreviated version of Motta's list of what was "hip" and "square" in Brazil at the end of 1968.

Hip	Square
Dom Helder	Dom Sigaud
pure gin	champagne
guitar	piano
Rogério Duprat	Maestro Carioca
wet hair	hairspray
England	France
Bob Dylan	Frank Sinatra
pamphlet	editorial
marijuana	psychoanalysis
Guevara	Kosygin
Stokely Carmichael	Lyndon Johnson
America	Europe
student leader	politician from Minas Gerais
"E proibido proibir"	"Caminhando"
João Gilberto	Jair Rodrigues
guerrilla movement	protest march
Chacrinha	Flávio Cavalcanti
Paulinho da Viola	Zé Keti
Teatro Oficina	Teatro Copacabana

Motta's Brazilian version used some of Mailer's material but mostly referenced the local context.[63] Ironically, this list was published on December 13, 1968, the day President Costa e Silva signed the Fifth Institutional Act (AI-5), which authorized the regime to impose strict censorship over the media, to temporarily close the federal Congress and state and municipal assemblies, to suspend the political rights of individuals, to nullify elected and appointed mandates, to dismiss government employees, and to suspend habeas corpus in cases involving "national security."[64] In short, AI-5 provided the regime with legal and institutional means to suppress all oppositional activities, regardless of whether they were "hip" or "square."

On the day after the promulgation of AI-5, the national magazine O Cruzeiro featured a long article called "Marginália: Arte e cultura na idade da pedrada" (Art and culture in the stone-throwing age), which focused on a wide range of artistic manifestations in some way connected to the tropicalist movement. A color photograph of Caetano Veloso wearing one of Hélio Oiticica's parangolés adorned the first page of the article. It opened with the slogans of a generation: "What is new today might be dead tomorrow. Down with prejudice. Art and culture as a totality. A new aesthetic. A new moral. Communicate through polemics. We're no longer in the Stone Age. We're in the 'Stone-throwing Age.' Which world is this? Fission. Fossil. Down with elite culture. 'Art is suspended etiquette.' No more swallowing of finished works. Participate. Culture without gods. From the bottom up. Everything has changed. Imagination in power. Third World. Art, chewing gum. Artist, Quixote. Marginal, marginália. The rebels think so." [65] The popular press no longer understood Tropicália simply as the recycling of kitsch icons of Brazilian culture. The article featured short statements by key figures such as Rogério Duarte (an instigator of the Bahian group), experimental writer José Agrippino de Paula, cartoonists Ziraldo and Jaguar, filmmakers Glauber Rocha and Rogério Sganzerla, actor Renato Borghi (who played Abelardo I in O rei da vela), the concrete poets, as well as the Bahian group—Veloso, Gil, Torquato Neto, and José Carlos Capinan. It was a summa Tropicália for a mass audience as well as the swan song of the movement.

In retrospect, the promulgation of AI-5 and the subsequent denouement of the tropicalist movement seemed to have marked the end of the "sixties" as a cultural period in Brazil. The decade had begun with radical and optimistic experiments in political mobilization and cultural activism bolstered by a left-wing populist government. It ended with the consolidation of hardline authoritarianism, the marginalization of moderate civilian and military leaders, and the brutal suppression of opposition movements. The subsequent five years are typically referred to as the anos de chumbo (leaden years) or simply o sufoco (the suffocation), terms that described the restrictive atmosphere acutely experienced by opponents of military rule. This period saw the liquidation of the guerrilla movement, an operation that depended heavily on the use of torture, as well as the forced exile of left-wing professors, journalists, and artists. Under Emílio Garrastazú Médici, who assumed the presidency in October 1969, authoritarian rule reached its zenith in Brazil.

Veloso and Gil were imprisoned for two months in Rio de Janeiro and then placed under house arrest in Salvador before being allowed to leave the country. On the eve of their departure, they were permitted to perform a live concert in Salvador, which was later released as the LP *Barra 69*. As a musical movement, Tropicália effectively ended with their arrest, but its aesthetics and strategies continued to orient and inform cultural production in Brazil. In 1969, Gal Costa released her first solo album featuring some of her hits from the tropicalist period and compositions by Jards Macalé and Jorge Ben, two allies from Rio, and by Jovem Guarda stars Roberto Carlos and Erasmo Carlos (plate 5). With the arrest and subsequent exile of Veloso and Gil, Gal Costa became the most prominent performer of the tropicalist group.

In the same year, Jorge Ben (he later changed his stage name to Jorge Benjor) released his own tropicalist-inspired album. An Afro-Brazilian singer-songwriter from Rio de Janeiro, Ben had forged a unique sound mixing bossa nova, samba, and rhythm and blues in the early 1960s. He gained mass popularity in 1963 with the pop samba "Mas que nada" (Oh, come on), which became an international hit with interpretations by Sérgio Mendes and Miriam Makeba. During the peak years of the televised musical festivals, Jorge Ben fell out of favor with the public, occupying an ambiguous position between the MPB group and the Jovem Guarda. His career was resuscitated in 1968 when he allied with the tropicalists and appeared several times on their program "Divino Maravilhoso."

Jorge Ben's 1969 album cover features a black and white drawing of him framed by a colorful psychedelic montage of cartoon female superheroes, samba musicians, tropical plants, and a Brazilian flag (plate 6). With a toucan perched on his shoulder, Ben holds an acoustic guitar bearing the insignia of his favorite soccer team, Flamengo. The broken shackles around his wrist pay homage to national and international black struggles. Several of the songs from the album made explicit references to Afro-Brazilian history and contemporary life in the *favelas*. The entire album is deeply influenced by African American soul music and its ethos of racial pride, self-determination, and collective struggle. This ethos is best exemplified in the soul-samba "Take it easy my brother Charles," a song of advice for a young black man with the bilingual refrain: "take it easy my brother Charles / take it easy *meu irmão de côr* (my brother of color)." On "Crioula" (Black woman), he sings the praises of a black woman who works in the street market but who is also the queen of carnival. He identifies her as "a child of African nobles / who by a geographic mistake / was born in Brazil on carnival day." The last verse quotes a line from the back cover of Gilberto Gil's 1968 solo album: "And as the poet Gil once said / black is the sum of all the colors / you black woman are colorful by nature." Jorge Ben's celebration of black female beauty and the affirmation of racial pride linked to African nobility anticipated one of the dominant themes in Afro-Brazilian music of the following decade. As Veloso has observed, "Jorge Ben was not only the first great black composer coming out of bossa nova . . . but, more importantly, the first to make this fact determine his style."[66]

Following the tropicalist experience, Os Mutantes continued to explore their tongue-in-cheek aural concoctions of psychedelic rock, pop rock, blues, and several Brazilian genres before drifting into more "serious" and less interesting realms of progressive rock in the 1970s. Their best work was registered on the three records recorded between 1968 and 1970. As the back-up group for many of the recordings and performances of Gil and Veloso, Os Mutantes had been a key component in the hybrid tropicalist sound. In 1969, they were invited to participate in the influential festival for MIDEM in Paris, where they were enthusiastically received as a vanguardist rock band on par with the Beatles.[67] Back in São Paulo, Os Mutantes received a lucrative contract to film four television commercials for Shell Oil for the Brazilian market. The commercials featured brief narrative tableaus based on songs by Os Mutantes, such as "Caminhante Noturno" (Night walker), "Não vá se perder por aí" (Don't get lost out there), and "Dom Quixote," a song that had been altered by censors at the 1968 TV Record festival.[68] In 1969 they also staged a musical, Planeta dos Mutantes (Planet of the mutants), cowritten with José Agrippino de Paula, author of the experimental novel Panamérica. Os Mutantes had emerged as the most acclaimed rock group in Brazil, achieving both critical and commercial success until Rita Lee left the band in 1972 to pursue a solo career.

Veloso, once released and placed under house arrest in Salvador, went to work on his second solo album, recorded in June 1969 on the eve of his departure for London. Arranged by Rogério Duprat, the album featured a diverse mix of songs including a traditional samba from Bahia ("Marinheiro só"), a vanguardist composition informed by concrete poetry ("Acrilírico"), an irreverent Argentine tango from the 1930s ("Cambalache"), an original Portuguese fado ("Os argonautas"), a tropicalistlike rock song ("Não identificado"), two original compositions in English ("The Empty Boat" and "Lost in the Paradise"), and an upbeat *frevo* ("Atrás do trio elétrico"), which would become a standard of the Bahian carnival.

The 1969 album might be regarded as Veloso's personal reading of the tropicalist experience in that it featured the kind of hybrid juxtapositions typical of the movement in its collective phase, but without the overarching concern for allegorizing Brazilian modernity. Veloso's distance from the social and political problems of contemporary society is palpable; most of the songs related to personal and existential concerns. A good example of this is Veloso's *fado* "Os argonautas" (The argonauts), a song that invokes the figure of the explorer-navigator in a maritime adventure fraught with anguish. The refrain cites Portuguese modernist poet Fernando Pessoa—"Navegar é preciso. Viver não é preciso" (Sailing is necessary. Living is not.)—yet the final refrain ends simply with "viver," suggesting a more affirmative vision of quotidian existence.[69]

Other songs on the same album alluded to or rekindled the heated debates surrounding Brazilian popular music. His "Não identificado" (Unidentified), for example, starts off as a soft and jazzy romantic pop song, with the first-person narrative voice proclaiming the intention of writing a "simple Brazilian tune" for a woman: "I'm going to make a romantic *iê-iê-iê* / a sentimental anticomputer." The following line, however, parodies the genre of romantic balladeering as the narrative voice announces that his love song is "to be recorded in a flying saucer" so that his passion may shine "like an unidentified object" in the night sky over a provincial city. At this point, the tempo picks up and the romantic love song is submerged under the howl of a distorted electric guitar. The final refrain ends with the repetition of "like an unidentified object," a line that simultaneously conveys the distance and ambiguity of his love as well as the indeterminacy of the song itself. Drawing equally from the traditions of the rural *seresteiros* (romantic balladeers) and from the most up-to-date acid rock of the late 1960s, the song proposes a hybrid musical aesthetic that plays with the sort of tensions between national/international, acoustic/electric, rural/urban, and terrestrial/cosmic that had defined tropicalist practice.

The most controversial song on the album was not even Veloso's composition but rather a stripped-down, somewhat lethargic version of Chico Buarque's "Carolina," a heavily orchestrated romantic bossa featured on his third album. As a result of the incident at the 1968 TV Record Festival in which Gil supposedly jeered his song, Buarque was at the time estranged from the tropicalists. With this in mind, critics read Veloso's version of "Carolina" as a parody of Chico Buarque's lyricism. In an interview published in the satiric weekly *O Pasquim*, Buarque expressed a sense of exasperation regarding his real or imagined conflict with tropicalists, arguing that he had never been an orthodox defender of purity in Brazilian popular music.[70] Buarque explained that he didn't like Veloso's interpretation of "Carolina" primarily for technical reasons but was ultimately unsure if it was, in fact, recorded in bad faith. It is clear from the interview, however, that Veloso's version irritated Buarque.

In the same interview, Luiz Carlos Maciel, an early champion of Tropicália and a journalist for *O Pasquim* sought to explain Veloso's position. He had been corresponding regularly with Veloso, who was then exiled in London and also writing for *O Pasquim*.[71] Maciel related Veloso's insistence that his version of "Carolina" was totally sincere, founded on a profound identification with the lyricism of Brazilian song. Veloso himself wrote a cryptic dispatch for *O Pasquim* in which he attempted to clarify his intentions, but the text was not published at the time.[72] In this essay, he proposed that the figure of Carolina in Buarque's song might be understood as the "antimuse" of Tropicália, symbolizing the sort of romantic lyricism that the movement sought to critique. Yet Veloso argued that the tropicalist moment had passed and multiple creative avenues had opened up, making it possible and necessary to reread Buarque's song without irony. According to this interpretation, Veloso's "Carolina" would be more like a pastiche in which Buarque's music was simply assimilated as one personal style among many without any pretensions of "transcending" it. The controversy over "Carolina" provides a good example of the ambiguities of tropicalist song, in which the line between sincerity and sarcasm, complicity and critique, was often blurred.

Gilberto Gil's artistic response to his ordeal in prison was considerably more upbeat and defiant. He began to practice yoga and macrobiotics, which he continued to pursue in subsequent years. While under house arrest in 1969 he also recorded an album that featured several songs he composed in prison. Like Veloso's post-tropicalist album, Gil's 1969 recording was later orchestrated and arranged by Rogério Duprat, featuring the same lineup of rock musicians. It remains his most audacious foray into rhythm and blues, psychedelic rock, and experimental electronic music.

On the 1969 album Gil also intensified his exploration into the relationship between technology and human consciousness. In several of the songs he composed while he was in prison, technology becomes a human surrogate. He later explained: "The fact that my existential condition had been violated and I had been denied liberty of action and movement, of control over space and time, of will and decision perhaps led me to dream of substitutes and unconsciously think of mental and physical extensions of human beings."[73] In one such song, "Cérebro Eletrônico" (Electronic brain), a first-person subject questions the limits of cybernetic technology, describing a computer that can do everything but still cannot talk, walk, ponder the existence of God, or express emotion. The electronic brain can do nothing to stop the subject's "inevitable journey to death," a fact that paradoxically gives meaning and substance to life. On "Futurível" (Futurable), however, space-age technology becomes the vehicle for entering a new, more enlightened stage of human consciousness. The poetic voice is that of a scientist or extraterrestrial being who transforms humans into pure energy, transporting them light-years away to be reconstituted as shiny, happy, more intelligent robots: "The mutant is happier / happy because in the new mutation / happiness is made of metal." The utopian desire to reconcile technological advances and personal spirituality frequently resurfaced in Gil's later compositions.

Gil's 1969 album also featured his most experimental recording, "Objeto semi-identificado" (Semi-identified object), an esoteric verbal collage derived from his conversations with Rogério Duarte, a Bahian philosopher and graphic artist who was one of the principal interlocutors of the tropicalist group. In the studio, composer-arranger Rogério Duprat later added a sound montage of dissonant tones, buzzes, echo effects, tape loops, and musical fragments reminiscent of adventure films and marching bands. The sound montage also cited fragments of other songs by Gil, such as "Cultura e Civilização" (Culture and civilization), a countercultural rock anthem later featured on Gal Costa's second album.[74] It begins with a sloganlike refrain, repeated several times throughout the song, that expresses a fundamental ambivalence toward culture and civilization in the enlightened, universalist sense (i.e., arts and humanities): "Culture and civilization / let them be damned / or not." In the following lines, Gil proposes an understanding of culture as the ordinary practices of everyday life. He invokes aspects of his life in Bahia such as chatting and drinking genipap liqueur with friends at the St. John's winter festival, eating cilantro, and letting his hair grow out "like a lion's mane." The tropicalist project had ended, and Gil was beginning to explore themes of personal identity.

TROPICÁLIA OTHERWISE

Fredric Jameson has argued that 1960s political and cultural radicalism in Europe and the United States was inspired, in part, by anticolonial or anti-imperialist liberation struggles in the Third World.[75] Political vanguardism in Brazil emerged from the radical nationalism of the 1950s, the CPC experiment, and other social movements of the João Goulart period. It was also influenced by anti-imperialist discourses and practices throughout Latin America (especially Cuba), Africa, and Asia. In short, Brazil was both a generator and consumer of what Jameson calls "third-worldism." The 1960s also saw the articulation of new individual and collective identities based on race, ethnicity, gender, and sexual orientation in the United States and Europe. Jameson relates the emergence of these new "subjects of history" to "something like a crisis in the more universal category that had hitherto seemed to subsume all the varieties of social resistance, namely the classical conception of social class."[76] The crisis that Jameson describes was in some ways similar to the dilemma of the Brazilian Left at the end of the 1960s.

Rogério Duarte, an intellectual mentor of the tropicalists, later remembered the Brazilian context: "At that time there was an elitist vision that embraced a purist pseudonationalism tied to the notion of 'our good negroes, our authentic samba,' as if everything was stagnate and not subject to transformation. The international moment during the time of Tropicalismo was basically informed by a third-worldist vision that was receptive to black and African perspectives. On the aesthetic level, the official white ethnocentrism began to lose power."[77]

The radical social and cultural movements of the early 1960s had attempted to introduce a class-based critique but were limited by paternalistic and, at times, ethnocentric populism. The traditional Left in Brazil, represented foremost by the Communist Party, paid scant attention to issues of racial and sexual inequality, focusing their efforts on anti-imperialist resistance and the class struggle. In a 1979 interview, Veloso claimed that he had felt alienated from left-wing politics since the early 1960s, when he was studying at the University of Bahia:

I always thought that it was obvious that we needed social justice and I wanted to be in favor of those who wanted social justice. In principle, I thought the leftists were good and intelligent and the others bad and stupid. At the same time, I felt a little alone, strange, because I wasn't able to enter any party, not even those university groups. I always felt a little put off by the disdain with which they treated things like sex, religion, race, male-female relations. . . . They were not only considered lesser questions, they were nonexistent and sometimes even harmful. Everything was considered alienated, petit-bourgeois, even though everyone in the university was, in fact, petit-bourgeois.[78]

Aside from responding to military authoritarianism, the tropicalists also introduced discourses that had been previously ignored or underestimated by the Brazilian Left. Liv Sovik has detected in Tropicália a specifically postmodern sensibility that evokes the quotidian life of "internal others"—social, racial, and sexual subalterns—without exalting them as the source of cultural authenticity and revolutionary transformation.[79] The tropicalists did not consciously inaugurate a cultural politics of difference in Brazil, but they did contribute to emerging discourses and practices focused on these new subjectivities. Gilberto Gil's position was especially significant in this regard. As shown above, Gil began to claim affinities with international black music during the final months of 1968, most notably during the eliminatory rounds of FIC when he performed "Questão de ordem."

Before leaving Brazil for exile in London, Gil made a live recording of "Aquele abraço" (That embrace), a euphoric samba that was featured on his 1969 solo album. The title and refrain of the song was an expression used on a popular television program with which the prison guards greeted Gil while he was under arrest in early 1969.[80] It was an exuberant assertion of joy in the face of the despair caused by military repression. He dedicated the song to Dorival Caymmi, João Gilberto, and Caetano Veloso, three Bahian composer-musicians that were central to the elaboration of distinct moments in Brazilian song: the golden age of radio, bossa nova, and Tropicália. In the song, he sends an "embrace" to the city of Rio de Janeiro, the prisoners of the Realengo penitentiary, the fans of the Flamengo soccer club, the girl from the *favela*, the samba school of Portela, the Band of Ipanema, Chacrinha, and finally, all of the Brazilian people. His imminent departure for London made the song even more poignant and endearing to the public. Even a government agency found the song appealing and useful despite the fact that Gil was a persona non grata in Brazil. While Gil was being deported, the state-owned petroleum company Petrobrás used "Aquele abraço" in an advertisement campaign that exalted national industrial progress.[81]

While in London, Gil was awarded in absentia the prestigious "Golfinho de Ouro" (Golden Dolphin) by the Museu da Imagem e do Som (Museum of Image and Sound) in Rio de Janeiro for "Aquele abraço." Established in 1967 and sponsored by the state secretary of tourism, the "Golfinho de Ouro" was given for seven categories: visual arts, cinema, theater, literature, popular music, art music, and sports. The "Golfinho de Ouro" awards were established to promote Brazilian arts and generate good publicity for the state government.[82] Gil was not a likely candidate for the award, which had previously been given to Chico Buarque and Paulinho da Viola, since officials of the museum had been critical of tropicalist music.

In a scathing critique of the museum that was later published in O Pasquim, Gil rejected the award: "I find it difficult to believe that this museum would award someone who was clearly against its asphyxiating, moralist, stupid, and reactionary cultural paternalism in relation to Brazilian music. . . . And I have no doubt that the museum really thinks that 'Aquele abraço' is a samba of penitence for the sins committed against 'sacred Brazilian music.' " What starts off as a diatribe against the museum for its folkloric conception of Brazilian popular music develops into a more profound critique of paternalism and racism in Brazilian society:

> I have no reason not to refuse a prize awarded to a samba that (the museum) supposes was made to defend the "purity" of Brazilian popular music. . . . Let it be clear . . . that "Aquele abraço" doesn't mean that I've been "regenerated," that I've become a "good negro samba player," which they want from all blacks who really "know their place." I don't know what my place is and I'm nowhere at all; I'm not *serving the table of the white masters* any more and I'm no longer sad in Brazil, which they are transforming into the slave quarters. Maybe for this reason God has taken me from there and put me on a cold, empty street where at least I can sing like a bird. The birds don't warble like those over there, but they *still* warble.[83]

Once again Gil referenced the Romantic poem by Gonçalves Dias, "Song of Exile," which expressed longing to hear warbling of the tropical birds in Brazil. With the intensification of repression under the hard-line Médici regime, Gil's ironic reference to the poem was particularly astute. In London, musicians didn't sing like the Brazilians, but at least they could sing without fear of censorship and arrest.

The argument that imperialist domination and military rule enslaved all Brazilian people, regardless of race, had been made by left-wing artists and intellectuals during the 1960s. Teatro de Arena's 1965 stage production Arena conta Zumbi, for example, allegorized the resistance to military rule based on the story of Zumbi, the heroic leader of a settlement of runaway slaves, or quilombo, during the seventeenth century.[84] Gil's comment about the "white masters" who were transforming Brazil into "slave quarters" may be interpreted, on one level, as a denunciation of oppression in general. Yet his references to "blacks who know their place" also suggests a specific critique of racial hierarchies that were reinforced by authoritarian rule.

Given the history of samba and state power since the 1930s, his rejection of prevailing notions of authenticity also constituted a critique of *mestiço* Brazil as it was institutionalized by the state. This certainly does not mean that Gil was repudiating *mestiçagem* as a cultural reality in Brazil, or that he was attempting to stake out a space of purity for Afro-Brazilian culture. The tropicalists, like most other artists and intellectuals, celebrated cultural syncretism in Brazil. His statement might be read instead as a critique of what Carlos Guilherme Mota has called the "ideology of Brazilian culture," which tends to efface conflict and difference in its construction of a homogeneous and unified national identity.[85] The stereotypical figure of the "good negro samba player," which Gil denounced, had emblematic status as the bearer of cultural authenticity in the national imaginary. As described in Chapter 1, samba was associated, above all, with *brasilidade* and rarely served as a vehicle for racial protest. Gil suspected that "Aquele abraço" was embraced by the cultural elite precisely because, as a samba, it could be situated within an accepted repertoire of cultural practices by blacks who "knew their place" in Brazilian society. By refusing the discourse of *brasilidade*, he positions himself on the margins of national identity. Gil insists that he is "nowhere at all." His rejection of "purity" is especially prescient in its questioning of the limits imposed on black artists in the name of racial or cultural authenticity, an issue taken up years later by African and Afro-diasporic musicians around the world.[86]

CONCLUSION

Tropicália coalesced as a movement in 1968, during a period of intense political and cultural turmoil. At the outset it was interpreted as a tongue-in-cheek embrace of kitsch and bad taste in Brazilian culture. The tropicalists consciously recycled anachronistic material such as melodramatic pre–bossa nova styles. Their readings of dated material combined a mixture of parody, which often involved an ironic critique, and pastiche, which suggested a measure of identification and complicity. Military authorities were generally indifferent to tropicalist recordings but grew increasingly alarmed by the group's irreverent televised performances and "happenings." These performances also exacerbated tensions with left-wing nationalists, who were critical of the tropicalists' flirtation with commercialism and mass culture. In an impassioned defense of the movement and an attack on the "policing of Brazilian popular music," Veloso responded to his critics by arguing that he and Gil "had the courage to enter all of the structures and leave them."

Toward the end of the movement, the tropicalists also began to embrace international countercultural movements, a move that was given greater impetus with the exile of Gil and Veloso to London in 1969. Around this time, they also began to articulate positions that occasionally dissented from consecrated discourses on national identity. Gil in particular played a key role in introducing international black musical and sartorial styles into tropicalist performance. This turn to Afro-diasporic culture toward the end of the tropicalist movement would orient much of his work during the following decade.

5

TROPICÁLIA,
COUNTERCULTURE, &
AFRO–DIASPORIC
CONNECTIONS

s a collective project, Tropicália ended in December 1968, yet it inspired emerging artists and groups loosely identified with a "post-tropicalist" current in MPB. For the original Bahian group and their allies in Rio and São Paulo, the tropicalist experience continued to orient their work in a diffuse and nonprogrammatic fashion. With the Fifth Institutional Act and the hardening of military rule, the cultural and political context had been radically changed. Despite the context of repression and censorship, Brazilian popular music was arguably the most resilient area of cultural production. Artists identified with the second wave of bossa nova, many of whom gained national recognition in the televised music festivals of the 1960s, achieved artistic maturity, producing in some cases the best work of their careers. Elis Regina, Maria Bethânia, and Gal Costa were consecrated as the leading divas of MPB. Milton Nascimento and his "Corner Club" produced astonishing fusions of contemporary jazz, rock, samba, Latin American *nueva canción*, and traditional musical styles from Minas Gerais. A new generation of "university singers," such as Ivan Lins, Luiz Gonzaga Jr., and João Bosco, came into the national spotlight on the TV Globo program "Som Livre Exportação." Female artists such as Joyce, Sueli Costa, and Marlui Miranda garnered critical acclaim not just as singers but also as composers.[1] After returning from exile in 1972, Gilberto Gil and Caetano Veloso consolidated their positions as popular artists and public intellectuals. Tom Zé, whose post-tropicalist work will be discussed in Chapter 6, continued to compose and record but remained on the margins of mainstream MPB.

Throughout the 1970s, the tropicalist movement continued to influence cultural production in Brazil, especially in the area of popular music. Artists who had previously criticized the cultural strategies and aesthetic innovations of the tropicalist group began to dialogue with the movement and its legacy. For the most part, the nationalist anxieties that informed debates surrounding the "direction of popular music" subsided as artists engaged a diverse range of musical and cultural information from local and international sources. Conflicts and rivalries of the 1960s receded, making possible collaborations that were previously unthinkable. In 1970, for example, the MPB singer Elis Regina recorded a duo with soul singer Tim Maia, who was formerly allied with the Jovem Guarda. The use of electric instruments and rock-informed musical arrangements no longer generated much controversy. The field of MPB became simultaneously less contentious and more heterogeneous as artists pursued individual projects with less anxiety over issues of cultural nationalism.

In the early 1970s, the tropicalist experience was also the primary reference point for urban middle-class youths identified with an incipient Brazilian counterculture. Although criticized for not articulating collective opposition to military rule, countercultural artists and adherents proposed new discourses and practices that attempted to resist authoritarian social control. Later in the decade, countercultural practices in Brazil took other forms, converging in some instances with new social and cultural movements. Gil and Veloso maintained a particularly fruitful dialogue with urban Afro-Brazilian musical countercultures, which became their primary source of cultural and political inspiration in the years following the tropicalist experience.[2]

FRESTAS: CONTESTING THE REGIME

With the establishment of blanket censorship and the ascension of military hard-liners, the lively cultural context of the 1960s gave way to what some critics described as a *vazio cultural* (cultural void) in the early 1970s. After the promulgation of the AI-5 in December 1968, the military regime intensified its efforts to silence the opposition and to closely monitor cultural production. More than thirty films and nearly a hundred plays were prohibited from exhibition between 1969 and 1971. Popular music was also a target for censors, who interdicted hundreds of songs annually during the early 1970s.[3] Before recording a song, artists were obliged to submit their compositions to the *Serviço de Censura Federal* (Federal Censorship Service) for approval. Censorship obviously intervened in the creative process of some composers, forcing lyricists to craft ever more subtle and ambiguous poetic commentaries on daily life under military rule. As José Miguel Wisnik has argued, popular music developed into a "network of messages" that circulated among artists and their audiences, often under the radar of censors.[4]

The undisputed master of political critique and double entendre was Chico Buarque, the erstwhile festival star of the mid-1960s. Aside from a brief period of self-exile in 1969–70, Buarque remained in Brazil and quickly established himself as a leading voice of protest in Brazilian popular music. Given his stature as a critically acclaimed and commercially successful singer-songwriter, he became the target for censors. In one 1971 interview, he complained that he was afraid to send new compositions to the censors because at that time they approved roughly one out of every three of his songs, forcing him to practice a form of "self-censorship."[5] After having several songs prohibited, Buarque began submitting compositions under the pseudonym Julinho de Adelaide in order to lead the censors astray. Amazingly, his exultant protest samba "Apesar de você" (In spite of you) was initially approved by censors and released in May 1971, and it sold 100,000 copies before authorities banned it. The song was later included on his 1978 album *Chico Buarque*. Thinly veiled as the bitter invective of a spurned lover, the lyrics were obviously directed at the military regime: "You invented sadness / now have the decency to dis-invent it." Much in the vein of sixties protest music, the song invokes a day of future redemption, a hope and a promise expressed in the refrain: "In spite of you, tomorrow will be another day."

The former tropicalists were relatively less affected by censorship, largely because their music was generally not associated with political protest. Nevertheless, both Gil and Veloso composed songs that were critical of the regime after they returned from exile in the early seventies. This period also marked the public reconciliation of the tropicalists and Chico Buarque, after several years of estrangement. In 1972, Buarque and Veloso recorded a live album, *Chico e Caetano juntos e ao vivo*, in which they sang each other's songs. Gil and Buarque cowrote an important protest ballad, "Cálice" (Chalice), which was also featured on Buarque's 1978 album. The refrain cites a biblical passage from the book of Mark: "Pai, afasta de mim este cálice" (Father, take away this cup from me). In Portuguese, the word *cálice* is a homophone of the imperative *cale-se* ("shut up"), linking the Catholic rite to the context of political censorship and repression.[6] When Buarque and Gil first performed the song, police agents unplugged the microphone, unwittingly dramatizing the song's message as they literally forced the musicians to "shut up." Veloso also composed songs for Buarque, including "Festa imodesta" (Immodest party), a rousing samba that invokes the figure of the *malandro*, the archetypal hustler who operates on the margins of society, relying on crafty ruses to allude authorities: "tudo aquilo / que o malandro pronuncia / que o otário silencia / passa pela fresta da cesta / e resta a vida" (all that / the *malandros* proclaim / and the idiots suppress / slips through the breaches in the basket / and life goes on). Under the regime of censorship, censored artists like Buarque had to adopt the artful strategies of the *malandro*, communicating through the *frestas*, or "breaches," in the censorious sieve of the regime.[7]

SONGS OF EXILE

Under the Médici regime, the coercive and ideological power of the military reached an apex. Between 1968 and 1974, Brazil's economy grew at an average rate of nearly 11 percent, aided by the dramatic expansion of industrial, agricultural, and mineral exports and facilitated by the suppression of labor demands. The so-called economic miracle exacted a toll on the working poor by privileging growth over collective welfare and exacerbating socioeconomic inequality. Yet the regime carefully constructed a public relations campaign around the concept of "Brasil Grande" (Great Brasil), drawing attention to the nation's vast natural and industrial resources that were fueling the economic boom. The hard-line regime capitalized on Brazil's victory at the 1970 World Cup Soccer Championship in Mexico City, becoming the first national team to win three titles. The rallying march for the World Cup team, "Pra Frente, Brasil" (Onward, Brazil), was appropriated by the regime and performed by military bands at official parades. Billboard images of the soccer star Pelé carried the regime's own boosterish slogan, "Ninguém segura mais este país" (Nobody will hold back the country now).[8] For opponents of military rule who rejected the patriotic hoopla, the regime had another motto: "Brasil: Ame-o ou Deixe-o." This motto echoed the "love it or leave it" slogan hurled at Vietnam protesters in the United States.[9]

In the late 1960s and early 1970s, the regime's motto had real consequences for thousands of Brazilians who were expelled from the country or chose voluntary exile to escape arrest and harassment. Exiles included opposition politicians, student leaders, former guerrillas, prominent academics, writers, and artists. Several of the most important artists identified with the tropicalist movement sought refuge and work abroad. Glauber Rocha, the director of *Terra em transe*, worked in Europe and Africa between 1969 and 1976, producing four films, including *Der Leone Have Sept Cabeças*, an allegory of colonialism and its demise in the Third World, which he filmed in the Republic of Congo.[10] José Celso, the director of Teatro Oficina, sought exile in Europe in 1974 after suffering arrest and torture by the São Paulo police. He traveled to Mozambique in 1975 to film a documentary called *25*, about the nation's independence from Portugal after a prolonged anticolonial struggle.[11] Throughout the 1970s, the radical conceptual artist Hélio Oiticica divided his time between Rio and New York, where he continued his work with ambient and experiential art.

By 1970, many of the top stars of MPB who had emerged in the 1960s were living abroad for both political and professional reasons. Working conditions for Brazilian artists were poor as the national recording industry became increasingly dominated by foreign artists. Some Brazilian artists even adopted anglicized stage names and recorded pop songs in English, while others recorded Portuguese-language versions of international hits.[12] Meanwhile, many acclaimed singer-songwriters of the fifties and sixties pursued careers abroad. Bossa nova exporters Sérgio Mendes and Oscar Castro-Neves moved to Los Angeles in the mid-1960s, where they were later joined by Edu Lobo, organist Walter Wanderley, accordionist-arranger Sivuca, percussionist Airto Moreira, and vocalist Flora Purim. Other bossa nova artists, such as João Gilberto, Carlos Lyra, and Leni Andrade, lived for a time in Mexico, while Vinícius de Moraes and Dori Caymmi moved to Uruguay. Chico Buarque lived and worked in Rome for over a year, participating in a concert tour of Italy with Toquinho (Antônio Pecci Filho) and African American entertainer Josephine Baker. Other musicians were forced to leave Brazil for political reasons. Geraldo Vandré, the author of the famous protest anthem "Caminhando" followed the trajectory of many left-wing exiles, fleeing first to Chile and then later to Europe.

Gilberto Gil and Caetano Veloso lived and worked in London from July 1969 until January 1972. Veloso was allowed to return twice in 1971 to celebrate his parents' fortieth wedding anniversary and then to record a televised music special on TV Tupi with Gal Costa and João Gilberto. During the first visit, Veloso was detained for several hours in the Galeão airport in Rio, as police agents tried unsuccessfully to force him to write a song in support of the Transamazonic Highway, a development project in keeping with the regime's discourse on "Brasil Grande." Each visit occasioned adulatory coverage in the national press, further consecrating Veloso and Gil as martyred heroes.

Despite these two visits, Veloso's exile in London was fraught with anguish, especially during the first year. He sent regular communiqués for publication in the satirical review *O Pasquim*. Many of his dispatches related his quotidian experiences in "swinging London" and reported on the local music scene, such as the famous Isle of Wight festival, which he attended with Gil.[13] In one early letter to *O Pasquim*, he referred to his ordeal in prison, ironically citing Gil's samba "Aquele abraço" as a gesture of defiance toward the military authorities: "Perhaps some guys in Brazil wanted to annihilate me; perhaps everything happened by chance. But now I want to send 'that embrace' to whomever wanted to annihilate me because they succeeded. Gilberto Gil and I send these guys that embrace from London. Not very deserving because now we know that it wasn't so difficult. But others will come. We are dead. He is more alive than we are."[14] Veloso has explained that the last line was an oblique reference to Carlos Marighella, the guerrilla leader who was assassinated by security forces soon after the Bahians had arrived in London. The cover of one Brazilian magazine had featured a photo of Marighella's corpse next to the photos of Gil and Veloso in exile.[15]

Several songs from Veloso's first recording from exile, such as "In the Hot Sun of a Christmas Day," also alluded to the repressive atmosphere of Brazil during the holiday before he was arrested: "machine gun / in the hot sun of a Christmas day / they killed someone else / in the hot sun of a Christmas day." Aside from new compositions in English, Veloso recorded a long and melancholic version of "Asa Branca" (1947), the classic *baião* by Luiz Gonzaga and Humberto Teixeira that narrates the story of a rural migrant who is forced to leave his lover during a blistering drought in the northeastern backlands. The narrator promises to return as soon as the green of his lover's eyes spreads out over the fields. Given Veloso's own location, his recording was readily interpreted as a poignant song of exile expressing his longing to return to Brazil.

Gilberto Gil's existential and artistic response to life in exile was considerably more buoyant. Almost from the beginning, he immersed himself in the vibrant cultural scene of London. His fourth solo album (1971) featured new songs in English performed in a soulful folk-rock style somewhat reminiscent of Richie Havens or an acoustic Jimi Hendrix. The liner notes informed the British public that Gil was a frequent visitor to the most fashionable music halls and clubs of the day: "Something has rubbed off, for the sounds and songs on this album introduce a subtle Latin pulse and folk-rock feeling which is unlike, and as fascinating as, anything we have yet heard." Gil's London album was synchronized with the international counterculture, featuring songs like "The Three Mushrooms," which alluded to his experimentation with hallucinogens to stimulate artistic invention.[16]

While in London, Veloso and Gil first heard reggae, a musical form that had emerged in Jamaica in the late 1960s and quickly spread throughout the Caribbean diaspora. Although considerably more privileged than most Caribbean immigrants, they identified with their struggle for rights and respect in British society. Gil's experiences of rejection and alienation were registered in a song written with Jorge Mautner called "Babylon," a term used by Rastafarians to denote a place of exile outside of the African homeland: "When I first came to Babylon I felt so lonely / I felt so lonely and people came along to mistreat me / calling me so many names in the street." For his part, Veloso became the first Brazilian artist to make explicit reference to reggae in the song "Nine out of Ten," featured on *Transa* (1972): "I walk down Portobello Road to the sound of reggae / I'm alive." Although both artists still evidenced greater musical affinities with Anglo-American folk-rock, their condition as political exiles from a peripheral country in contact with Caribbean immigrants opened up new perspectives on the African diaspora that they further explored later in the 1970s.

COLLAGES AND PALIMPSESTS

While in London, Veloso initiated new musical experiments that further radicalized the collage aesthetics of Tropicália. His second album recorded in London, *Transa*, featured original folk-rock compositions in English containing brief citations from the history of Brazilian song. Whereas his previous albums had featured integral versions or "covers" of songs, cited either as a parody or as a pastiche, *Transa* created a "mosaic of references" without a hint of ironic distance.[17] The first track, "You Don't Know Me," cited material from the 1960s, including "Maria Moita" (Lyra-Moraes), "Reza" (Lobo-Guerra), and his own "Saudosismo." In "It's a Long Way" (a homage to the Beatles' "Long and Winding Road"), Veloso cited songs from his childhood, including Dorival Caymmi's "A lenda do Abaeté." By using a collage technique, Veloso invoked diverse spatial and temporal points of reference, moving continuously from the present to the past, from London to Rio and Salvador.

The most ambitious song on *Transa* was "Triste Bahia" (Sad Bahia), based on "A cidade da Bahia" (The city of Bahia), a seventeenth-century sonnet by baroque poet Gregório de Matos, which was itself a parody of a sonnet by Portuguese poet Francisco Rodrigues Lobo.[18] A notorious satirist of colonial Bahian society, especially of the mercantilist elite and the clergy, Matos was eventually exiled to the Portuguese colony of Angola, a source of slaves and a convenient place to exile outcasts and critics. In "A cidade da Bahia," Matos sarcastically laments the corruption and decadence of the Bahian capital under the control of avaricious Portuguese planters and merchants. The sonnet allegorizes Bahia as a city in ruins following the decline of the sugar industry.

Veloso's "Triste Bahia" is also allegorical, presenting a collage of diverse historical referents that never coalesce as a cohesive totality. Yet unlike Matos's baroque sonnet, "Triste Bahia" goes beyond the melancholic gaze by excavating the "ruins of history" and exposing the African foundations of Bahian culture and society. No other region of Brazil was quite so dependent on African slaves as Bahia. After abolition, former slaves and their descendants occupied subaltern positions in the local economy, while manifestations of Afro-Bahian culture, such as Candomblé and *capoeira*, were disparaged, subject to official control, and often suppressed. Until 1976, for example, Candomblé temples in Salvador were required to register with the police and obtain clearance for public festivals. "Triste Bahia" is best understood as a sonic quilt composed of heterogeneous musical and poetic fragments. Its spatial referent is Bahia, especially Salvador and the *recôncavo*, the region surrounding All Saints Bay where Veloso grew up. The temporal scope is expansive, with references to the colonial era, the nineteenth century, and the present.

This multitemporal historical perspective finds echoes in the formal properties of the song, consisting of several layers of overlapping polyrhythms. Opening with the staccato notes of a *berimbau* and a salvo of *atabaques* (Afro-Brazilian drums), the introduction is reminiscent of convocational rites that initiate the dance/fight *capoeira*. Veloso sings the first stanzas of Matos's sonnet over the slow pulsations of a *capoeira* rhythm accompanied by an acoustic guitar. His mournful lament is abruptly interrupted by a reference to Vicente Pastinha, an acclaimed master of *capoeira de Angola*, the most traditional form: "Pastinha já foi à África / pra mostrar capoeira do Brasil" (Pastinha went to Africa / to show *capoeira* of Brazil). In this line Veloso refers to Pastinha's trip to Africa in 1966 to represent Brazil in the first International Black Arts Festival in Dakar, Senegal.

With the reference to Pastinha, the tempo picks up and the baroque elegy to "sad Bahia" cedes to call-and-response chanting of *capoeira*. At this point Veloso quotes directly from Pastinha's famous *ladainha*, or solo chant, which expresses disillusionment with the world: "I'm already fed up / with life here on earth / oh mama, I'm going to the moon / together with my wife / we'll set up a little ranch / made of straw thatch." [19] The whimsical verse pays homage to Pastinha but also intimates Veloso's own sense of alienation while living in exile. The tempo increases with the addition of more rhythmic layers, including *ijexá* (a rhythm used by Afro-Bahian percussive groups called *afoxés*) and *samba-de-roda*. Veloso sings brief fragments of *afoxé* songs and traditional Bahian sambas. In one passage he cites a Catholic liturgical chant to the Virgin Mother, followed by a reference to a "white flag planted on strong wood," a common marker of a Candomblé temple. By the end of the song, the layers of rhythms are thick and fast, evoking the atmosphere of a Candomblé festival when devotees begin to fall into trance and receive the Yoruba deities, or *orixás*. Veloso's "Triste Bahia" brilliantly enacts what Robert Stam has called "palimpsest aesthetics," a layered ensemble of superimposed or juxtaposed cultural traces from different times and places.[20] Although it begins with Matos's lament for Bahia, Veloso's song suggests the possibility for regeneration through Afro-Brazilian expressive cultures.

Veloso further radicalized his experiments with collage and palimpsest aesthetics on *Araçá azul* (Blue araçá), his first postexile recording from 1972. An araçá is a tropical fruit that Veloso gathered from the trees when he was a child, but there is no such thing as a blue araçá. It evokes memories of a past that never existed, or one that is obscured and unknown. In the hauntingly beautiful title track, Veloso identifies *araçá azul* as a "secret dream" and a "toy." Indeed, Polygram had given Veloso free reign to "play" in the studio and create a highly personal and cryptic album. *Araçá azul* was his most experimental album and proved to be inaccessible for all but the most adventurous listeners. It became the most refunded or exchanged record in the history of the Brazilian recording industry.[21]

During the tropicalist phase, Veloso had become a popular media star, championing pop music as a cultural product for mass consumption. It was precisely his status as a consecrated artist that allowed him to make an experimental album with little popular appeal. He ironically quips on one song: "I make my destiny, I don't ask for it / I'm entitled to the other side / I put all my failures / on the hit parade." *Araçá azul* was not so much a renunciation of his youthful enthusiasm for culture industry as an assertion of his continuing interest in exploring the "other side" (i.e., vanguard experimentalism and traditional musical practices) of popular music.[22] A personal homage to the Brazilian avant-garde, especially Oswald de Andrade and the concrete poets of São Paulo, *Araçá azul* represented a continuation of the vanguardist experiments initiated during the period of Tropicália. Structured as a mosaic of musical fragments including bossa nova, rock, sonic "found objects" from the streets of São Paulo, duodecophonic arrangements by Rogério Duprat, and Afro-Bahian *samba-de-roda*, *Araçá azul* has been aptly described as a "cubist album."[23] For the samba recordings, Veloso invited Edith Oliveira, a woman from his hometown, to sing and play percussion with a knife and porcelain plate.

Collage aesthetics are best demonstrated in "Sugarcane Fields Forever," an obvious allusion to the Beatles' "Strawberry Fields Forever" from 1967. Alternating between traditional Afro-Bahian sambas, dissonant orchestral sounds, bossa nova, and rock jingles, the constituent elements are never synthesized into a stable fusion but rather remain suspended in a state of dialogic tension. Just when the listener is getting used to the shrill voice of Edith Oliveira, a cacophonous orchestra abruptly intervenes, only to be succeeded by soft bossa nova, which itself is interrupted by the return of *samba-de-roda*. The song cannot be consumed passively; it never allows the listener to "get into a groove." Instead, it invites reflection on the affinities and connections between vanguard experimentation, traditional popular music, and contemporary urban forms such as rock and bossa nova.

Like his reworking of Gregório de Matos's baroque sonnet, "Sugarcane Fields Forever" also excavates Bahian history. While the Beatles' strawberry fields conjure a bucolic paradise that is ideal for hallucinogenic trips, Veloso's sugarcane fields serve as a reminder of Bahian plantation life based on the labor of African slaves. Yet he also alludes to an embodied history of miscegenation and cultural hybridity that constitutes his own identity. In one bossa nova interlude, he repeatedly intones: "Sou um mulato no sentido lato, um mulato democrático do litoral (I'm a mulatto in the broad sense, a democratic mulatto from the littoral). Referring to racial, political, and regional identities, Veloso's self-affirmation as a "democratic mulatto" from the Bahian coast implicitly called into question the pretensions of the military regime that disingenuously claimed to be democratic, while also alluding to the racial dimensions of any struggle for democracy in Brazil.

Araçá azul is often regarded as the terminal experience of Veloso's tropicalist phase.[24] It revisited and radicalized the poetic and musical experiments of Tropicália that had been interrupted by the military regime. On this album, Veloso accentuated the productive juxtapositions first explored in 1968 between popular music and vanguard experimentalism, the archaic and the ultramodern, and the rural and the urban. Yet bearing in mind that the tropicalists were also engaged in the production of "pop music" for mass consumption, *Araçá azul* seems rather like an anomaly in Veloso's oeuvre. His subsequent work, while not excessively commercial, was more readily assimilated into the mainstream popular music market.

COUNTERCULTURAL BRAZIL

Gil and Veloso returned to Brazil definitively in January 1972, during the most repressive phase of military rule. By that time, armed opposition had largely been liquidated and many political activists were either in jail or in exile. The lively and highly contested cultural terrain of the late 1960s had given way to political disillusionment and social malaise. With nearly all avenues of organized political opposition cut off, middle-class urban youth turned to more personal and "spiritual" quests, often aided by drug consumption, psychoanalysis, macrobiotics, and non-Western religions. As elsewhere in the world, the Brazilian counterculture produced its own repertory of fashions and linguistic codes to mark distinctions between those who were *bacana* (hip) and those who were *careta* (square). Although Caetano Veloso liked to claim that he was *careta* (in part, because he didn't use drugs), he became a countercultural trendsetter with his long hair and androgynous outfits.

The new countercultural sensibility, often called *desbunde* (dropout), or *curtição* (trip out), found expression in alternative journals such as *Flor do mal*, *Bondinho*, *Verbo Encantado*, and a short-lived Brazilian edition of *Rolling Stone*. Meanwhile, a new generation of post–Cinema Novo directors made low-budget films known as *cinema do lixo* (garbage cinema), or simply *urdigrudi* (i.e., underground). Just as the fast-paced and media-saturated São Paulo had been the site of the tropicalist movement, Rio de Janeiro became the epicenter of the new countercultural sensibility. Artists, intellectuals, and hangers-on congregated at fashionable beach hangouts of Ipanema that had names like "Hippilândia" (Hippieland), "Dunas do Barato" (Groovy dunes), and the "Monte da Gal," named for its most famous denizen, Gal Costa.

Together with international countercultural materials, which circulated in the form of magazines, books, films, and sound recordings, Tropicália was the primary point of reference for the Brazilian counterculture in the early 1970s. Several of the former tropicalists emerged as leading cultural icons of the countercultural scene. The lyricist Torquato Neto, for example, circulated in the milieu of underground filmmakers who had positioned themselves against the consecrated directors of Cinema Novo. Before committing suicide in 1972, he had maintained a regular column in the Rio edition of *Última Hora* named after his most famous tropicalist lyric, "Geléia geral." Together with Waly Salomão and Hélio Oiticica, Torquato Neto organized the *Navilouca* (Ship of fools), a collection of poems, prose, and visual arts featuring the major proponents of the Brazilian counterculture.

Gal Costa became the focus of media attention, emerging as the leading voice of the Brazilian counterculture. Her albums from this period continued in the tropicalist vein, featuring a mixture of hard rock, blues, samba, and bossa nova–style readings of Brazilian classics. In 1969, she began working with Waly Salomão and Jards Macalé, a singer-songwriter from Rio who had been an interlocutor of the tropicalist group. Salomão and Macalé penned "Vapor Barato," a countercultural anthem recorded by Gal Costa on her 1971 live album *Gal Fatal, A todo vapor*. An acoustic blues ballad in the style of Janis Joplin, the song portrays a hippie dropout wearing "red jeans, a general's coat, and lots of rings" who is leaving her "honey-baby" to embark on a personal quest of self-discovery.

By this time, other artists and bands identified with the post-tropicalist Brazilian counterculture had also emerged. In 1968, another young cohort of musicians and songwriters from Salvador coalesced to form the group Novos Baianos (New Bahians). Led by singer-songwriter Moraes Moreira, lyricist Luiz Galvão, guitarist Pepeu Gomes, and vocalists Paulinho Boca de Cantor and Baby Consuelo, the Novos Baianos developed a distinct sound, aptly described as a meeting of the Bahian carnival and Woodstock.[25] Mixing the high-speed *frevo* rhythm of the *trios elétricos*, guitar-driven rock, and bossa nova, the group had a major impact on Bahian pop music in the 1970s and beyond. For a time, the group lived together in a semirural alternative community in Rio de Janeiro state and functioned as a musical collective. Unlike the tropicalists, however, the Novos Baianos never proposed any sort of "movement" aimed at critiquing musical traditions and cultural ideologies.

Another Bahian musician who emerged as a central figure of the Brazilian counterculture was Raul Seixas, a long-haired, bearded rocker who combined Elvis Presley–style rock 'n' roll with northeastern forms such as *baião* and *capoeira* music. Raul is somewhat unique among his generational cohort in that he seemed to have entirely ignored bossa nova, jazz-samba, Tropicália, and even the rock innovations of Os Mutantes. Seixas consciously positioned himself outside of the MPB camp, declaring flatly in one song from 1974 that he had "nothing to do with the evolutionary line of Brazilian popular music," a reference to Caetano Veloso's famous statement of 1966. Veloso himself has argued that all that was not American in Raul Seixas was Bahian, suggesting that his musical trajectory from northeast Brazil to the United States bypassed Rio and São Paulo, the traditional centers of cultural influence.[26]

Seixas was most famous for his radically nonconformist songs and performative gestures, which included exhorting a crowd of fans to throw away their identity papers and take off their clothes during one concert.[27] With lyricist Paulo Coelho (who later gained international fame with his novels of spiritual questing), Seixas composed some of the great rock anthems of the Brazilian counterculture such as "Ouro de tolo" (Fool's gold), in which he ironizes his pop star fame, "Metamorfose ambulante" (Moving metamorphosis), an impassioned defense of constant change and self-contradiction, and "Sociedade Alternativa," a call for establishing an "alternative society" during the period of military rule.[28]

The countercultural ethos also found expression in artists who destabilized gender distinctions and, in some cases, openly affirmed their homosexuality. Ney Matogrosso, the lead vocalist of the band Secos Molhados, was the supreme avatar of this transgendered gay sensibility. With a high-pitched contratenor voice, he performed on stage in high-camp style, scantily clad, fully made-up, and adorned with feathers.[29] Matogrosso gained national attention around the same time that Caetano Veloso launched his experimental album *Araçá azul*. The inside of the fold-out album cover announces that *Araçá azul* is "a record for *entendidos*," a multivalent term that conventionally refers to those who are "in the know" but is also used colloquially to refer to gays. Although the recordings make no explicit references to sexuality, the album cover photo of Veloso's scrawny and pale body in front of a mirror suggests gender and sexual ambiguity.

As exiled leaders of a cultural movement widely regarded as the inaugural moment of a Brazilian counterculture, Veloso and Gil were received with enthusiasm and anticipation when they returned from exile. Yet both musicians made it clear that they had no intention of leading a movement or speaking for the new counterculture. Upon arriving, Veloso announced to the press: "I don't want to assume any leadership role. I only want to sing my songs so that people see that we continue singing and working. There is no more hope for organizing people around a common ideal."[30] Gil also expressed ambivalence regarding expectations that he articulate a position of cultural and political leadership. In one interview, he remarked, "There was a time in my life in which I felt that I had political obligations with society in the sense of contributing most intensely to desired transformations. And to some extent I still think and act this way, but I have been greatly disillusioned, I learned that we can't do so much. We can do other things, but not necessarily transform the world from one day to the next." [31]

Gil evidenced the most personal interest in the ethos and lifestyle of the counterculture. He followed a macrobiotic diet, continued to use marijuana and hallucinogens, and indulged his audiences with references to his personal spiritual quests. Gil's first postexile album, Expresso 2222, best captured the mixture of political disillusionment and personal liberation among the participants in Brazil's countercultural scene. His song "Oriente," written in the countercultural haven of Ibiza, Spain, while he was still exiled, is emblematic of Gil's work in the early seventies. A slow and meditative song, "Oriente" evokes the sound of an Indian raga, opening with the exhortation: "Se oriente rapaz / pela constelação do Cruzeiro do Sul" (Orient yourself, man / by the constellation of the Southern Cross). The phrase, "orient yourself" is multivalent, suggesting that self-discovery, or personal orientation, may be found in the Orient. During this period, countercultural youth throughout the West were attracted to Eastern religions and philosophies. Gil has noted that the reference to the Southern Cross, a national symbol shown on the Brazilian flag, was an expression of his "longing for the Southern Hemisphere." [32] It simultaneously evokes his home and serves as a celestial guide to other points on the globe.

In the United States, countercultural movements have been subject to numerous conflicting interpretations. Theodore Rosnak has argued that the counterculture was produced by "technocracy's children," a uniquely affluent generation that came of age during the 1960s struggle for civil rights and the widespread protests against the war in Vietnam. For Rosnak, the primary significance of the counterculture was its rejection of the military-industrial complex with its profoundly destructive and anti-ecological vision for eternal economic growth. The counterculture was an "exploration of the politics of consciousness" that called for new ways of understanding sexuality, community, nature, and the individual psyche. [33] Other critics have argued that the counterculture, with its image of youthful rebellion and its message of nonconformity, was proper to the development of a robust and segmented consumer culture. Drawing on numerous examples from the advertising industry, Thomas Frank has shown that Madison Avenue executives played key roles in the invention and marketing of countercultural styles and the promotion of "hip consumerism" in the United States. [34]

Although influenced by American and European phenomena, the middle-class Brazilian counterculture emerged under different historical circumstances. Brazil was a relatively poor and unevenly developed society living under a brutal military regime. Certain aspects of countercultural style frequently appeared in fashion magazines, but there was relatively little attempt to promote "hip consumerism" in the early 1970s. On the other hand, the anti-technological and ecological critique identified by Rosnak had less salience than the critique of military violence and social control.

The antiauthoritarianism of the Brazilian counterculture did not take the form of consciousness-raising and collective action that characterized protest movements of the 1960s. For this reason, some observers criticized the phenomenon as a form of depoliticized escapism. In an analysis of the "AI-5 generation," for example, Luciano Martins has argued that the Brazilian counterculture was "an expression of alienation produced by authoritarianism." [35] More sympathetic analyses of the counterculture, however, have drawn attention to its resistance to institutionalized culture, technocratic rationality, and myriad forms of social control under military rule. The anti-imperialist imperatives that oriented revolutionary discourse of the 1960s became less relevant as artists questioned the very notion of a unitary "national culture." Silviano Santiago has argued that the counterculture "integrated into a universal context those values that were marginalized during the construction of Brazilian culture." [36] There was an attempt to critique national culture from the margins, drawing inspiration from international countercultures and internally marginalized communities in Brazil.

SWEET BARBARIANS

Heloísa Buarque de Hollanda has noted that the urban countercultural milieu of the early 1970s tended to identify less with the *povo* or revolutionary proletariat and more with racial and sexual minorities.[37] These communities seemed to offer symbolic refuge to hippies and other countercultural adherents who felt alienated from the patriotic discourse of the "economic miracle" touted by the military regime. In the early 1970s, many of them gravitated to Bahia, which they regarded as a privileged site of telluric and ludic pleasure away from the fast-paced life of Rio and São Paulo. Veloso remembers that "Salvador—with its electric and liberated carnival, with its deserted beaches and beach villages, with its colonial architecture and its Afro-Brazilian religions—became the preferred city of the *desbundados* (dropouts)." [38] After returning from exile, Veloso and Gil soon emerged as central figures in the Bahian carnival. In 1972, Veloso performed on his own *trio elétrico* called the

Caetanave (Caetano ship), a moving soundstage in the form of a spaceship. He composed several new *frevos*, an up-tempo musical style originally from Pernambuco that was used by the *trios elétricos*. The following year, Gil joined the Filhos de Gandhi (The Sons of Gandhi), a venerated *afoxé* group founded in 1949 by black stevedores that had almost become defunct. He composed a popular homage to the *afoxé*, titled "Filhos de Gandhi," which invokes all of the *orixás* to descend during carnival to see the group parade.[39] Gil's partici- pation in the Filhos de Gandhi sparked a revival of the group, which became a celebrated symbol of the Bahian carnival.

During this time, Antônio Risério observed a reciprocal exchange of dis- courses, practices, and styles between the largely middle-class countercul- ture and the working-class black youth in Bahia.[40] There was a resurgence of pop songs celebrating Afro-Brazilian culture, particularly the Candomblé religion, a thematic current developed by Dorival Caymmi beginning in the late 1930s.[41] The confluence of countercultural and Afro-diasporic perspec- tives was dramatized in 1976, when Gil, Veloso, Gal Costa, and Maria Bethânia embarked on a national tour to promote *Doces Bárbaros* (Sweet barbarians), a double album reuniting the original Bahian group that first coalesced in Sal- vador in 1964. *Doces Bárbaros* synthesized the cosmology of Candomblé with astrology, a spiritual practice that became popular in Brazil in the 1970s.

Likening themselves to barbarians invading Rome, the Bahian group set out to "conquer" the capital cities of Brazil, announcing in Veloso's title track: "with love in our hearts / we prepare the invasion / filled with joy / we enter the beloved city." Instead of conquering the city by force, the sweet barbari- ans proposed to overtake the city by turning it into a Dionysian space of per- petual carnival. Using the lingo of Brazilian hippies, the refrain announces the radiation of "alto astral, altas transas, lindas canções / afoxés, astronaves, aves, cordões" (good vibes, groovy times, lovely songs / *afoxés*, spaceships, birds, *cordões*). Invoking Yoruba deities of Candomblé, the *orixás*, the sweet barbarians proposed an insurgency with the help of the "sword of Ogun," the "blessing of Olorun," and the "lightning bolts of Yansã." Another popu- lar song from the album, "São João, Xangô Menino" (St. John, Xangô child), celebrates religious syncretism in Bahia in which each *orixá* is identified with a specific Catholic saint. What began as a strategic response to the official persecution and suppression of African religion in Brazil evolved into a new Afro-diasporic religion with its own pantheon of African, Catholic, indige- nous divinities. In this song, Veloso and Gil referenced the winter festival for St. John, often associated with Xangô, the *orixá* of fire and thunder. Dur- ing their tour, the sweet barbarians performed several other songs celebrating Candomblé that were not included on the *Doces Bárbaros* album, including "Oração para Mãe Menininha" (1972), Dorival Caymmi's classic tribute to the most famous Candomblé priestess of the century, and "As ayabás" (Veloso-Gil), based on the sacred rhythms of the female *orixás*. Although none of the four Bahians had been raised within Afro-Brazilian religious traditions, they became increasingly involved with Candomblé during the 1970s.

Whereas the *Doces Bárbaros* tracks discussed above take Bahia as its main point of reference, Gil's "Chuck Berry Fields Forever," another allusion to the Beatles' hit, outlined the Afro-Atlantic connections of popular music. In a sense, the song is a diasporic coda to Veloso's earlier composition about Bahia, "Sugarcane Fields Forever." Set to 1950s-style rock 'n' roll, the song described in mythical terms the transnational genesis of rock music in Africa, Latin America, and the United States. In Brazil, as elsewhere in the world, rock music is typically imagined as the cultural domain of white working- and middle-class youth. With the emergence of Elvis Presley as the first international rock star, and the subsequent British invasion, the Afro-diasporic origins of rock 'n' roll were largely obscured. In Gil's song, Chuck Berry, the African American rock 'n' roll innovator, serves as an emblem of this erasure. Gil portrays the emergence of rock 'n' roll as a gendered collision between a feminine Europe and a masculine Africa:

> Vertigem verga a virgem branca tomba sob o sol
> rachado em mil raios pelo machado de Xangô
> E assim gerados, a rumba, o mambo, o samba, o rhythm'n'blues
> tornaram-se ancestrais, os pais de rock and roll

> Struck with vertigo the white virgin stumbles in the sun
> split into a thousand rays of light by the ax of Xangô this is how
> rumba, mambo, samba, and rhythm and blues were born
> they became the ancestors, the parents of rock 'n' roll

European culture, represented here as a "white virgin," is torn asunder by Xangô, a warrior deity in Yoruba religion, generating a panoply of diasporic rhythms in Cuba, Brazil, and the United States that would become the roots of modern rock. In this mythical story, the sweet barbarians are cast as the four horsemen of the "após-calipso" (postcalypso), a clever pun referring to the Trinidadian rhythm, another prerock diasporic form. Despite its problematic gender politics, "Chuck Berry Fields Forever" is interesting in that it refuses to construct African culture as a passive victim of European domination.[42] It is also notable for insisting on the transnational, diasporic genesis of rock, locating it beside other Afro-Atlantic musical cultures.

The Doces Bárbaros tour was emblematic of the Brazilian counterculture of the 1970s, expressing the aspirations and fantasies of a generation of urban middle-class youth under the dictatorship. In one statement, Veloso affirmed that the Bahian group was not interested in arguing about laws, morals, religion, politics, or aesthetics. The sweet barbarians sought instead to radiate "an immense charge of vital light" on each city they "invaded."[43] The untimely denouement of the tour was equally emblematic of countercultural Brazil under the military regime. During their visit to Florianopolis, the capital of Santa Catarina, local police agents invaded their hotel rooms in search of illicit drugs. Gilberto Gil and the group's drummer were arrested for possession of marijuana and subsequently interned in a sanitarium.

Gil turned this untimely event into an opportunity to provoke a public discussion regarding drug use. While interned, he gave an interview in which he stated his position on drug use: "I think it's important, it's something that has been discussed on a deep cultural level all over the world. Why not here in Brazil? Why maintain all of this obscurantism, this fear of modernity, this fear of being in the world today?"[44] Of course, drug use certainly was not being discussed "all over the world," but it certainly was a debated issue in parts of Western Europe and the United States. Under the governorship of Jerry Brown, for example, California legalized the possession of small amounts of marijuana for personal consumption in 1975, a fact that did not go unnoticed by the Brazilian press after Gil was detained.[45] Gil attempted to turn his ordeal into a principled referendum on drug consumption and its policing, which he proposed as a dilemma of modernity and not as a question of morality and criminality. His reference to the Sartrean notion of "being-in-the-world" recalls the tropicalists' previously outlined position on the influence of foreign technologies and styles on Brazilian popular music. Like electrified rock music, drug experimentation was central to international countercultural practices and discourses that many Brazilians were absorbing.

AFRO-BRAZILIAN COUNTERCULTURES

Focusing primarily on the Anglophone North Atlantic, Paul Gilroy has emphasized the role of popular music in the genesis and development of a Black Atlantic "counterculture of modernity" that is positioned simultaneously

within and against the Enlightenment legacy of the West.[46] Gilroy empha-
sizes the dialogic and multidirectional flow of culture in the Afro-Atlantic
world and cites popular music as a key vehicle for these transnational ex-
changes. Together with Cuba, Jamaica, and the United States, Brazil has been
a key producer and receiver of musical forms of the Afro-Atlantic world. In the
1970s these transnational cultural flows were particularly significant for the
development of new forms of urban Brazilian music that denounced racial
inequalities, affirmed historical and cultural connections with Africa, and articulated a black collective identity. As elsewhere in the Afro-Atlantic world,
popular music in Brazil has served as the primary vehicle for the circulation
of oppositional values that draw from myriad transnational sources.[47]

Well-established figures of MPB contributed to these developments. Of
particular importance was the work of Jorge Ben, a key ally of the tropicalists
who had forged a unique personal style combining urban samba with rhythm
and blues. In the early 1970s he produced several compositions that explored
themes in Afro-Brazilian history. His song "Zumbi" (1974) pays homage to
the leader of the famous quilombo of Palmares, a large seventeenth-century
maroon settlement. Although not a song of protest against military rule, it
expressed a measure of racial pride and political defiance. Jorge Ben achieved
enormous success in 1976 with "Xica da Silva," an irresistible funk-samba
that was featured as the theme song to Carlos Diegues's film about the black
mistress of a wealthy diamond merchant in eighteenth-century Minas Gerais.

The 1970s saw the proliferation of commodified forms of African American popular culture throughout the Third World, with especially strong resonance in postcolonial African and Caribbean nations. In several different
contexts, soul music, blaxploitation films, and African American sports luminaries had a significant impact on African and diasporic youth, generating
expressions that were often at odds with state-sanctioned national cultures.[48]
Young Afro-Brazilians appropriated these cultural products and icons to challenge the nationalist ethos of brasilidade, which tended to obfuscate racial
discrimination and inequality by exalting the mestiço ethos. Transnational,
diasporic cultures often served to critique established modernist notions of
national identity. As discussed in Chapter 1, samba has been for the most part
complicit in reproducing the ideology of racial democracy since the 1930s.
When urban Afro-Brazilian youth began to openly challenge racial hegemony
in the 1970s, they often turned to other forms of diasporic music as the most
effective vehicle for racial affirmation.

In the mid-1970s, a cultural movement dubbed "Black Rio" or "Black Soul"
emerged in the working-class neighborhoods of Rio de Janeiro's North Zone.

Inspired directly by the black-consciousness movement in the United States and its attendant musical, visual, and sartorial styles, the movement was quickly reproduced in other Brazilian capitals, such as São Paulo, Belo Horizonte, and Salvador. The English word "black" entered into the lexicon of Afro-Brazilian youth as a marker of personal and collective identity. The Black Soul movement revolved primarily around dance parties, attracting thousands of youths with Afro hairstyles in platform shoes and bell-bottom slacks. Disc jockeys with portable sound systems played the latest soul and funk hits from the United States.[49] Record companies began investing in established singers like Tim Maia, Cassiano, and Luiz Melodia, and local funk-samba fusion groups such as Banda Black Rio.

On one level, the Black Soul movement was a commercial enterprise based on the recognition of urban black communities as potentially lucrative markets for multinational companies and their Brazilian affiliates. Yet it also gave impetus to an emergent black-consciousness movement in Brazil spearheaded by Movimento Negro Unificado (MNU, Unified Black Movement), which was founded in 1978 following the death of a young black worker while in police custody in São Paulo. The Black Soul movement underscored transnational cultural affinities, often with political implications, that attracted many Afro-Brazilian youth. As Jorge Watusi, an Afro-Brazilian artist-activist wryly observed of the Black Soul phenomenon in Salvador, "[C]onsciousness came as a fashion."[50] The expression of racial consciousness in the Black Soul movement was based more on style, both musical and visual, than on the lyrical content of the dance songs.

The Black Soul movement was criticized in the Brazilian press from several angles. Conservative critics allied with the military regime, such as Gilberto Freyre, charged that soul music was an insidious importation of African American cultural and political discourses that were irrelevant to Brazil's "racial democracy."[51] Some Afro-Brazilian activists, including samba musicians, criticized the movement for its lack of cultural authenticity. Middle-class blacks also expressed some anxiety about the movement, fearing that it would generate racial tension. Traditional leftists critiqued Black Soul on the grounds that it was mere entertainment, produced and commodified by multinational capital, which diverted attention from class politics. The soul movement was ultimately ambiguous: if on one hand it was a commodified product backed by multinational recording companies, it also advanced a self-conscious diasporic identity among young Afro-Brazilians.

In Salvador, Bahia, the Black Soul movement had particular repercussions, contributing to a local phenomenon known as *blackitude baiana*.[52] Between

1974 and 1980, new carnival organizations known as *blocos afros*, such as Ilê Aiyê, Malê Debalê, Olodum, and Muzenza, emerged to protest racial inequality and promote Afro-Brazilian culture. These developments were inspired as much by local cultural practices, like Candomblé and samba, as by transnational phenomena such as Pan-Africanism, anticolonial liberation movements (particularly in Lusophone Africa), and Black Power, as well as soul, funk, and, later, reggae and rap music.[53] Almost from the beginning, the new Afro-Bahian music was transnational and diasporic in terms of musical and discursive values.

Gil and Veloso invested their considerable cultural capital to these new Afro-Brazilian cultural movements, both in published interviews and in their recordings. Countering the denunciations of Black Soul in the national press, Veloso supported the movement in terms of identity politics: "I like seeing Brazilian blacks identify with American blacks. I adore Black Rio. I think the blacks are affirming themselves more as blacks than as Brazilians and this is important."[54] Lélia Gonzales, one of the founding leaders of the Unified Black Movement claimed that Gil gave a "big boost" to the organization by performing at MNU-sponsored events when other artists refused for fear of being associated with a movement perceived as radical and divisive.[55] While other artists and commentators criticized these movements, often on the grounds that they were not authentically Brazilian, the tropicalists championed them as an expression of Afro-diasporic modernity and as a vital component of the general critique of authoritarianism in Brazil.

REINVENTING BRAZIL

Under pressure from moderate sectors of civil society, the military regime initiated a period of *distensão* (decompression) in the mid- to late-1970s. New possibilities and imperatives came into focus with the emergence of independent social and political movements representing blacks, women, gays, and labor. This period also marked the resurfacing of public controversy among various sectors of the left-wing opposition. Many of these debates concerning the role of artists and intellectuals, the social and political efficacy of art, and the relationship among cultural producers, media industries, and the state had already been rehearsed in the 1960s. The touchstone for the most heated polemics was an interview given in August 1978 by filmmaker Carlos Diegues, who invoked the specter of "ideological patrols" to denounce his critics from the orthodox Left. Mainstream and alternative newspapers and magazines immediately seized upon the trope and began soliciting opinions from public intellectuals and artists. Two university professors compiled a collection of their own interviews relating to the polemic.

Several people interviewed had recently returned from abroad following the passage of an amnesty bill for political exiles in August 1979. Many were skeptical of revolutionary projects and critical of ideological positions that had predominated in the 1960s. Fernando Gabeira, a former urban guerrilla involved in the kidnapping of the American ambassador in 1969, stated: "In the 1960s I criticized my position as a petit-bourgeois intellectual; now in the 1970s, I'm advancing this self-criticism, analyzing my position as a *macho latino*, as a white guy, and as an intellectual." [56] At a time when opponents of the military regime were raising questions about intellectual authority, racial privilege, gender identity, and sexual orientation, the tropicalist movement was a key point of reference.

In the late 1970s, both Veloso and Gil composed and recorded songs that expressed gender ambiguity and homosociability that intervened directly in debates concerning sexuality in Brazil. In Gil's "Pai e mãe" (Father and mother) (1975), he expresses homosocial affection as an extension of filial love for his father: "I spent a lot of time / learning to kiss / other men, like I kiss my father." He subsequently recorded "Superhomem (A canção)" (Superman [The song]) (1979), in which he claimed and affirmed his "feminine" side. After confessing that he had once believed that "being a man was enough," he goes on to proclaim that the "the womanly part of me / that I'd suppressed until then / is the best side / I have in me now / and is what makes me live." Veloso was even more explicit in presenting an androgynous persona on stage and in public, and his lyrics occasionally touched upon homoerotic desire. One his most famous songs, "Menino do Rio" (Boy from Rio) (1979), is dedicated to a young surfer from Rio with an "eternally flirtatious heart." The song ends with the declaration, "[W]hen I see you I desire your desire." These homoerotic overtures were ultimately ambiguous since both artists were married, insisted on their heterosexuality, and also produced numerous love songs for women. Yet the sexual ambiguity of their songs and performances (especially Veloso's) contributed in a diffuse way to a critique of traditional masculinity in Brazil.

Gil and Veloso participated more decisively in the movement to affirm Afro-Brazilian culture and its connections with Africa and other points in the diaspora. In 1977, they joined a delegation of 160 representatives to the Second International Festival of Black Art and Culture (FESTAC), a major international event involving seventy-five countries. Along with a large contingent of visual artists, filmmakers, and university professors, the Brazilian delegation included a Candomblé priestess, Olga de Alaketo, the dance troupe of the Federal University of Bahia, and saxophonist Paulo Moura.[57] Under the aegis of the Ministries of Foreign Relations and Education, Brazil's official participation in this international cultural event was fraught with ambiguities and contradictions. Participation in FESTAC served the interests of the Brazilian government, which was eager to capitalize on historical and cultural connections with West Africa. Vocal critics of Brazilian race relations, like artist-activist Abdias do Nascimento, were excluded from the official Brazilian delegation.[58] Yet the festival also gave impetus to the Afro-diasporic turn in Brazilian popular music. Gil and Veloso subsequently recorded albums inspired by their experiences in West Africa and by the new Afro-Brazilian cultural movements.

Veloso's 1977 album, Bicho, featured a song based on Nigerian juju music, "Two Naira Fifty Kobo" (a typical cab fare in Lagos at that time), that invokes a divine force that "speaks Tupi, speaks Yoruba" and affirms the cultural affinities between Brazil and Nigeria. Bicho also included several upbeat disco-inflected songs like "Odara," a Yoruba term commonly used by Candomblé practitioners to signify "good" or "positive." In Veloso's song, "odara" signifies a state of rapture achieved through dancing: "deixe eu dançar / pro meu corpo ficar odara / minha cara / minha cuca ficar odara" (let me dance / so that my body becomes odara / my face / my head becomes odara). Such use of the term "odara" owed much to a romantic countercultural imagination that typically associated black culture with corporal liberation and collective exaltation. On the other hand, songs like "Odara" located Afro-Brazilian culture at the very center of Brazilian modernity, instead of assigning it a premodern role as the bearer of cultural purity. Veloso promoted the album with a series of performances with Banda Black Rio called the "Bicho Baile Show," and he actively encouraged audiences to dance, which was unusual for MPB concerts.

In the other dance song of the album, "Gente" (People), Veloso celebrates the life force of humans striving to survive, to satisfy corporal desires, and to attain spiritual fulfillment even under the most adverse circumstances. The disarming naïveté of its simple platitudes such as the verse "gente é pra brilhar não pra morrer de fome" (people are made to shine not die of hunger) divided critics. Such verses elicited ridicule from skeptics yet also appeared as slogans of social critique spray-painted on city walls. Bicho also included the hits "O leãozinho" (The lion cub), a precious homage to Veloso's astrological sign, and "Tigresa" (Tigress), inspired by the emerging movie star Sonia Braga.

In assessing the controversy over Veloso's album, one critic pointedly asked: "Must a composer adorn his verses with exhortations of social activism, or does he have a right to simply live in a universe populated by butterflies, felines, lion cubs, and beautiful people?" [59] Veloso's most acerbic critics were his former allies from *O Pasquim*, the leftist satiric journal of Rio de Janeiro. The celebrated cartoonist of *O Pasquim*, Henfil, quipped that Veloso was the leader of the "Odara Patrol." Veloso appropriated the moniker and responded by accusing his critics of anti-Bahian prejudice, going so far as compare them to white South Africans under apartheid. [60]

In the same year, Gil produced *Refavela*, a brilliant and far-reaching reflection on Africa and Afro-Brazilians within a contemporary diasporic perspective. The album cover featured a close-up photo of Gil wearing an embroidered skull cap and Candomblé beads. It was the second in a series of albums titled with the prefix *re*, suggesting a period of reinvention and regeneration for the artist and for the nation as it entered a period of gradual political opening. His 1975 album, *Refazenda*, synthesized diverse personal meditations on nature, spiritual renewal, and his rural northeastern heritage. In contrast, *Refavela* was dedicated to the black urban countercultures of Rio de Janeiro and Salvador.

The title track celebrated *favelas* as the loci of quotidian struggles, social activism, and emerging cultural movements like Black Rio. "Refavela" challenged familiar notions of the *favela* as a space of crime and social anomie by suggesting how its inhabitants participate in the economic and cultural life of the city. The song opens with an acoustic guitar and a West African talking drum followed by a salvo of Candomblé percussion and an exultant chant-refrain in the Yoruba language. Combining elements of funk, reggae, Nigerian juju, and Afro-Bahian rhythms, the musical style is sui generis, reflecting the transnational scope of the song.

With specific references to the Black Rio movement, "Refavela" locates young urban Afro-Brazilians in a diasporic "counterculture of modernity," to use Gilroy's term. One stanza, for example, describes the "paradoxical" relationship between the local and the transnational in diasporic culture: "a refavela / revela a escola de samba paradoxal / brasileirinho pelo sotaque / mas de língua internacional" (the refavela / reveals the paradoxical samba school / quite Brazilian in its accent / but international in its language). "Refavela" is a verbal and musical collage of social and cultural references, including shantytowns, residential projects, samba schools, and dance halls. As one of the final stanzas proclaims, the song is an allegory of black urban life in the 1970s. [61]

On the same album, Gil recorded a funk-pop version of Ilê Aiyê's 1975 car-nival song "Que bloco é esse?" (What group is this?), a defiant affirmation of the "black world" in the face of racial prejudice. Mixing wry humor with racial politics, the song enacted a symbolic reversal of *branqueamento* (whiten-ing), a pernicious ideology of racial progress based on Eurocentric models of beauty and modernity:

> branco se você soubesse
> o valor que preto tem,
> tu tomava um banho de piche
> e ficava preto também
>
> white, if you understood
> the value of blacks,
> you would bathe in tar
> and become black too

Gil's recording was particularly timely since Ilê Aiyê was often rebuked in the local press for its pointed critiques of racism in Bahian society. Other com-positions from Gil's *Refavela* underscored the historic and contemporary cul-tural connections between West Africa and Brazil, especially Bahia. The funk-inflected "Babá Apalá," for example, tells the story of Aganjú, a manifestation of the *orixá* of thunder, Xangô, and his ancestral connection to contemporary Afro-Brazilians. English versions of these songs were later recorded on the 1979 album *Nightingale*, Gil's first attempt to break into the U.S. pop market.

Refavela provoked controversy in the popular press, suggesting that this kind of gesture of racial affirmation posed some difficulties for sectors of the Brazilian critical establishment. Two years later, in an interview with *Jornegro*, an Afro-Brazilian monthly from São Paulo, Gil interpreted the unfavorable reactions to *Refavela*, underscoring the tension between national and dias-poric articulations of racial identity that were implicit in the denominations "negro" and "black," respectively: "The press came down hard on me be-cause the attitude of the album was *black* and at the time most journalists were against *black*, not against *negro*, but against *black*, the consciousness that is connected to the international sphere and isn't just Brazilian." [62] Writing for *Veja*, Tarik de Souza labeled Gil's effort "*rebobagem*" (restupidity) and in-terpreted the album as an imitation of soul music with "confused lyrics." [63] He seemed particularly incensed that Gil would "reduce to merely soul" Tom Jobim's canonical bossa nova composition "Samba do avião" (Song of the jet). Other critics ridiculed Gil's new personal aesthetic when he began wearing braids with cowrie shells and West African dashikis. Lélia Gonzales of the MNU remarked at the time that Gilberto Gil "is a guy who disturbs" because he intervenes on the "symbolic" level.[64] In other words, Gil's critique of authoritarianism, racism, and the universalist pretensions of "national identity" depended less on his verbal statements than on his open affirmation of an African or Afro-diasporic musical and sartorial aesthetic.

Gil's greatest hit of his career, "Não chore mais," a Portuguese version of Bob Marley's reggae ballad "No Woman, No Cry," came in 1979. His version coincided with the beginning of political opening and was associated with a popular movement calling for amnesty for political exiles. According to Gil, the song sought to associate Jamaican Rastafaris and Brazilian hippies who were persecuted for smoking marijuana.[65] But it is also a ballad of mourning for the victims of authoritarian rule and a song of hope urging Brazilians to focus on the future:

> amigos presos
> amigos sumindo assim
> pra nunca mais tais recordações
> retratos do mal em si
> melhor é deixar pra trás

> friends arrested
> friends just disappearing
> forever
> these memories
> portraits of evil incarnate
> better to leave it all behind

At the end of the song, the tempo speeds up to a danceable beat as Gil intones *tudo, tudo, tudo vai dar pé*, an almost literal translation of Bob Marley's "everything is gonna be all right." The overall effect of the song is to situate democratic aspirations in Brazil within the context of Third World and Afro-diasporic struggles. In 1980, Gil toured the major Brazilian capitals with reggae superstar Jimmy Cliff. The recording of Marley's song and the subsequent tour with Cliff positioned Gil as the leading exponent of reggae in Brazil. His ongoing forays into reggae music contributed decisively to the expansion and indigenization of reggae throughout Brazil in the 1980s and 1990s.

Surrounded by local fans, Gilberto Gil (right) and Candomblé priestess (center)
welcome Jimmy Cliff (left) at the airport in Salvador, 1980. Gil and Cliff are wearing
carnival attire of the *bloco afro* Ilê Aiyê and are holding fabric of the *afoxé* Badauê.
(A Tarde)

CONCLUSION

Throughout the 1970s, the tropicalist group contributed in diverse ways to
youth countercultures that were concerned less with conventional political
protest than with the articulation of new personal and collective identities.
Gilberto Gil, Caetano Veloso, and Jorge Ben were positioned at the inter-
section of middle-class countercultural phenomena such as the *desbunde* and
emergent Afro-diasporic movements involving soul, reggae, and new black
carnival music from Bahia. These cultural phenomena participated, however
diffusely, in a broad initiative in civil society advocating the return of democratic rule in Brazil. Central to this widespread call for *abertura* (opening)
were new "social movements," including grassroots labor activism, which

led to the foundation of the Worker's Party (PT), an Afro-Brazilian movement (MNU), a gay movement (SOMOS), and various feminist organizations.

In "Pipoca moderna" (Modern popcorn), from his 1975 album *Jóia*, Caetano Veloso referenced the emergence of diffuse yet irrepressible forms of agitation against authoritarian rule. Originally composed as an instrumental piece by Sebastião Biano for A Banda de Pífanos de Caruaru, a fife-and-drum ensemble from rural Pernambuco, Veloso added alliterative verses that denounced the violence of military rule in lines such as "era nê de nunca mais" (it was n of never more). In the onomatopoeic refrain, the heating and popping of corn suggest the willy-nilly emergence of opposition forces: "pipoca ali aqui / pipoca além / desanoitece a manhã / tudo mudou" (popcorn there here / popcorn beyond / night ends morning comes / all has changed). Although frequently criticized for not being "political," the former tropicalists inspired and contributed to several social and cultural movements that were beginning to emerge, popcornlike, to contest authoritarianism in Brazil.

6

TRACES OF
TROPICÁLIA

Throughout the seventies and eighties, the tropicalists remained acutely sensitive to the ongoing transformations and innovations in Brazilian and international musics. Their early experiments with electric instruments and rock music set the stage for a "boom" in Brazilian rock in the 1980s. Their creative appropriation of reggae, disco, soul, juju, and Afro-Bahian forms contributed to several Afro-Brazilian musical movements during the same period. The tropicalists also contributed substantially to the dissolution of cultural hierarchies by producing music for mass consumption while making use of literary and musical techniques formerly associated with the realm of "high art." They have developed a compelling model for syncretic or hybrid cultural production in Brazil, generating a tradition of their own in Brazilian popular music. During the 1990s, the tropicalists maintained a ubiquitous presence in the national media, continued to produce innovative work, and were often acknowledged as a major influence on emerging artists. Gil and Veloso in particular have exercised tremendous influence over the field of Brazilian popular music that surpasses their popularity in terms of record sales. The 1990s also witnessed renewed critical and popular interest in Tom Zé, the most radical innovator of the tropicalist group, who struggled for many years on the margins of MPB. His extraordinary artistic and professional comeback has brought into focus dimensions of Tropicália that previously had been ignored.

The issues and imperatives surrounding cultural production in Brazil have, of course, changed since the era of Tropicália. By the end of the century, there was considerably less anxiety in relation to the cultural hegemony of the United States. The range of musical production accepted as "Brazilian" has expanded and now includes all sorts of styles that originated elsewhere, such as rock, reggae, funk, rap, and metal, as well as new hybrids generated in dialogue with Brazilian traditions. In many ways, the tropicalist experience and its aftershocks helped to create the conditions of possibility for the proliferation of these hybrid styles. Progressive artists have also relinquished the role of political vanguard guiding the *povo* toward social revolution. This does not mean, of course, that Brazilian popular music has become apolitical or acritical, only that its claims tend to be less redemptive. Gone is the figure of the protest singer with an acoustic guitar singing truth to power as epitomized by Geraldo Vandré. In his place, however, are myriad artists and groups engaging modern media technologies and articulating forceful critiques of social inequality, racism, sexism, police violence, environmental depredations, political corruption, and other dilemmas of contemporary Brazilian society. Although extremely heterogeneous, much of this music is indebted, however indirectly, to the tropicalist experience of the 1960s.

TROPICÁLIA REPRISE

Perhaps the first self-conscious reevaluation of the tropicalist moment came in 1989 with the release of Caetano Veloso's album *Estrangeiro* (Foreigner), which was recorded and produced in New York by Peter Sherer and Arto Lindsay, two prominent denizens of the New York art-rock music scene. Hélio Eichbauer's magnificent expressionist backdrop for the second act of Teatro Oficina's 1967 production of *O rei da vela* (discussed in Chapter 3) was used as the album cover and as the stage scenery for Veloso's live performances. The title track of the album invoked the vision of Brazil as seen from the perspective of foreigners such as Cole Porter, Claude Levi-Strauss, and Paul Gauguin, who all visited Rio. For Veloso, the estranged, out-of-place perspective of the foreigner frames his own sense of alienation as he wanders the streets: "and I, less a stranger to the place than to the time / continue more alone walking against the wind." The textual reference to his first pop hit from the tropicalist period, "Alegria, alegria," reinscribes the lonely urban subject who is "walking against the wind" into the contemporary context.[1]

Unlike the young artist of "Alegria, alegria," the first-person narrator of "O estrangeiro" feels out of step with the present and estranged from the urban space through which he passes. The dystopian world that Veloso invokes in "O estrangeiro" is sustained by reactionary ideologies and extra-official violence, which are the legacy of authoritarian rule. Much like the tropicalist satires of military reason, Veloso cites the most retrograde discourses that proclaim that "the demented should receive shock treatment" and that "the white adult male should always be in command." The power elite in Veloso's song "recognize the necessary value of hypocritical acts / eliminate the Indians, expect nothing of the blacks."

The heavy dance beat and piercing guitar create a hard-edged, unsettling ambiance that challenges foreign perceptions of Brazilian music as suave and melodious. Veloso comments on this generalization and his own relationship to it in the final line of the song by paraphrasing Bob Dylan: "Some may like a soft Brazilian singer / but I have given up all attempts at perfection." This remark came from the liner notes of Bob Dylan's 1965 album *Bringing It All Back Home*, in which he first used electric rock to the dismay of folk purists. The Rio de Janeiro of the 1950s and 1960s that produced the "soft Brazilian singer" no longer exists, compelling the artist to create a brash aesthetic of imperfection.

Traces of the tropicalist experience are also present on Veloso's 1991 album, *Circuladô*. The general concept of the album is outlined in the opening track, "Fora da ordem" (Out of order), a pointed response to George Bush's triumphalist proclamation of a "new world order" following the collapse of Eastern bloc socialism. In this song, a first-person narrative voice allegorizes contemporary Brazil with fragmentary scenes from Rio and São Paulo, just as the 1968 song-manifesto "Tropicália" used Brasília to allegorize the nation under military rule. It opens with reference to the discovery of the dead body of a young drug dealer in the "ruins of a school still under construction," an allegorical image of social decay that suggests a link between youth crime and a lack of educational infrastructure. Subsequent references to homeless children roaming the streets at night, a heap of trash, and an open sewer in the upscale Leblon neighborhood in Rio complete the portrait of contemporary urban Brazil. This is the other side of the new world order backed by global capital and U.S. political and military power. Only ephemeral moments of pleasure relieve the despair as the artist engages in a quick flirtation with a male hooker in São Paulo and an affair with a "*mulata* acrobat" provoking a "plethora of joy, a Jorge Benjor show inside of us." In the end, there is no resolution or redemption, only "several possible beautiful harmonies without final judgment."

Although less explicit, some of Gil's songs written in the 1990s also revisited and updated tropicalist approaches to Brazilian culture. Like Veloso, he has produced a good deal of social critique addressing racism, poverty, corruption, and environmental destruction, yet his music tends to be more sanguine about contemporary life. His song "Parabolicamará," from his 1991 album, Parabolic, for example, celebrates the worldwide expansion of media technology as a force of global unity: "Today the world is very large / because the earth is so small / the size of a satellite dish." The song's title is a neologism referring to "parabolic antennas" and "camará" (comrade), a word commonly used in capoeira chants. Based on the rhythm and vocalization of capoeira music, the song echoes Gil's festival hit song "Domingo no parque," which helped to launch the "universal sound" in 1967. In its enthusiasm for the potentially liberating uses of technology, the song also recalls some of his compositions written in prison in 1969.

In the 1990s, Gil also became an enthusiastic proponent of the Internet and set up a sophisticated website that documents his musical activities, advocacy work, and conversations with leading Brazilian intellectuals. In a song from the album Quanta (1997), he likened the Internet to jangadas, the simple wooden rafts used by fishermen in northeastern Brazil. His cybernetic jangada guides his oriki (the sacred parable of his personal Yoruba divinity, or orixá) through a tide of information in order to reach a computer in Taipei. The final stanza of this song, called "Pela internet," (On the internet) cleverly parodies "Pelo telefone," a song from 1917 that is regarded as the first recorded samba. As in many of his tropicalist songs, modern technology functions as a vehicle for reflecting on tradition.

The fiftieth birthdays of Veloso and Gil in 1992 occasioned dozens of major retrospective tributes in the national press. TV Manchete ran a five-part documentary about Caetano Veloso covering all of the major phases in his artistic career, focusing especially on Tropicália. After years of composing, recording, and performing separately, Gil and Veloso reunited in 1993 to record Tropicália 2, a commemoration of the movement's twenty-fifth anniversary. The two Bahians toured Brazil, Europe, and the United States with the acoustic show "Tropicália Duo." Although there was an element of nostalgia in the album, the Bahian duo reaffirmed the ongoing relevance and vitality of the tropicalist project. In the 1960s, the tropicalists fused local genres such as samba and baião with rock and soul music. On Tropicália 2, the Bahian duo mixed rap and samba-reggae, a hybrid rhythm of Bahia that emerged in the 1980s.

The album featured a mix of new compositions and innovative rereadings of material from the 1960s through the 1990s. Gil paid homage to one of

Caetano Veloso (left) and Gilberto Gil perform at the Avery Fisher Hall in New York City during their Tropicália Duo tour, 1994. (Claudia Thompson)

his inspirations, Jimi Hendrix, recording a version of his "Wait until Tomorrow." Veloso reprised Gil's "Tradição" (Tradition), a song about growing up in Salvador in the 1950s that originally appeared on Gil's album *Realce*. They also celebrated contemporary Afro-Bahian music with a rendition of "Nossa gente" (Our people), by the *bloco afro* Olodum. Several of the new songs were tributes to artists and movements that informed Tropicália. The *samba-enredo* "Cinema Novo" traces the history of Brazilian film from classics of the 1930s like Humberto Mauro's *Ganga bruta* to the Embrafilme superproductions of the 1970s like Carlos Diegues's *Xica da Silva*. They highlight the crucial intervention of Cinema Novo in the 1960s and its impact on other realms of Brazilian culture. Other tracks revisited their dialogues with the musical and poetic vanguards of São Paulo, as in Gil's concrete poem put to music ("Dada") and Veloso's digitally sampled sound collage of Brazilian radio singers of the twentieth century ("Rap popcreto"). A more personal homage appeared in Gil's "Baião atemporal," a northeastern *baião* that tells the story of "someone from the Santana family" (a reference to Tom Zé's extended family) who leaves the rural town of Irará on a *pau-de-arara* (flatbed truck) headed for the city.

Tropicália 2 was not simply a nostalgic and self-congratulatory project. As with most of Veloso's and Gil's work, it also contained heavy doses of social criticism. The opening track, "Haiti," for example, is a powerful denunciation of state-sponsored violence against black urban youth. For this song, Veloso and Gil experimented with rap music, a genre that gained a large following among Afro-Brazilian urban youth during the 1990s. Brief rhythmic quotations of samba-reggae fill out the slow rap beat and sparse arrangements. Veloso's lyric documents a scene he witnessed at the 1993 Femadum (Olodum's annual music festival), where he received the "Olodum Citizenship" award presented each year to artists who have contributed to the struggle for racial and social justice. Given the high-minded civic purpose of the Femadum event, Veloso left outraged by incidents of police violence he witnessed from the stage set up in front of the Casa de Jorge Amado, a building that overlooks Pelourinho square in the historic section of Salvador. In the song, he describes a line of mostly black police beating up young blacks, *mulatos*, and poor whites. Veloso's privileged point of view from the stage allows him to witness the brutal police repression of youth who are identified and stigmatized as much by their blackness as by their poverty. Olodum's public rehearsals in Pelourinho square have long been sites of petty crime, fist fights, and violent confrontations with baton-wielding police. But this time, Veloso draws attention to the "eyes of the whole world watching the square":

> não importa nada
> nem o traço do sobrado
> nem a lente do "Fantástico"
> nem o disco de Paul Simon
> ninguém, ninguém é cidadão

> nothing matters:
> not even the contours of the villa
> not even the lens of "Fantástico"
> not even Paul Simon's record
> nobody, nobody is a citizen

He references the majestic colonial villa that houses a museum dedicated to the life and works of Jorge Amado, Bahia's most consecrated novelist; the film crew of "Fantástico," a popular nationally televised program; and, finally,

Olodum's acclaimed collaboration with Paul Simon. Despite the group's connections to people and institutions that wield economic and cultural power on the local, national, and international levels, flagrant assaults on basic rights continue to oppress Olodum's core constituency.

In following the stanzas of "Haiti," Veloso denounces a broad range of social and political injustices, including the lack of funding for education, the massacre of mostly black inmates in a São Paulo prison, and the U.S. blockade against Cuba. "Haiti" is a polyvalent song that comments on several issues relating to citizenship in Brazil and to global conflicts and dilemmas. The refrain compares Bahia and, later in the song, Brazil in general, to the Haiti of 1993 under the brutal military regime of Raoul Cedrás. It is a parody of the refrain from Veloso's 1979 hit "Menino do Rio" (Boy from Rio), written for a surfer boy in Rio de Janeiro: "Let Hawaii be here, all that you dream of." Over a melodic citation of the original refrain, he changes the geographic point of reference: "Think about Haiti, pray for Haiti / Haiti is here, Haiti is not here." The fusion of rap with samba-reggae, two musical idioms associated with racial protest, further underscores the Afro-diasporic paradigm that structures the song. As Barbara Browning has noted, "Haiti is here—you could be in Port-au-Prince—but also in L.A., in Kingston, in Havana, in Lagos."[2] As the leading track on the album, "Haiti" set the tone for the entire album, which updated the tropicalist project in light of subsequent developments in Brazilian popular music.

TICKLING TRADITIONS: TOM ZÉ

Perhaps the most remarkable phenomenon of the tropicalist revival in the 1990s was the professional resurrection of Tom Zé. Following the tropicalist movement, Tom Zé continued to compose and record, but his career trajectory was markedly different from those of his Bahian cohorts. In the 1970s, while Gil, Veloso, Gal Costa, and Maria Bethânia enjoyed commercial success and critical acclaim, Tom Zé slipped into near obscurity. Unlike the other Bahians, he stayed in São Paulo, remaining on the margins of the MPB industry and the countercultural scene, which were based primarily in Rio de Janeiro. In the Brazilian press, he has been described as an "errant navigator" who took several "wrong turns" that compromised his professional career.[3] Tom Zé explored the more experimental implications of Tropicália, selectively appropriating elements of contemporary avant-garde music, folk music from the rural *sertão*, modern samba, and rock. His artistic trajectory may have been "errant" in terms of commercial appeal, but it also yielded some of the most innovative and uncompromising popular music of the late twentieth century. When some of his songs from the 1970s were compiled on CD nearly twenty years later, they sounded "cutting edge" to audiences in Brazil, Europe, and the United States.

Tom Zé's career was revived in the early 1990s after David Byrne, an influential New York–based rock artist and producer, serendipitously discovered *Estudando o samba* (1975) while purchasing records in Rio.[4] Drawing primarily from this album and from *Todos os olhos* (All of the eyes) (1973), Byrne produced a compilation on his Luaka Bop label titled, with intended irony, *The Best of Tom Zé: Massive Hits*. The compilation received high marks from North American and European music critics, eliciting comparisons with John Zorn, Frank Zappa, and Captain Beefheart, as well as with Byrne himself. Writing for the *New York Times*, one critic wrote: "Never have American audiences been treated to a more thrilling display of the vigorous intelligence that tends to lurk beneath Brazilian pop's pretty surfaces."[5] In 1991 it remained for several weeks on the *Billboard* chart in the Adult Alternative category and placed fourth in the *Downbeat* critic's poll for the World Beat Album of the Year.

With the marketing of Tom Zé's music, audiences outside of Brazil began to take note of the diversity of Brazilian popular music. Tom Zé gained a substantial following in Europe and the United States, most notably among listeners who were not Brazilian-music enthusiasts but were drawn to his unorthodox experiments in pop music. Brazilians also began to take note of a key tropicalist who for years had been neglected by the music industry and the media. After years of playing to small audiences of musicians, university students, and cognoscenti, he began to achieve greater recognition in Brazil among younger audiences. In April 1999, Tom Zé performed at the Pro-Rock music festival in Recife, which showcased emerging artists from the Northeast. He was received enthusiastically by a crowd of 5,000 young rock fans, many of whom were likely unaware of his participation in the tropicalist movement.[6]

Tom Zé lost a mass audience in the early 1970s, but he continued to garner acclaim among fellow artists and critics in Brazil. He had profound impact on young musicians such as Itamar Assumpção, Arrigo Barnabé, and Walter Franco, who were loosely identified with a post-tropicalist Paulista vanguard.[7] His music also caught the attention of avant-garde composers in Brazil who admired his use of unusual time signatures, polytonality, and calculated dissonance. Hans-Joachim Koellreutter, the German composer who introduced duodecophonic technique to Brazil in the 1940s, claimed in a video documentary about Tom Zé that he "represents a new way of thinking [about music] whose characteristics we still do not comprehend."[8] Perhaps more than any other Brazilian musician, Tom Zé has contributed to the dissolution of barriers between erudite and popular music.

Like the Brazilian jazz instrumentalist Hermeto Paschoal, Tom Zé is a sound inventor who has experimented relentlessly and often playfully with a wide range of natural and mechanical materials from everyday life. Drawing on his training at the University of Bahia with the Swiss musician-inventor Walter Smetak, he began to create his own instruments in the 1970s. In 1978, he founded the Hertz Orchestra, in which musicians played a variety of invented and "found" instruments. One contraption, the HertZé, was a primitive analog version of what would later be called a sampler. It involved a series of tape recordings of different radio frequencies connected to a panel of buttons. Each button accessed a different tape player, allowing the instrumentalist to produce brief bursts of aleatoric sounds from various recordings. Other musicians played electric appliances and tools (blender, washing machine, floor polisher, saws), while Tom Zé maintained the basic rhythmic structure by striking an *agogô* (a percussive metal bell) to a high-power blade sharpener, producing a high-pitched metallic sound. The Hertz equipment was inadvertently destroyed in the late 1970s but was reconstructed in the late 1990s. When Tom Zé began touring again in the 1990s, he dedicated a portion of his shows to these sonorous experiments with electric tools. Wearing a hard hat, thick leather gloves, industrial goggles, and a raincoat, he would create on stage a factory shop floor atmosphere that presented musical invention as a "craft" similar to any other form of construction.

In conjunction with his formal experiments in music, Tom Zé also continued to explore vanguardist poetics in dialogue with the concrete poets of São Paulo, creating what one critic called "poemúsica."[9] With Augusto de Campos, he cowrote "Cademar" (1973), a lyric consisting of one basic phrase that is fractured into phonemic clusters, producing two separate questions without response: "Ô ô cadê mar/ia que não vem (1. where is the ocean? it's going not coming. 2. where is Maria/she's not coming)." In other songs, Tom Zé used concrete techniques to reconfigure discursive meaning with homophonic translations. He often used this type of linguistic play as a vehicle for humor, best exemplified by the rock composition "Jimmy, rende-se" (Give in, Jimmy) (1970), which in Brazilian Portuguese sounds like "Jimi Hendrix." Other lines such as "Bob dica, diga" (Bob saying say), "Billy Rolleyflex" (a type of camera), and "Janis Chopp" (Janis draft beer) approximated the phonetic equivalents of Bob Dylan, Billy Holiday, and Janis Joplin. The ironic humor

Tom Zé and John Herndon of Tortoise in Chicago, 1999. (Christopher Dunn)

of the song depended on the transformation of these consciously "mispronounced" names of consecrated American entertainers into banal expressions and consumer items of everyday life in Brazil.

The question of musical "tradition" in Brazilian song has been central to Tom Zé's work since the era of Tropicália. As shown in previous chapters, the tropicalists were deeply engaged with the tradition of Brazilian song, but they also aimed to subvert it through calculated use of parody and satire. Of all the tropicalists, Tom Zé was perhaps most explicit in his critique of tradition, particularly when it was used to accuse artists of inauthenticity or alienation from Brazilian culture. On one song from his first album, "Quero sambar meu bem" (I want to samba my dear), he embraced samba as a source of pleasure yet also rejected its status as a mummified object of melancholic contemplation for musical traditionalists:

> quero sambar também
> mas eu não quero
> andar na fossa
> cultivando tradição embalsamada

I want to samba too
but I don't want
to wallow in the pits
cultivating embalmed tradition

In other compositions, Tom Zé alluded to ways in which tradition has been constructed or "invented" in the process of national formation. As rich and vibrant as Brazilian musical tradition may be, it also inspires exaggerated reverence and timidity that ultimately impedes innovation. One of his repertory shows from 1971, for example, was provocatively titled "Com quantos quilos de medo se faz uma tradição?" (How many kilos of fear does it take to make a tradition?), which is a line from his song "Sr. Cidadão" (Mr. Citizen). The implication of this critique is multivalent, referring simultaneously to creative strictures imposed by "tradition" but also to the social conventions maintained by the "senhor-cidadão," described by Marilena Chaui as the conservative bourgeois subject who "preserves citizenship as a class privilege." [10] The critique of tradition is directed specifically at Brazilian musicians in "Complexo de Épico" (Epic complex), from *Todos os olhos.* In this song, Tom Zé playfully admonished Brazilian composers for doing everything—speaking, seeming, being, smiling, crying, playing, and loving—with "such seriousness." Time-honored musical traditions seem to hover over Brazilian composers like frail specters from the past: "It's as if some nightmare / were haunting our rhythms / in a wheelchair."

It would be a mistake, however, to conclude that Tom Zé has sought a total rupture with the past. Instead, he has maintained a dialogue with musical and literary traditions that in some cases reveal sincere affection. The song "Augusta, Angélica, e Consolação" (1973), for example, is a whimsical tribute to Adoniran Barbosa, the Italo-Brazilian master of *samba paulistano,* a form that typically documented the dreary, fog-covered urban cityscape of São Paulo with great pathos. Like his 1968 hit "São São Paulo," it was also an homage to his adopted city. The lyrics anthropomorphize a trio of famous avenues of downtown São Paulo, rendering them as three women with distinct personalities. The women embody the characteristics of the avenues that bear their names. Augusta used to be the site of upscale shops, while Angélica Avenue had many medical offices. In Tom Zé's song, the former "spends her money on imported clothes," while the other one "smelled like a doctor's office" and always canceled appointments. As the name suggests, only Consolação gave him solace in the urban solitude of São Paulo. Tom Zé further developed his peculiar rereading of the tradition of Brazilian song on an album from 1975, suggestively titled *Estudando o samba* (Studying the samba). He explored several forms of samba, including rural and urban forms from São Paulo, *samba-de-roda*, *samba-canção*, *maxixe*, and bossa nova, while introducing elements of vanguard music and concrete poetry.[11]

In 1992, Luaka Bop issued *The Hips of Tradition*, a CD of mostly new material that made explicit reference to the diverse traditions that informed his creative process. Nearly every song was accompanied by a brief reference to a literary work, including texts by canonical authors such as Cervantes, Guimarães Rosa, William Faulkner, Thomas Mann, and the Brazilian concrete poets, as well as to linguist Stanislaw Len and children's author Elfeas Andreato. Some songs were inspired by young rock musicians in Brazil or simply by the "difficulty of daily life in São Paulo." In the liner notes, Tom Zé describes his music as a mixture of Beethoven, vanguard composer Arnold Schoenberg, and Jackson do Pandeiro, a satirical singer-songwriter from northeastern Brazil noted for his richly textured hybrid rhythms that drew from both regional and international sources. Jackson do Pandeiro is best known for his recording of "Chiclete com banana" (Chiclets with bananas), an ironic commentary on the uneven exchange of musical influences between Brazil and the United States.[12] Taking cues from Jackson do Pandeiro, Tom Zé used a diverse range of musical sources, including northeastern forms such as *embolada* and *baião*, as well as reggae, rock, and funk.

Unlike his earlier songs, in which "tradition" was invoked as a burden that produced conformity, the songs on this album engage "tradition" as a productive interlocutor in constant dialogue with innovation. In the song "Tatuarambá," a neologism that combines "samba" and "tattoo," he opens with the exhortation sung in English "to expose the hips of tradition / to the burning iron of ads." As a body part that provides support and generates sensual movement, "hips" simultaneously connote stability and activity. For Tom Zé, musical traditions are not to be preserved and revered deferentially but rather disassembled and perpetually reconstituted using new musical and poetic information. This is an operation that is both playful and painful, as suggested in the last line of the song, in which he proposes "tickling traditions / itching, scratching the tradition."

Tom Zé further developed his meditation on tradition on the CD *Fabrication Defect: Com defeito de fabricação*, a project that explicitly foregrounded intertextuality, a concept drawn from literary theory that posits that all texts maintain a dialogic relationship with other texts. The acknowledgment of intertextuality undermines any claim that a given text, or any other form of cultural expression, is original and self-contained. Every text necessarily plagiarizes other texts to some degree. Tom Zé uses the term *arrastão* to describe the social and cultural implications of intertextuality in the Brazilian context. Typically used to describe a type of dragnet used by fishermen, *arrastão* entered the Brazilian colloquial lexicon to refer to a coordinated disturbance in a crowded public space, allowing thieves to make off with money and valuables. In the early 1990s, the *arrastões* sparked panic and fury among the residents of the South Zone of Rio and contributed to the vilification of the predominantly black working-class *galeras* (loosely organized gangs) associated with the funk and hip-hop movements, who were accused of instigating melees on the beach.[13]

In Tom Zé's songs and liner notes, the *arrastão* functions as polyvalent metaphor for musical practices that use parody, pastiche, and other forms of citation to generate an "aesthetics of plagiarism." He proposes the concept as a strategy for recycling "sonorous civilized trash" collected from the everyday noises of contemporary life. His formulation recalls the *estética do lixo* (aesthetics of garbage) of the post-tropicalist underground filmmakers of the sixties and seventies who recycled the material and symbolic detritus of a peripheral industrial society.[14] As a strategy for literary and cultural production, *arrastão* also updates Oswald de Andrade's *antropofagia*, which recommended the cannibalization of the colonizers' cultural heritage. In a similar vein, Tom Zé proposes "an aesthetic of *arrastão* that ambushes the universe of well-known and traditional music." Tom Zé has distanced himself, however, from cannibalist aesthetics: "I never read Oswald de Andrade . . . I didn't listen to international pop of the 1960s or the 1950s because I didn't have time while I was studying at the music school at the University of Bahia. I wasn't able to engage in cannibalist leisure. I brought different elements from the songs and dances from my primitive world together with the Vienna School; everything after Schoenberg: atonality, polytonality, duodecophonism, serialism." [15] Although much of Tom Zé's work suggests a sensibility that is akin to Oswaldian-tropicalist *antropofagia*, his frame of reference is a secular tradition of intertextual musical and literary appropriation.

As in his previous album, each song makes musical or discursive references to diverse texts, compositions, styles, and genres. The appropriated or "plagiarized" material from the album forms a dense web of multitemporal literary and musical references, including Saint Augustine, Provençal troubadours, Father Antônio Vieira (a famous colonial era priest), Gustave Flaubert, Alfred Nobel, Jorge Luis Borges, the concrete poets of São Paulo, Tchaikovsky, Rimsky Korsakov, Italian Renaissance music, *pagode* samba, rural *caipira* music, northeastern accordion players, and his own contemporaries, Gilberto Gil and Caetano Veloso. On the opening track, "Gene," he even "plagiarized" a few lines from "Escolinha de robô" (Preschool for robots), one of his own songs from the early 1970s. At the end of his manifestolike statement, he proclaims the end of the composers' era and the beginning of the "plagio-combinator era."

Central to Tom Zé's project is the figure of the android, a humanlike automaton exploited as cheap labor that is regulated and controlled by transnational capital. According to his formulation, these entities, which are manufactured for the sole purpose of producing surplus capital, have "fabrication defects." He explains: "The Third World has a huge and rapidly increasing population. These people have been converted into a kind of 'android,' almost always illiterates. . . . But these androids reveal some inborn 'defects': They think, dance, and dream—things that are very dangerous to the First World bosses." Agency is restored through everyday cultural practices, even though they may be ultimately commodified for mass consumption.

The best example of Tom Zé's *arrastão* aesthetics is the song "Esteticar," which makes reference to the theory behind the entire project in the refrain: "hold on to your seats milord / this mulatto *baião* / tuxedo-izes itself / in the aesthetics of the *arrastão*." The song is a modified *baião* that assumes the voice of a poor northeastern migrant in São Paulo who challenges the prejudices of the rich and powerful: "you think I'm an android laborer / a mere mongoloid mongrel *mameluco*." By referencing *mamelucos*, an archaic term used to describe people of African and indigenous descent, he calls attention to the discrimination against northeastern migrants, especially those who are darkskinned, who live in a city that is dominated by Euro-Brazilians.

Tom Zé further elaborated the concept of *arrastão* on the CD *Jogos de armar* (Building blocks) (2000), a recording that proposed a set of practices based on the theory outlined in *Fabrication Defect*. Each song was conceived explicitly as a work to be plagiarized by other musicians. It came with an auxiliary CD containing tracks of the constitutive fragments from each of the songs in order to facilitate the appropriation of rhythmic patterns, melodies, and vocal choruses for other recordings. Many of these sounds were made using the reconstructed versions of instruments first built in 1978, such as the HertZé. Several lyrics even contain "verses for possible collaboration" that are not used in the recorded version. According to the liner notes, each track is a "song-module open to innumerable versions, receptive to interference by amateurs and professionals." Since each song was already conceived as a plagiarized *arrastão* of another song or style, the CD sought to engender a collaborative intertextual chain of musical citations.[16]

Even before the recording of *Jogos de armar*, the music of Tom Zé had already been sampled and reconfigured by musicians in the United States. Soon after the release of *Fabrication Defect*, several of its compositions were recorded by key figures in the experimental music scene such as John McIntire of Tortoise, Sean Lennon and Yuka Honda of Cibbo Mato, and the group High Llamas. The remix album *Postmodern Platos* (1999) was particularly apposite of Tom Zé's project for recombinant "plagio-combinator" aesthetics. This collaboration coincided with a late-1990s tropicalist vogue in the United States.

TROPICALIST INTERNATIONAL

Unlike bossa nova, the music of Tropicália never received much attention outside of Brazil in the late 1960s.[17] There are several possible reasons for this lack of attention. First, tropicalist music bore little resemblance to bossa nova and was therefore ignored by European and North American jazz enthusiasts, the principal consumers of Brazilian music abroad. Second, the movement coincided with a boom in Anglo-American rock connected to vibrant counter-cultural movements focused almost entirely on national or First World contexts. Third, the market for international popular music was extremely small in the 1960s. Twenty years would pass before the development of the "world music" phenomenon. Even with the emergence of "world music" as a marketing category, Tropicália was an unlikely candidate for international acclaim since it often confounded metropolitan stereotypes about what popular music from other countries should sound like. Finally, Tropicália was itself a cultural movement that was concerned primarily with the national context. The tropicalists evidenced little interest in developing their careers outside of Brazil, as many bossa nova musicians were doing at the time. Veloso and Gil worked in England in the early 1970s but enjoyed limited popular success and returned to Brazil as soon as conditions permitted. Although they eventually attracted audiences abroad, the tropicalist experience of the 1960s had never been a point of reference for foreign listeners in the way that bossa nova had been for international fans of Tom Jobim and João Gilberto.

This situation changed in the 1990s. In 1989, David Byrne's Luaka Bop label released *Beleza Tropical*, a highly successful compilation of Brazilian popular music that featured Veloso, Gil, and Gal Costa and contained liner notes describing the tropicalist movement. The liner notes to Tom Zé's subsequent compilation also introduced him as a veteran of the tropicalist movement. In 1991, Caetano Veloso published a long article in the *New York Times* about Carmen Miranda that explained her significance for the tropicalists. It was this article that prompted one New York–based publisher to encourage Veloso to write his tropicalist memoir, *Verdade tropical*. By this time, references to Tropicália turned up regularly in journalistic writing about Brazilian music in the United States.[18]

At some point in the mid-1990s, tropicalist recordings of the late 1960s began to circulate among U.S. musicians, critics, and cognoscenti seeking new directions in popular music.[19] With the commercial mainstreaming of post–punk rock (i.e., Seattle "grunge") in the early 1990s, the category of "alternative rock" seemed increasingly obsolete. Many rock artists turned to rap and hip-hop for inspiration, incorporating heavy funk beats, turntable scratching, and digital sampling into their music. Other groups developed a postmodern aesthetic based on ironic pastiches of a wide variety of music including film scores, lounge music, and other obscurities mined from the history of popular music from around the world.[20]

With the development of these so-called postrock trends in British and American popular music, the conditions were right for the enthusiastic reception of tropicalist music outside of Brazil. By the late 1990s, most of the tropicalist albums had been reissued on CD and were readily available in the United States and Europe.[21] One critic from the *New York Times* remarked: "Word has got around that some of the revered underground rock bands of the moment, particularly Stereolab and Tortoise, love these albums; they talk about them in fanzine interviews."[22] The tropicalists were hailed as precursors of the metropolitan groups pursuing an aesthetic based on the ironic appropriation, juxtaposition, and recycling of dated material from diverse sources. Musicians and critics have expressed a sense of "finally catching up" to the sort of recombinant and hybrid music developed in Brazil over thirty years ago.[23] Tropicália had become the latest incarnation of Oswald de Andrade's "poetry for export."

Perhaps the best examples of the sort of ironic cannibalizing that was typical of Tropicália can be heard in the recordings of Os Mutantes, the defunct avant-garde rock band from São Paulo. Their music drew indiscriminately from psychedelic rock, blues-rock, iê-iê-iê, the Beatles, bossa nova, French and Italian pop, Latin music, and a host of Brazilian forms. In many of their songs, Os Mutantes gleefully played with awkward and humorous "mistranslations" of metropolitan pop, conveying a sense of affection and ironic distance in relation to Anglo-American rock.[24] One of the most acclaimed pop iconoclasts of the 1990s, Beck, has expressed a sense of wonder after having first heard Os Mutantes, with their ironic mix-and-(mis)match concoctions that predated his own collage aesthetic by thirty years.[25] In 1998, he released an album entitled *Mutations*, featuring the radio single "Tropicália," a samba reminiscent of Gil's "Aquele abraço" and Jorge Ben's soul-sambas from the early 1970s. The lyrics of the song are also redolent of the allegorical poetics of Veloso's "Tropicália" of 1968, but from a decidedly metropolitan point of view. Beck's "Tropicália" is told from the perspective of a disillusioned expatriate living in a place that "reeks of tropical charms . . . where tourists snore and decay."

The tropicalist vogue in the United States reached an apex in the summer of 1999. Several mainstream and specialized magazines featured articles about the movement and the current activities of the major participants. Tom Zé, Caetano Veloso, and Gilberto Gil performed throughout the United States, where they drew large audiences and elicited rave reviews in music magazines and mainstream newspapers. Caetano Veloso toured with a twelve-piece band featuring brass and rhythm sections, presenting material from his studio album *Livro* and the follow-up live album *Prenda Minha*. Gilberto Gil and his band presented material from his 1997 double CD *Quanta* and the subsequent live album *Quanta Live*. Meanwhile, Tom Zé performed in several American cities with Tortoise, an instrumental group from Chicago.

In the summer of 2000, the group Portastatic (a side project of Mac Mc-Caughan of the band Superchunk) released an EP of Brazilian songs, *De Mel, de Melão*, featuring wonderfully inventive covers of "Baby" and "Objeto Não-identificado," two tropicalist era classics by Caetano Veloso. McCaughan explained in the liner notes that he was inspired to record the songs because "the energy, emotion, and pure melodies conceived by the original artists are universally exciting." The recording was well received by Tropicália enthusiasts throughout the United States. One on-line music critic rejoiced, presumably with a measure of irony: "Bless globalization. On Portastatic's delicious new EP, Superchunk's Mac McCaughan takes cues from Brazil's Tropicália new wave of the late '60s, who at the time were taking cues from the acid and pop movements of America and England. And now, thirty years later, college kids can interpret the lyrics with help of online translation engines as they sit in an Internet café munching on cashew satay sticks." [26] Brazilian critics noted with interest the Tropicália vogue among rock musicians in the United States and Europe. Writing for the *Folha de São Paulo*, Hermano Vianna cautiously speculated that "the place of Brazilian culture in the 'concert of nations' has undergone a small but decisive transformation with the so-called 'cult' of tropicalism." [27] After discussing the trend with one American observer, Vianna concluded that Tropicália was not received abroad as an exotic curio of "world music." Instead, it was "celebrated as if it were a vanguard school within the long history of rock or international pop music." Yet

Gilberto Gil performs in New Orleans, 1999. (Christopher Dunn)

metropolitan readings of Tropicália as a precursor to a global postmodern musical aesthetic are often oblivious to the movement's critical intent and impact in Brazil.

TROPICÁLIA AND CONTEMPORARY BRAZILIAN MUSIC

Tom Zé once remarked that the legacy of Tropicália has more to with the "architecture" of music-making than with the imitation of style. By architecture, he was referring to the way that artists make use of local and international influences, new production technologies, and mechanisms of media diffusion at any given historical moment. Referring to the vanguardist gesture that formally ended the movement in late 1968, Tom Zé continued: "The things of Tropicalismo cannot be imitated, they have been exhausted and buried." [28] Any formal revival of the late-1960s "universal sound" would inevitably be overburdened with nostalgic kitsch. In the last ten years, however, the tropicalist experience has been renovated, appropriated, and rearticulated in surprising ways.

In 1992, Veloso's 1967 hit "Alegria, alegria" was unexpectedly revived as a protest song by middle-class urban youth who took to the streets to denounce a corruption scandal involving Fernando Collor de Melo. A neoliberal politico from the Northeast, Collor was the first directly elected president of the New Republic after the end of military rule. Veloso's song had been selected as the theme for *Anos rebeldes* (Rebellious years), a popular miniseries that aired nightly for six weeks on TV Globo. Written by Gilberto Braga, *Anos rebeldes* was the first *telenovela* to dramatize political and cultural conflicts under military rule from the time of the coup in 1964 until 1979, when the Amnesty Law allowed for the return of political exiles. Several episodes dealing with the hothouse atmosphere of 1968 featured archival footage of mass demonstrations in Rio de Janeiro and ensuing battles with police battalions. The series revisited the lively debates surrounding MPB through characters who argued over the relative merits of protest music, rock, and MPB, with references to Caetano Veloso, Chico Buarque, and Geraldo Vandré. In one scene, the principal male protagonist and his girlfriend engaged in a heated argument about the results of the 1968 Festival Internacional da Canção in which Tom Jobim and Chico Buarque were jeered by the audience after winning, despite the overwhelming popular support for Geraldo Vandré's hymn of resistance, "Caminhando."

The popularity of the series was likely related to its representation of political struggle against authoritarianism at a time when the nation was disenchanted with the New Republic and disgusted by the corruption scandal.[29] *Anos rebeldes* also introduced middle-class Brazilian youths to the political and cultural debates that had animated their parents' generation. Many young protesters found inspiration in the series as they took to the streets to demand Collor's impeachment, which occurred several months after the series was broadcast. Street marches often included a mobile sound system playing "Alegria, alegria" in repeating loops as the demonstrators sang along. In an ironic twist, Veloso's first tropicalist hit about a solitary *flaneur* who was disengaged from political debates was reconfigured as a collective protest anthem twenty-five years later.

Throughout the 1990s, Tropicália was the subject of several public commemorations, most notably during carnival. In 1994, the famous samba school Mangueira of Rio de Janeiro paid tribute to the "sweet barbarians" (Gil, Veloso, Gal Costa, and Maria Bethânia), the four most consecrated Bahian artists who have mostly resided in Rio de Janeiro since the 1970s. Mangueira's 1994 *samba-enredo* "Atrás da verde-e-rosa só não vai quem já morreu" (Behind the pink and green only those who've died don't follow) was an homage to Veloso's "Atrás do trio elétrico," composed while he was under house arrest in 1969.[30] The samba theme also alluded to key moments in the early artistic career of the *grupo baiano*, such as Bethânia's acclaimed 1965 performance on the Opinião shows, Veloso's "Alegria, alegria," Gil's "Domingo no parque," and Costa's 1969 rock hit "Meu nome é Gal" (My name is Gal). Veloso would return the gesture several years later in a song from his album *Livro* (1997), which proclaimed that Mangueira was "where Rio was the most Bahian."

The *bloco afro* Olodum from Salvador also celebrated Tropicália and its legacy in the Bahian carnival of 1994. Combining social critique with pop appeal, Olodum had gained national and international fame in the late eighties and early nineties with its percussive fusions of samba, reggae, and other Afro-Caribbean rhythms. In the 1980s, the group had emerged as a prominent advocate for black cultural and political affirmation. Following a much publicized collaboration with Paul Simon on his album *Rhythm of the Saints*, Olodum attracted an international following and later went on to collaborate with Michael Jackson on the song "They Don't Care About Us." Beginning in the early 1990s, Olodum changed its ensemble format by adding electric instrumentation to its *bateria* (drum corps) in an effort to compete in the local pop market. The group continued to perform and record songs of political and racial protest but also expanded its range of themes. Whereas much of their work from the eighties referenced the histories and heroes of black struggles in Brazil and Africa, their hit song of 1994, "Alegria geral" (General joy) (an allusion to "Alegria, alegria" and "Geléia geral"), unabashedly proclaimed: "Olodum is hippie / Olodum is pop / Olodum is reggae / Olodum is rock / Olodum has flipped out." Another song from the same album, *O Movimento*, contemplated the technological modernization of two famous Candomblé temples often associated with premodern African tradition: "parabolic antennas in Gantuá / computers in Opô Afonjá / tropicalists poets of light." Olodum chose the legacy of Tropicália as a platform to underscore the modernity and vitality of Afro-Bahian culture. The tropicalist turn in Olodum's music and discourse yielded ambiguous results. For some critics, it compromised the group's position as a leading voice of black consciousness in Bahia. On the other hand, this move also allowed the group to articulate its message to a wider audience in the local and national pop markets.[31]

As described in the opening paragraphs of this book, the commemorative hoopla around Tropicália in Brazil reached an apex in 1998, the thirtieth anniversary of the movement. In conjunction with carnival activities, the city government and the local tourist board sponsored a commemorative event,

"30 Years of Tropicália," involving visual arts exhibitions, dramatic readings, and lectures in the Museum of Modern Art of Bahia.[32] Artists and critics remarked in the press that Tropicália had a profound impact on the contemporary Bahian carnival, with trios elétricos playing everything from frevo to hard rock and blocos afros pounding out new hybrid rhythms such as samba-reggae.[33] Veloso has claimed that the new "electrified, rockified, cubanized, jamaicanized, popified" carnival of Bahia grew out of the tropicalist experience in marked opposition to the more famous carnival of Rio de Janeiro, which is still dominated by the samba schools.[34] The Bahian pop music of the 1990s to which Veloso refers is typically called axé music, a moniker that combines the Yoruba term for "life-giving force" and the English noun. The tropicalist carnival occasioned the recording of new versions of tropicalist classics by blocos afros and contemporary proponents of axé music.[35] During carnival, axé bands and percussion troupes played tropicalist songs throughout the city. Gil commanded a special trio elétrico (dubbed the "Trio Eletrônico") that featured guest stars such as Milton Nascimento, Djavan, Elba Ramalho, Carlinhos Brown, and the leading female vocalist of the tropicalist movement, Gal Costa. As Gil, Veloso, and Costa performed their hits from the tropicalist period, privileged celebrants such as the renowned novelist Jorge Amado and the patriarch of Bahian politics, Antônio Carlos Magalhães, cheered from the VIP stands above the avenue.[36]

As in any commemorative or retrospective celebration, the Tropicália carnival tended to flatten the contours of cultural memory into readily consumable icons and styles while other aspects of the movement were all but effaced. City avenues were festooned with cartoonish banners of Veloso, Gil, and Costa, large figurines of Carmen Miranda, and kitsch symbols of life in the tropics involving bananas and pineapples. References to Tom Zé and other tropicalists were conspicuously absent. The 1998 carnival celebration tended to foreground the more overtly kitsch representations of "life in the tropics" that had been an object of tropicalist satire in early 1968. It was not so much a false representation of Tropicália as a celebratory one that ignored the movement's critique of Brazilian society. A complex set of historical references was collapsed into festive representations largely devoid of critical distance.

The influence of Tropicália extends beyond the commemorative homages discussed above. Many of the most acclaimed artists to emerge on the national scene in the 1990s, often referred to as the nova geração, or new generation, of Brazilian popular music, evidence affinities with the tropicalist project. Brazilian popular music of the 1990s was characterized by the nationalization of musical practices of exogenous origin (such as rock, reggae, rap, and funk) and the emergence of new hybrids that combine genres from national and international sources. This is not particularly novel since the appropriation of foreign styles has been central to the genesis of Brazilian popular music since the nineteenth century. As Christina Magaldi has shown, the novelty lies in how these new musics are positioned in relation to essentialist notions of "national culture" or *brasilidade* (Brazilianness). She argues that *brasilidade* has ceased to play a central role in the production and consumption of popular music and that exogenous musical forms have been "used and re-interpreted in the Brazilian scene to articulate local social and ethnic allegiances."[37] Genres such as rock, rap, and reggae have effectively become indigenized so that they are experienced as part of a larger repertoire of practices recognized and accepted as Brazilian.

Much of the current popular music produced today bears the mark of Tropicália and countercultural sounds of the early 1970s. Songs from this period have been covered by artists such as Marisa Monte, Daúde, and Andrea Marquee. Other singer-songwriters have taken cues from what Tom Zé calls the "architecture" of Tropicália to produce new experiments in pop music that involve vanguardist poetics and musical techniques. Arnaldo Antunes, formerly of the rock band Os Titãs, has pursued the convergence of Brazilian song and concrete poetry first explored by the tropicalists. Carlinhos Brown, the cosmopolitan pop star from Bahia, has developed a decidedly hybrid aesthetic drawing from several forms from northeast Brazil, as well as reggae, funk, and techno dance music. Another young Bahian pop musician, Lucas Santtana, made an explicit homage to the tropicalists on his debut album, *EletroBenDodô*. His album opens with a digital sample of the first measure of Veloso's "Tropicália" layered over a distorted electric guitar and a samba rhythm played on the *pandeiro* (tambourine).

Perhaps the best examples of contemporary music oriented by the strategies of Tropicália come from Recife, the capital of Pernambuco in northeast Brazil. In the 1990s, Recife was home to *mangue beat* (swamp beat), a musical movement that combined local forms such as *baião*, *embolada*, and *maracatú* with elements of heavy metal, rap, funk, and reggae. Before the untimely death of its leader, the most acclaimed band of the *mangue* movement was the multiracial group Chico Science & Nação Zumbi. The liner notes to their first album, *Da lama ao caos*, contained a playful manifesto that suggested affinities with Tropicália, seventies counterculture, and Afro-diasporic music: "Mangueboys and manguegirls are individuals interested in comics, interactive TV, hip-hop, street music, John Coltrane, nonvirtual sex, ethnic conflict, and all advances in applied chemistry that relate to the alteration and expansion of consciousness." The band's second album, *Afrociberdélia*, included sampled riffs of tropicalist recordings, vocal tracks by Gilberto Gil, and a version of Jorge Mautner's post-tropicalist anthem from the mid-1970s, "Maracatú atômico," which fused the *maracatú* rhythm with drum-and-bass dance music.

Hermano Vianna has referred to the music of Chico Science & Nação Zumbi as "a kind of postmodern musical interpretation of Recife's famous native son, Gilberto Freyre." [38] Indeed, one song from this album, "Etnia" (Ethnicity), theorizes the production of hybrid music that reflects and celebrates Brazil's *mestiço* cultural and racial identity: "we are all together a miscegenation / and we cannot flee from our ethnicity / Indians, whites, blacks, and *mestiços*." The song certainly celebrates a *mestiço* national identity and reaffirms the cultural unity of a heterogeneous nation. Yet it also embraces transnational hybrid forms ("it's hip-hop in my *embolada*") that do not conform to any narrowly defined cultural nationalism. The band's name, "Zumbi Nation," would even suggest alternative forms of nationhood based on the experience of Palmares, the seventeenth-century *quilombo* of runaway African slaves, indigenous peoples, and marginalized whites who lived together under the leadership of a black warrior, Zumbi. The band embraced a radically democratic, utopian form of "Brazilianness" informed by the history of Afro-Brazilian struggles.

Of course, artists that achieved recognition in the 1990s have also endeavored to distinguish themselves from the tropicalists in terms of style, repertoire, uses of technology, and appropriations of international musical material. One successful singer-songwriter, Chico César, has even claimed that the tropicalists have had a stifling effect on his generation. MPB artists that emerged in the 1960s have indeed maintained an extraordinary degree of influence that far exceeds the popularity and cultural prestige of their generational counterparts in the United States and Europe. César has suggested that the tropicalists have effectively "sold out" to commercial interests and have ceased to produce anything novel: "Today Caetano Veloso is a pop star. Gilberto Gil is merely a great artist. And Gal Costa became a lady dedicated to singing bossa nova. Even Tom Zé, who went for years without recognition, became a media darling after receiving the blessing of David Byrne." [39] Given the fact that César has also enjoyed considerable success as a pop artist both at home and abroad, his resentment seems rather misplaced, especially in relation to Tom Zé, who has remained on the margins of mainstream popular music in Brazil.

The publication of Caetano Veloso's memoir, *Verdade tropical*, in 1997 occasioned yet another round of debates concerning the movement, its legacy, and its contemporary relevance. The *Folha de São Paulo* dedicated an entire issue of the Sunday arts section to the tropicalist movement and Veloso's interpretation of it. Most reviewers regarded the memoir as an insightful contribution to interminable debates surrounding Brazilian modernity, national identity, popular music, and cultural production under authoritarian rule. Yet others criticized it as a pretentious and self-aggrandizing narrative written to consolidate Veloso's hegemonic position in Brazilian culture. In marked contrast to his enthusiastic analysis of the tropicalists in 1977, Gilberto Vasconcellos sarcastically quipped that Veloso had written the memoir "with an eye on a post in the Brazilian Academy of Letters." [40] It is unlikely that Veloso had the academy in mind as he was writing his memoirs, but Vasconcellos's ironic gibe begs the question. Given the complexity and variety of Veloso's poetic *oeuvre*, why shouldn't he be nominated to Brazil's most prestigious literary establishment? Why shouldn't Gilberto Gil be nominated to the institution he satirized so brilliantly on his album cover from 1968?

Liv Sovik has argued that Tropicália is "canonical pop," whose formal strategies have become standard practice in the Brazilian arts. The eclectic mixtures and pastiches of local and global material together with lyrical juxtapositions of contradictory social realities are no longer as effective as they were in the 1960s. The debate surrounding Tropicália, Sovik notes, has become "a way of speaking about other things." [41] In the late 1960s, Tropicália was the touchstone for controversy over culture and politics under military rule. The 1990s' debates over the movement tend to reference globalization and its impact on Brazilian culture, economy, and politics. Both Veloso and Gil have in the past publicly supported the president of Brazil, Fernando Henrique Cardoso, a former sociologist noted for his work on dependency theory who became a proponent of free-market neoliberalism. In one interview, Cardoso praised the tropicalist duo for their "universal" qualities and characterized Chico Buarque, who has maintained steadfast support for the left-wing opposition, as a "conventional" artist of the "traditional elite." [42] There is, of course, a measure of bad faith in this statement, given that Buarque has consistently opposed the interests of both the traditional and neoliberal elites throughout his career.

Critics of Veloso, on the other hand, have claimed that he is complicit with the postdictatorial neoliberal order. In the article cited above, Vasconcellos charged that Veloso's market success and critical acclaim were legacies of military rule: "After the owner of the TV Globo network and the president of the Republic, perhaps the tropicalist singer has been the greatest beneficiary of the coup of '64." Vasconcellos echoes the previously cited critique by José Ramos Tinhorão, who claimed that Tropicália was the cultural vanguard of the military regime. Although Veloso has indeed enjoyed a successful career since the 1960s, his present status is clearly not a function of conservative modernization under military rule and the neoliberal transition under Collor and Cardoso. Like many other MPB artists, Veloso certainly benefited from the institutional expansion of the culture industry since the 1960s, but he has also consistently articulated trenchant critiques of contemporary Brazilian society.

Veloso is undoubtedly a consecrated artist in Brazil, and Tropicália has, as Sovik has argued, entered into the canon of Brazilian culture. In a 1999 poll taken by the national magazine IstoÉ, however, Chico Buarque was elected the "Brazilian of the Century" in the realm of music by a jury of critics and musicians.[43] He was followed by Tom Jobim, Vinícius de Moraes, and Milton Nascimento. The leading articulators of Tropicália, Caetano Veloso and Gilberto Gil, were elected fifth and tenth, respectively. Tropicália may be canonical, but there is no consensus regarding its legacy in Brazilian culture.

CONCLUSION: TROPICÁLIA AND BRASILIDADE

The tropicalist project was articulated during a period of intense political and cultural conflict in Brazil. It simultaneously critiqued the military rule and the national-popular project of the Brazilian Left. The tropicalists' ambiguous position led to a curious situation in which they were severely criticized by the Left yet ultimately persecuted by the military regime as subversives. Tropicália also intervened in debates relating to the question of Brazilian modernity and nationality as theorized and represented in the various currents and phases of modernismo, a project oriented by the twin imperatives of formal experimentation and cultural nationalism.

If we were to periodize Brazilian modernismo, there are compelling reasons for marking its beginning in 1922, when a modernismo coalesced, and ending in 1968, with Tropicália. In his analysis of cinema, Ismail Xavier has identified late-1960s cultural production in Brazil as a "frontier situation" marking the "final stage" of modernism and the beginning of a "postmodern condition" in Brazil.[44] The tropicalist movement confounds any attempt to label it either as "modernist" or as "postmodernist." In its questioning of populist nationalism, its engagement with mass culture and consumer society, and its embrace of pop aesthetics and kitsch iconography, Tropicália seems to be manifestly postmodern. Yet the tropicalist movement was also indebted to Oswald de Andrade's iconoclastic project of cultural cannibalism of the 1920s, the concrete poets' international vanguardism of the 1950s, and, to some extent, the "romantic revolutionary" protest culture of the 1960s. Veloso's injunction to "reclaim the evolutionary line" of Brazilian popular music certainly suggests a teleological outlook often associated with high modernism. The tropicalist experience suggests that modernist and postmodernist practices and strategies in Brazil frequently operate simultaneously in a continuum rather than as a tidy succession of stages or conditions.

The fundamental ambiguities of the tropicalist project are particularly notable in relation to brasilidade, the modernist discourse on national identity. In the 1960s, the tropicalists critiqued and satirized the various discourses of brasilidade, whether in its progressive "nationalist-participant" or conservative patriotic forms. Veloso's memoir is filled with disparaging references to os nacionalistas in Brazil during the 1960s. Against the essentialisms of the regime and its opposition, the tropicalists proposed an allegory of Brazil that was contradictory and fragmentary. Later, they would embrace countercultural practices that were positioned against or on the margins of dominant constructions of "national culture." Their engagement with reggae, soul, funk, hip-hop, and the music of the Bahian blocos afros allied them with cultural phenomena that underscored the specificity of the Afro-Brazilian experience in a context of marked racial inequality. Some of Tom Zé's work has similar resonances in the way it denounces race- and class-based discrimination against northeastern migrants in São Paulo.

Yet the tropicalists have also manifested a profound commitment to the "modern tradition" of Brazilian culture. They have deep knowledge of Brazilian popular music, from the "golden age" of radio in the 1930s and 1940s to contemporary hip-hop from São Paulo; from the samba tradition to the rock boom of the 1980s; from bossa nova to contemporary Afro-Bahian pop. Although it theorized and practiced the "cannibalization" of international culture, Tropicália and its legacy should not be construed merely as a celebration of globalization. Marcelo Ridenti has argued that the tropicalists, especially Veloso, have oscillated like a pendulum between "critical internationalism," emphasizing a productive engagement with contemporary cultural trends abroad, and "radical nationalism," focused on the affirmation of Brazilian expressive cultures.[45] The movement of this pendulum marks the contours of what Ridenti calls brasilidade tropicalista, a reformulation of cultural nationalism attentive to aesthetic renovation, mass media expansion, and cultural movements in the international sphere.

In recent years, the more nationalistic dimensions of the tropicalist project have gained ascendance, particularly in Caetano Veloso's public discourse. He has even articulated a position on race and nationality that would have pleased Gilberto Freyre. In 1999, he told one American journalist that "a nation cannot exist without a myth. I think Freyre has been very important to the building of our best myth as a nation, the myth of racial democracy." [46] For many Afro-Brazilian activists and critics of race relations, this statement would most likely seem naive, if not insidious. One could argue that it is the worst myth precisely because it is complicit in maintaining elite white hegemony by camouflaging racial inequality. Yet Veloso is not unaware of the implications of this embrace of the myth of racial democracy, nor is he interested in maintaining the racial status quo. Veloso's position is instead a utopian gesture consistent with his ideas about Brazil's relation to Western modernity and its specific contribution to this project as a Portuguese-speaking and multiracial American nation. Veloso has written that his desire to outline new utopias compensates for his "participation in the creation of a feeling of disenchantment" during the tropicalist movement.[47] From the ruins of his generation's emancipatory projects, new ones may indeed emerge, although at present utopian energies are not on the rise in Brazil.

As a cultural movement that emerged during a period of political and cultural crisis, Tropicália maintained an ambivalent if not antagonistic relationship with brasilidade as it had been articulated since the 1930s. The very notion of a unitary "Brazilian culture" became untenable due, in part, to the tropicalist intervention. By undermining prevailing notions of authenticity, it opened up new directions in popular music and ushered in diverse countercultural practices that were in dialogue with related phenomena in the international sphere. In doing so, Tropicália helped to redefine the cultural and political imperatives of a generation that came of age in somber times.

NOTES

INTRODUCTION

1. Fabio Schivartche, " 'Doutor' Caetano recebe título sobre trio elétrico," *Folha de São Paulo*, Feb. 20, 1998. The quotations that follow in the text are from this article.
2. See Martins, "A geração AI-5."
3. In Latin America, the contemporary usage of hybridity is particularly indebted to the formulations of Néstor García Canclini in his book *Hybrid Cultures*.
4. Bourdieu, "Field of Cultural Production," 37.
5. These articles were later published in a volume of essays written by diverse authors about popular and "erudite" music in Brazil and abroad. See Augusto de Campos, *Balanço da bossa*.
6. This article was later published in Brazil as "Cultura e Política, 1964–1969," in *O pai de família*, 61–91. An English translation of this essay appears in Schwarz's *Misplaced Ideas*.
7. Schwarz, *Misplaced Ideas*, 140.
8. Ibid., 144.
9. Favaretto, *Tropicália*, 108.
10. Santiago, "Fazendo perguntas com o martelo," 1–13.
11. Buarque de Hollanda, *Impressões de viagem*.
12. See Veloso, *Alegria, alegria*, and Gil, *Gilberto Gil*.
13. Examples of these three types of books are, respectively, Buarque de Hollanda and Gonçalves, *Cultura e participação nos anos 60*; Paiano, *Tropicalismo*; and Lima, *Marginália*.
14. Calado, *A divina comédia dos Mutantes* and *Tropicália*.
15. The most famous example of this literature is Fernando Gabeira's *O que é isso, companheiro?*.
16. Béhague, "Bossa and Bossas," 216; "Brazilian Musical Values of the 1960s and 1970s."
17. Perrone, *Masters of Contemporary Brazilian Song*. For a useful introduction to the multi-faceted tradition of Brazilian song, see McGowen and Pessanha, *Brazilian Sound*.
18. Johnson, *Cinema Novo X 5*; George, *Modern Brazilian Stage*. Other sources on Brazilian film include an edited volume by Johnson and Stam, *Brazilian Cinema*; Stam, *Tropical Multiculturalism*; and Xavier, *Allegories of Underdevelopment*.
19. There was no kinship between Oswald de Andrade and Mário de Andrade. For the sake of clarity I will refer to them either by full or by first names.
20. Augusto de Campos, *Balanço da bossa*, 207.
21. Veloso, *Verdade tropical*, 105.
22. Ibid., 192.
23. Mário Chamie, "O trópico entrópico de Tropicália," *Estado de São Paulo, Suplemento Literário*, Apr. 4, 1968.
24. For a particularly useful English-language introduction to tropicalist music with an extensive annotated discography, readers should consult Slipcue (slipcue.com).
25. Stam, *Tropical Multiculturalism*, 361–63.

CHAPTER ONE

1. Ortiz, *A moderna tradição brasileira*, 13–14.
2. *Modernismo* was the Brazilian analogue to similar artistic movements throughout Spanish America that were typically referred to as *las vanguardias*. In Spanish America *modernismo* denotes late-nineteenth-century aestheticism roughly equivalent to Parnassianism in Brazil.
3. Bosi, *História concisa*, 385–86.
4. Torgovnick, *Gone Primitive*, 8.
5. See, for example, Johnson, "Tupy or Not Tupy," 46.
6. Oswald de Andrade, "Manifesto da Poesia Pau-Brasil," in Teles, *Vanguarda européia e modernismo brasileiro*, 326–31. Cited below by author. For a useful English translation, see Stella M. de Sá Rego, "Manifesto of Pau-Brasil Poetry," *Latin American Literary Review* 14, no. 27 (1986), 184–87.
7. Santiago, "Fazendo perguntas com o martelo," 6.
8. Oswald de Andrade, "Manifesto Antropófago," in Teles, *Vanguarda européia and modernismo brasileiro*, 353–60. For an excellent annotated translation, see Leslie Bary, "Oswald de Andrade's Cannibalist Manifesto," *Latin American Literary Review* 19, no. 38 (1991): 35–47.
9. See "Nhengaçu Verde Amarelo (Manifesto do Verde-amarelismo, ou da Escola da Anta)," in Teles, *Vanguarda européia e modernismo brasileiro*, 361–67.
10. José de Alencar (1829–77) was a writer and conservative politician during the reign of Dom Pedro II, the last emperor of Brazil. His first Indianist novel, *O Guaraní* (1857), inspired an opera, written by Brazilian composer Carlos Gomes, which was enthusiastically acclaimed after opening at Teatro Scala in Milan in 1870.
11. Johnson, "Brazilian Modernism," 204.
12. The *jabuti* is a type of tortoise in northern Brazil that appears as a wily and aggressive trickster figure in indigenous tales. See Bary, "Oswald de Andrade's Cannibalist Manifesto," 46, n. 23.
13. Nunes, "Antropofagia ao alcance de todos," 15–16.
14. Pindorama is the Tupi designation for Brazil that means "region of palm trees." See Bary, "Oswald de Andrade's Cannibalist Manifesto," 47, n. 28.
15. Helena, *Totens e tabus*, 164–65.
16. Haroldo de Campos, "Rule of Anthropophagy," 44.
17. Bary, "Civilization, Barbarism, 'Cannibalism,'" 98–99.
18. Roberto Schwarz, "Brazilian Culture: National by Elimination," in *Misplaced Ideas*, 9.
19. Mello e Souza, *O tupi e o alaúde*, 10–16. See also Reily, "Macunaíma's Music," 71–72.
20. For detailed analyses of the film version of *Macunaíma*, see Johnson, *Cinema Novo X 5*, 25–34; Stam, *Tropical Multiculturalism*, 239–47; and Xavier, *Allegories of Underdevelopment*, 133–53.
21. See Mello e Souza, *O tupi e o alaúde*, 74–75.
22. Unruh, *Latin American Vanguards*, 146–47.
23. Mário de Andrade, *Ensaio sobre a música brasileira*. This and subsequent citations are taken from pages 13–29 in the first section of the book. I will be using "art music" to refer to what in Brazil is called *música erudita* or *música artística*. This music is usually

created by composers with formal training in dialogue with the European classical tradition who occupy a position of prestige as producers of "high" art.

24. For an analogous case of elite use of popular music in Cuba, see Moore, *Nationalizing Blackness*.
25. Reily, "Macunaíma's Music," 74.
26. See Wisnik and Squeff, *O nacional e o popular na cultura brasileira*, 131.
27. Mário de Andrade, *Ensaio sobre a música brasileira*, 166–67.
28. Wisnik and Squeff, *O nacional e o popular na cultura brasileira*, 134.
29. For an account of elite racial ideology in Brazil, see Skidmore, *Black into White*.
30. Vianna, *Mystery of Samba*, 8.
31. See Carlos Nelson Coutinho, "As categorias de Gramsci e a realidade brasileira," in Coutinho and Nogueira, *Gramsci e a América Latina*, 108–10.
32. Getúlio Vargas later reinvented himself as a democratic populist and was elected president with a wide margin in 1950. Acrimonious political conflict and scandal plagued his presidency, and in 1954 he committed suicide in the presidential palace.
33. Johnson, "Institutionalization of Brazilian Modernism," 8–9.
34. For an exemplary piece of self-criticism, see Oswald de Andrade's 1933 preface to his experimental novel, *Serafim Ponte Grande*, written during the period of *antropofagia*.
35. See Wisnik and Squeff, *O nacional e o popular na cultura brasileira*, 179–90.
36. Mota, *Ideologia da cultura brasileira*, 27–33.
37. Ortiz, *Cultura brasileira e identidade nacional*, 41.
38. For a broad perspective on Brazilian popular music and internationalization, see introduction to Perrone and Dunn, *Brazilian Popular Music and Globalization*.
39. Carmen Miranda later recorded a samba, "Disseram que voltei americanizada" (They say I returned Americanized) (Luís Peixoto–Vicente Paiva), in which she responded to her critics. Caetano Veloso recorded this song on his 1992 live album, *Circuladô ao vivo*.
40. Mammí, "João Gilberto e o projeto utópico da bossa nova," 64.
41. Júlio Medaglia, "Balanço da bossa nova," in Augusto de Campos, *Balanço da bossa*, 81; Veloso, *Verdade tropical*, 226.
42. Castro, *Chega de Saudade*, 175. For testimonies regarding the magnitude of bossa nova's impact, see the chapter titled "Vidas," in Homem de Melo, *Música popular brasileira*, 13–62.
43. Treece, "Guns and Roses," 7.
44. Skidmore, *Politics in Brazil*, 164–67.
45. Ibid., 164–70.
46. Corbisier, *Formação e problema da cultura brasileira*, 78.
47. For a detailed discussion of Corbisier's work and the Hegelian dialectic, see Ortiz, *Cultura brasileira e identidade nacional*, 58.
48. Sodré, *Introdução á revolução brasileira*, 226.
49. Holston, *Modernist City*, 18.
50. Perrone, *Seven Faces*, 18.
51. Gullar, *Vanguarda e subdesenvolvimento*, 35.

52. Tinhorão, *Música popular: Um tema em debate*, 37–38.

53. See Tinhorão's critique in "Confronto: Música popular brasileira," *Revista Civilização Brasileira* 3 (July 1965): 307.

54. Ibid., 37.

55. José Ramos Tinhorão, "Bossa nova vive um drama: Não sabe quem é o pai," *Senhor* (Apr.–May 1963). Cited in Castro, *Chega de saudade*, 427.

56. Tinhorão, *Pequena história da música popular*, 245.

57. Caetano Veloso, "Primeira feira de balanço," in *Alegria, alegria*, 1. This article was originally published in the Bahian cultural review, *Ângulos*.

58. Augusto de Campos, *Balanço da bossa*, 143.

59. See Cardoso and Faletto, *Dependência e desenvolvimento na América Latina*, 25–30.

60. Tom Zé's song "Vaia de bêbado não vale" (Jeering of drunks doesn't count) was recorded in response to an incident in October 1999 in which bossa nova luminary João Gilberto was jeered by an elite audience during a concert to inaugurate the Credicard Hall in São Paulo.

61. Cited in Castro, *Chega de saudade*, 273.

62. "Triste é viver sem Tom Jobim," *Veja*, Dec. 14, 1994, 116–25.

63. See Veloso, "Carmen Mirandadada," *Folha de São Paulo*, Oct. 22, 1991, abridged and translated into English as "Caricature and Conqueror, Pride and Shame," *New York Times*, Oct. 20, 1991. A complete translation of the original article appears in Perrone and Dunn, *Brazilian Popular Music and Globalization*.

64. See Veloso's commentary on Carmen Miranda in Dunn, "Tropicalista Rebellion," 131–35.

CHAPTER TWO

1. Ortiz, *A moderna tradição brasileira*, 164.

2. García Canclini, *Hybrid Cultures*, 56.

3. Tatit, *O cancionista*, 275–76.

4. Maciel, *Geração em transe*, 73.

5. Ridenti, *Em busca do povo brasileiro*, 55–57.

6. For a detailed discussion of the Brazilian Left in the 1960s, see Ridenti, *O fantasma*, 25–29, and Skidmore, *Politics in Brazil*, 224–28.

7. Skidmore, *Politics in Brazil*, 284–93.

8. Walnice Nogueira Galvão, "As falas, os silêncios," 186.

9. See Ortiz, *Cultura brasileira e identidade nacional*, 75. Ortiz notes that the CPC's understanding of the "national-popular" was not coterminous with Gramsci's formulation in the *Prison Notebooks*, which understood culture as a struggle for hegemony and not as a question of alienation from "authentic" national expression.

10. Estevam, *A questão da cultura popular*, 90–94. A very useful abridged translation of Estevam's statement of principles appears in Johnson and Stam, *Brazilian Cinema*, 58–63.

11. Ibid., 93.

12. Perrone, *Seven Faces*, 75.

13. Cited in Berlinck, *O Centro Popular de Cultura da UNE*, 35.

14. The dramatist Oduvaldo Vianna Filho, for example, criticized the romantic pre-

tensions of consciousness-raising events and called for more aesthetic complexity in productions seeking to attract a mass audience. See Damasceno, *Cultural Space*, 106–8.

15. Roberto Schwarz, "Culture and Politics," in *Misplaced Ideas*, 135.

16. Ibid., 127.

17. Ridenti has critiqued Schwarz's analysis, arguing that "at the most, there was an outline of an alternative hegemony, or counterhegemony that was almost totally aborted and incorporated in a distorted fashion by the ruling order." See *O fantasma*, 91–92.

18. Pereira, " 'Persecution and Farce,' " 55.

19. Ortiz, *A moderna tradição brasileira*, 114–15.

20. This data was collected from the Seventh and Eighth General Censuses of 1960 and 1970 conducted by the IBGE (*Recenseamento Geral* and *Censo Demográfico*).

21. Sérgio Mattos, "O impacto da Revolução de 1964 no desenvolvimento da televisão," 32.

22. Ianni, *O colapso do populismo no Brasil*, 151.

23. For a critique of the construction of the Brazilian Northeast in the national imaginary, see Albuquerque, *A invenção do nordeste*.

24. See, for example, Veloso's own recollection of his intellectual formation in the interview "Conversa com Caetano Veloso," in Augusto de Campos, *Balanço da bossa*, 201.

25. Dunn, "Tom Zé," 116–18.

26. Veloso, *Verdade tropical*, 28.

27. See "Gilberto Gil," *Jornegro* 2, no. 7 (1979). I am grateful to Emanuelle Oliveira for sharing her collection of Afro-Brazilian journals from the 1970s with me.

28. For a splendid cultural history of Salvador during the 1950s and 1960s, see Risério, *Avant-garde na Bahia*. See also Maciel, *Geração em transe*, and Capinan, "Tropicalismo eppur si mueve."

29. Risério, *Avant-garde na Bahia*, 35.

30. Veloso, *Verdade tropical*, 59–60.

31. Other key academic and state institutions were established during this period, including a school of modern dance and the Center for Afro-Oriental Studies (CEAO) dedicated to studying historic and contemporary links between Africa and Bahia. Around this time, the state government invited Lina Bo Bardi, an Italian architect and industrial designer based in São Paulo, to found and direct the Museum of Modern Art of Bahia. See Risério, *Avant-garde na Bahia*. Rubim et al., "Salvador nos anos 50 e 60," 33.

32. Appleby, *Music of Brazil*, 163–64.

33. Augusto de Campos, "Smetak, para quem souber," in *Música e invenção*, 85–89.

34. See Dunn, "Tom Zé," 112.

35. "Clever Boy Samba" never appeared on a sound recording, but Veloso performed it on a TV Manchete program that commemorated his fiftieth birthday in 1992. For lyrics to the song, see "Caetano Veloso completa hoje 50 anos," *Folha de São Paulo-Ilustrada*, Aug. 7, 1992. A slightly different version appears in Calado, *Tropicália*, 119–20.

36. Calado, *Tropicália*, 52–55.

37. Carlos Coqueijo, "Bossa nova no Vila Velha," *Jornal da Bahia*, Dec. 6–7, 1964.

38. Augusto Boal subsequently directed two other musical dramas, *Arena conta Zumbi* (Arena tells of Zumbi), which was about the seventeenth-century runaway slave settlement, or *quilombo*, led by the Afro-Brazilian hero Zumbi, and *Arena conta Tiradentes* (Arena tells of Tiradentes), which dramatized the story of a failed movement for national independence in the late eighteenth century under the leadership of Tiradentes (the "tooth-puller"). See Claudia de Arruda Campos, *Zumbi, Tiradentes*, and Anderson, "Muses of Chaos and Destruction of *Arena conta Zumbi*."

39. Quoted in Buarque de Hollanda, *Impressões de viagem*, 32, and Damasceno, *Cultural Space*, 135.

40. Damasceno, *Cultural Space*, 136.

41. Ibid., 131–32.

42. Veloso, *Verdade tropical*, 74.

43. Buarque de Hollanda, *Impressões de viagem*, 35.

44. Mostaço, *Teatro e política*, 77.

45. Ruy Castro, "Eu fui a geração Paissandú," *Correio da Manhã*, Feb. 6, 1968.

46. To avoid confusion, critics usually use the abbreviation MPB to refer to this eclectic post–bossa nova pop to distinguish it from the larger field of *música popular brasileira* that denotes all popular music from Brazil.

47. See Augusto de Campos, "Conversa com Gilberto Gil," in *Balanço da bossa*, 191, and in Gil, *Gilberto Gil*, 25.

48. Barbosa, "Que caminho seguir na música popular brasileira?" 378.

49. Fonseca, *Caetano*, 29.

50. Augusto de Campos, "Boa Palavra sobre a música popular," in *Balanço da bossa*, 59–65. Campos's articles on Brazilian popular music during the late 1960s were originally published in *O Estado de São Paulo* and *Correio da Manhã*.

51. Augusto de Campos, *Balanço da bossa*, 62.

52. Napolitano, "A invenção da música popular brasileira," 99.

53. Calado, *Tropicália*, 114–15; Veloso, *Verdade tropical*, 139.

54. Original recordings from this program have been compiled on the CD collection *Elis Regina no Fino da Bossa*.

55. Later in the year, Gil hosted his own short-lived program, "Ensaio Geral" (General rehearsal) on TV Excelsior, which was an unsuccessful attempt to compete with TV Record's musical showcases. See Calado, *Tropicália*, 100.

56. Motta, *Noites tropicais*, 95, 100.

57. Carvalho, "Tupi or not Tupi MPB," 167.

58. Medeiros, *A aventura da Jovem Guarda*, 48.

59. Leite et al., *Gente nova, nova gente*, 86.

60. Wisnik, "O minuto e o milênio," in Bahiana et al., *Anos 70*, 21.

61. The weekly lists of IBOPE consistently registered hits by the Beatles, the Rolling Stones, Herb Alpert, Frank Sinatra, Jerry Adriani, The Mamas and the Papas, The Monkees, Johnny Rivers, Lovin' Spoonful, Miriam Makeba, Otis Redding, and Johnny Mathis, along with Brazilian pop stars Roberto Carlos, Agnaldo Timóteo, Wilson Simonal, and Wanderléa.

62. Calado, *Tropicália*, 107–8.
63. Tinhorão, *Música popular: Do gramafone ao rádio e TV*, 175–76.
64. Francisco Antônio Doria, "De vaias, festivais e revoluções," *Correio da Manhã*, Oct. 6, 1968. See also Miller, "Os festivais no Panorama da música popular brasileira," 236–37.
65. TV Excelsior also aired its own II Festival de Música Popular Brasileira, which was won by Geraldo Vandré with a slow samba, "Porta Estandarte" (Vandré-Lona).
66. On the eve of the festival, Roberto Carlos's "Esqueça" vied with Frank Sinatra's "Strangers in the Night." By the end of the month, both had fallen considerably in rank, while "A banda" and "Disparada" traded off first place from week to week. See IBOPE, "Gravações mais vendidas," Oct. 24–29, 1966.
67. Motta, *Noites tropicais*, 113.
68. Walnice Nogueira Galvão, "MMPB," 113.
69. Ibid., 95–96.
70. In this song, Walnice Nogueira Galvão notes a "complicity between the author and the public," ensuring that the song will be well received by progressive audiences. See Walnice Nogueira Galvão, "MMPB," 110.
71. Henrique Nunes, "A grande guerra da canção," *Manchete*, Oct. 21, 1967.
72. See IBOPE, "Indices de Assistência da TV," Oct. 1967.
73. See IBOPE, "Gravações mais vendidas," Nov. 6–11, 1967.
74. Augusto de Campos, "Festival de viola e violência," in *Balanço da bossa*, 128–29.
75. Ibid., 130.
76. Ricardo, *Quem quebrou meu violão*, 196.
77. See IBOPE, "Gravações mais vendidas," Dec. 11–16, 1967.
78. Aguiar, "Panorama da música popular brasileira," 151.
79. *O Sol* was published as a supplement of *Jornal dos Esportes*, a daily paper dedicated to sports. Veloso's fiancée at the time, Dedé Gadelha, wrote for *O Sol*, as did lyricist Torquato Neto. Its masthead proclaimed: "*O Sol*, a newspaper published for young people, founded on Youth Power, will tell you everything you need to know, without care for traditional styles and methods."
80. Perrone, *Masters of Contemporary Brazilian Song*, 52.
81. Walnice Nogueira Galvão, "MMPB," 112.
82. Concrete poet Décio Pignatari remarked that Gil's "Domingo no parque" recalled the technique of Sergei Eisenstein, while Veloso's "Alegria, alegria" had stylistic affinities with Jean-Luc Godard's cinematography. See Augusto de Campos, "A explosão de alegria, alegria," in *Balanço da bossa*, 153.
83. Antônio Carlos Cabral, "Domingo no parque e praxis na praça," *O Estado de São Paulo*, *Suplemento Literário*, Mar. 30, 1968. Led by Mário Chamie, *poesia-praxis* was a poetic vanguard of the 1960s that critiqued the rarified formalism of orthodox *poesia concreta*, allowing for semidiscursive verse oriented toward social and political themes. See Perrone, *Seven Faces*, 62–63.
84. García Canclini, *Hybrid Cultures*, 2–3.
85. Dirceu Soares, "A música é Gil, é pop," *Jornal da tarde*, Oct. 20, 1967; reprinted in Gil, *Gilberto Gil*, 17–18.
86. See Carlos Acuio, "Por que canta Caetano Veloso," *Manchete*, Dec. 16, 1967; re-

printed in Veloso, *Alegria, alegria*, 21–24. Note that *acarajé* is a typical Bahian street food of West African origin made with fried bean cakes.

87. Santaella, *Convergências*, 4.

88. Augusto de Campos, "Música popular de vanguarda," in *Balanço da bossa*, 290.

89. See Perrone, "From Noigandres to 'Milagre da Alegria,'" for examples of the tropicalists' subsequent use of concrete poetry.

90. Hamilton Almeida, "Quem é Caretano," *Bondinho*, Mar. 31 and Apr. 13, 1972; reprinted in Veloso, *Alegria, alegria*, 122–23.

91. "Manifesto Música Nova," *Invenção* 3 (1963); reprinted in *Arte em Revista* 1 (Jan.–Mar. 1979): 33–35, and in Mendes, *Uma odisséia musical*, 73–74.

92. Mendes's musical rendering of "Beba Coca-Cola" is featured on his CD *Surf, bola na rede, um pente de Istanbul e a música de Gilberto Mendes*.

93. Júlio Medaglia, "Música, não-música, anti-música," *Estado de São Paulo, Suplemento Literário*, Apr. 24, 1967.

94. Schwarz, "Nota sobre vanguarda e conformismo," 130.

95. Cited in Medaglia, "Música, não-música, anti-música."

96. Mendes, *Uma odisséia musical*, 61.

CHAPTER THREE

1. Dunn, "Tropicalista Rebellion," 123.

2. Ferreira, "Tropicalismo: retomada oswaldiana," 763.

3. Veloso, *Verdade tropical*, 247.

4. Buarque de Hollanda, *Impressões de viagem*, 55.

5. Xavier, *Allegories of Underdevelopment*, 50–51; Johnson, *Cinema Novo X 5*, 128–35.

6. Xavier, *Allegories of Underdevelopment*, 75.

7. See Robert Stam, "Land in Anguish," in Johnson and Stam, *Brazilian Cinema*, 152–53.

8. Veloso, *Alegria, alegria*, 123.

9. See Artaud's "Theatre and Cruelty" and "The Theater of Cruelty: First Manifesto" from *Theater and Its Double*, anthologized in *Antonin Artaud: Collected Works*.

10. Tite de Lemos, "A guinada de José Celso," *Revista Civilização Brasileira*, July 1968; reprinted in *Arte em Revista*. For a discussion of Oficina's use of Artaud, see Silva, *Oficina*, 160–63.

11. George, *Modern Brazilian Stage*, 76–78.

12. Oswald de Andrade, *O rei da vela*, 47.

13. Silva, *Oficina*, 145–46. For an analysis of the *chanchadas*, see Stam, *Tropical Multiculturalism*, 79–105.

14. Carlos Gomes (1836–96) was Brazil's most acclaimed opera composer. *Lo Schiavo* was first performed in the Teatro Lírico of Rio de Janeiro on October 27, 1889, a little more than a year after abolition and weeks before the fall of the monarchy. It was sponsored by and dedicated to Princess Isabel, who, on May 13, 1888, had signed the *Lei Aurea* (Golden Law) formally ending slavery. See *Enciclopédia da música brasileira*, 335.

15. See Graham Bruce, "Alma Brasileira: Music in the Films of Glauber Rocha," in Johnson and Stam, *Brazilian Cinema*.

16. "O sol ainda brilha?" *Veja*, Nov. 23, 1977, 74.

17. George, *Modern Brazilian Stage*, 63.

18. Ibid., 108.

19. Ibid., 64. See also Ventura, 1968, 229–37.

20. See Carlos Acuio, "Porque canta Caetano Veloso?" *Manchete*, Dec. 16, 1967; reprinted in Veloso, *Alegria, alegria*.

21. Veloso, *Verdade tropical*, 244.

22. Roberto Schwarz, "Culture and Politics," in *Misplaced Ideas*, 153.

23. Francis Paulino, "A influência de Paco Rabane na música popular brasileira, ou o tropicalismo maior de Charles Lloyd," *Última Hora-SP*, Oct. 27, 1968.

24. Boal, "Que você pensa do teatro brasileiro," 43–44.

25. Wilson Coutinho, "Esse teu olhar quando encontra o meu," 10.

26. Throughout the 1960s and 1970s, Hélio Oiticica wrote copious notations explaining the theory behind his work. An indispensable source on his work is the catalog of a 1992 international retrospective, *Hélio Oiticica*, including the artist's texts and essays by Guy Brett, Catherine David, Waly Salomão, and Haroldo de Campos. This catalog is available in Portuguese/French, English/Dutch, and Spanish/Catalan bilingual editions.

27. See Mário Pedrosa, "Programa ambiental," 103–4, and Brett, "O exercício experimental da liberdade," 222–23, in *Hélio Oiticica*; and Favaretto, *A invenção de Hélio Oiticica*, 168.

28. Oiticica, "Subterranean Tropicália Projects," in *Hélio Oiticica*, 143.

29. See Oiticica, "Bases fundamentais para uma definição do parangolé" and "Anotações sobre o parangolé," in *Hélio Oiticica*.

30. Oiticica, "Tropicália," in *Hélio Oiticica*, 124.

31. Risério, "Tropicalismo," 11.

32. Veloso, *Verdade tropical*, 244.

33. Avelar, *Untimely Present*, 68–77.

34. Benjamin, *Origin of German Tragic Drama*, 178.

35. See Luis Fernando Veríssimo's text in the retrospective illustrated volume *Glauco Rodrigues*, 33–35.

36. Dunn, "Tropicalista Rebellion," 130–31.

37. Augusto de Campos, *Balanço da bossa*, 162.

38. Benjamin, *Origin of German Tragic Drama*, 166.

39. Favaretto, *Tropicália*, 65–66.

40. Quoted in Julian Dibbell in "Notes on Carmen," *The Village Voice*, Oct. 29, 1991. See also Dunn, "Tropicalista Rebellion," 131–34.

41. See, for example, Santiago's discussion of parody and pastiche in Brazilian culture in "Permanência do discurso da tradição no modernismo," in Borheim et al., *Cultura brasileira*, 140–45.

42. See Jameson, *Postmodernism*, 17–18.

43. See Dunn, "Tropicalista Rebellion," 132.

44. Favaretto, *Tropicália*, 68.

45. See note on Manoel Barenbeim, who produced most of the tropicalist albums for Philips, in "Ele grava para milhares as canções dos festivais," *Veja*, Oct. 30, 1968.

46. Béhague, "Bossa and Bossas," 217.

47. Moehn, "In the Tropical Studio," 61–62.

48. Ruy Castro, "Uma geléia geral de vanguarda," *Correio da Manhã*, Sept. 21, 1968.

49. Veloso, *Verdade tropical*, 168.

50. The *geléia geral* trope was cited in *Invenção* 3 (June 1963) and *Invenção* 5 (Dec. 1966–Jan. 1967). See Veloso's discussion of the trope in *Verdade tropical*, 216.

51. Vasconcellos, *Música popular*, 18.

52. Favaretto, *Tropicália*, 94–95.

53. A good example of this type of poetry is Oswald de Andrade's "Biblioteca Nacional" (National Library). See Perrone, *Seven Faces*, 9–10.

54. García Canclini, *Hybrid Cultures*, 157.

55. Oswald de Andrade, *Obras completas*, 36.

56. Roberto Schwarz, "Culture and Politics," in *Misplaced Ideas*. Subsequent citations are from pages 139–44.

57. Jameson, "Third World Literature," 69.

58. Vasconcellos, *Música popular*, 53–59, and Hoisel, "Tropicalismo," 46.

59. Sartre, "Plea for Intellectuals," 259–77.

60. Dunn, "Tropicalista Rebellion," 121. In a 1968 interview, Veloso cited Sartre's *Search for a Method* as one of the few theoretical texts that he had read as a student. See Augusto de Campos, "Conversa com Caetano Veloso," in *Balanço da bossa*, 201.

61. Santiago, "Fazendo perguntas," 12.

62. Santiago, "Apesar de dependente, universal," in *Vale quanto pesa*, 15–18.

63. Ibid., 23–24.

64. Augusto de Campos, *Balanço da bossa*, 168.

65. García Canclini, *Hybrid Cultures*, 252.

66. Hoisel, *Supercaos*, 145–46.

67. Other examples include Os Mutantes' "Dom Quixote" (1969) and Veloso's "Clara" (1968). See Augusto de Campos, "Música popular de vanguarda," in *Balanço da bossa*, 283–92.

68. For Augusto de Campos's concretist transcription of "Batmacumba," see Perrone, *Masters of Contemporary Brazilian Song*, 62.

69. Augusto de Campos, *Balanço da bossa*, 287.

70. Pedro Alexandre Sanches, "Volta ao 'Tom Zé,' lado B da Tropicália," *Folha de São Paulo*, Aug. 30, 2000.

71. Adorno and Horkheimer, "Culture Industry," 139.

72. Favaretto, *Tropicália*, 93; Perrone, *Masters of Contemporary Brazilian Song*, 61.

73. Joseph Page has noted that Cubatão was designated a "national security zone" in 1968 (the same year "Parque industrial" was recorded), which further limited the political rights of its inhabitants. See Page, *Brazilians*, 281.

74. Dunn, "Tom Zé," 118.

75. Sérgio Garcia, "Aquele Abraço!" *Jornal do Brasil-Domingo* 18, no. 907 (Sept. 19, 1993).

76. Polari, *Em busca do tesouro*, 123; Ridenti, *O fantasma*, 71.

77. Gabeira, *O que é isso, companheiro?* 135. In Bruno Barreto's filmic adaptation of this memoir (distributed in the United States as *Four Days in September*), one of the characters claims that this cryptic reference can be detected "if you play that record

backwards." For documentary evidence of the impact of this song among political prisoners, see Ridenti, *Em busca do povo brasileiro*, 281.

78. Polari, *Em busca do tesouro*, 121.

79. Originally published in 1985 by the Archdiocese of São Paulo as *Brasil: Nunca Mais*, this report was subsequently translated and published in the United States as *Torture in Brazil*.

80. With the success of the Cuban Revolution, the *foco* theory for revolutionary struggle became popularized in parts of Latin America, including Brazil, during the 1960s.

81. Favaretto, *Tropicália*, 92.

82. Veloso's Lindonéia bears a striking resemblance to Macabéia, the poor, uneducated northeastern migrant who is the protagonist in Clarice Lispector's *A hora da estrela* (The hour of the star) (1977).

83. Décio Bar, "Acontece que ele é baiano," *Realidade* 3, no. 33 (Dec. 1968): 187–95.

84. Schwarz, "Culture and Politics," 143.

85. Augusto de Campos, *Balanço da bossa*, 170.

86. Sant'anna, *Música popular e moderna poesia brasileira*, 30.

87. Tinhorão, *Pequena história*, 267.

CHAPTER FOUR

1. Ricardo, *Quem quebrou meu violão*, 60.

2. See Jerônimo Teixeira, "O liquidificador de acarajés," in Maltz et al., *Antropofagismo e tropicalismo*, 41–72.

3. Motta, *Noites tropicais*, 193. Midani had pursued a similar marketing strategy for rock music in Mexico, where he was the president of Capitol Records before taking the job with Philips in Brazil. See Zolov, *Refried Elvis*, 112.

4. See "Entrevista: Caetano Veloso," *Imprensa* 8, no. 87 (Dec. 1994): 18.

5. See Santos, "Kitsch e cultura de massa no Brasil," 39–40.

6. Nelson Motta, "A cruzada tropicalista," *Última Hora–Rio*, Feb. 5, 1968. Motta discusses his tongue-in-cheek article in *Noites tropicais*, 169–70.

7. Skidmore, *Black into White*, 100.

8. It is interesting to note that the modernists of the cannibalist group, Oswald de Andrade and Tarsila do Amaral, had also cultivated a public relationship with the popular circus clown Piolim in the 1920s. See Silviano Santiago, "Caetano Veloso enquanto superastro," in *Uma literatura nos trópicos*, 149.

9. Anamaria Costábile, "Chacrinha, verdade ou mito que buzina o século XX," *Correio da Manhã*, Aug. 29, 1968.

10. Favaretto, *Tropicália*, 114–19.

11. Eli Halfoun, "Caetano ou Chacrinha?" *Última Hora–Rio*, Apr. 13, 1968.

12. In a survey conducted by Marplan, a polling service for *Jornal do Brasil*, respondents answered the following question: "Is Caetano Veloso a good artist?" Survey respondents were classified according to socioeconomic status. Among upper-, middle-, and lower-class respondents, Veloso received approval ratings of 50 percent, 47 percent, and 62 percent, respectively. The same survey also reported that 80 percent of all respondents disapproved of jeering at the 1968 FIC. See "Carioca reprova a vaia em festivais," *Jornal do Brasil*, Oct. 6, 1968.

13. Calado, *Tropicália*, 210–11.

14. Neto, *Os últimos dias de Paupéria*, 295–308.

15. Ibid., 301.

16. The most complete exposition of Freyre's Luso-tropicalism can be found in *O luso e o trópico* (1961), which was translated into English in the same year. For a concise discussion of this theory, see the chapter "Brazil as a European Civilization in the Tropics," in Freyre, *New World in the Tropics*.

17. Freyre, *New World in the Tropics*, 121.

18. Within months after the Bahian group had launched the tropicalist movement in São Paulo, a parallel movement emerged in Recife led by poets Jomard Muniz de Brito and Celso Marconi. Gil and Veloso were signatories to a tropicalist manifesto written by the Pernambucan group in April 1968 that denounced the "cultural morass of the provinces" and the "intellectual menopause" of "our old professors." The Recife tropicalists were particularly critical of conservative champions of traditional northeastern folklore such as dramatist and novelist Ariano Suassuna. I am grateful to Durval Muniz de Albuquerque Jr. for this information.

19. See Mário Chamie, "O trópico entrópico de Tropicália," *Estado de São Paulo, Suplemento Literário*, Apr. 4, 1968.

20. Quoted in Calado, *Tropicália*, 201.

21. Nelson Motta, "Para onde vai Gilberto Gil?" *Última Hora–Rio*, Oct. 14, 1968.

22. Both of these singles were featured as bonus tracks added to Gil's 1968 album included in the remastered box set *Ensaio Geral*, released in 1998.

23. Motta, *Noites tropicais*, 175.

24. Hélio Oiticica, "O sentido de vanguarda do grupo baiano," *Correio da manhã*, Oct. 24, 1968.

25. Author interview with Gilberto Gil, May 23, 1995.

26. "Gil está falando de vaias e festivais," *Jornal da Tarde*, Sept. 28, 1968; reprinted in Gil, *Gilberto Gil*, 33–35.

27. For a discussion of Guilherme Araújo's role in tropicalist style, see Silviano Santiago, "Caetano Veloso enquanto super-astro," in *Uma literatura nos trópicos*, 143–47.

28. Sant'anna, "Tropicalismo! Tropicalismo! Abre as asas sobre nós," *Jornal do Brasil*, Mar. 2, 1968; reprinted in his collection of essays, *Música popular e moderna poesia brasileira*, 88–96.

29. See Nick Nesbitt's useful discussion of the neologism "negritude" in Appiah and Gates, *Africana*, 1404–8.

30. The studio and live recordings of "É proibido proibir" are featured in the collection *Caetano Veloso: Singles* (1999).

31. See Luiz Carlos Maciel, "É proibido proibir," *Correio da Manhã*, Oct. 11, 1968.

32. See "O 'hippie' proibido dos tropicalistas," *Veja*, Oct. 23, 1968. In this short profile of Danduran, he is misidentified as "Johnny Grass."

33. See Dunn, "Tropicalista Rebellion," 126.

34. For a useful transcription of Caetano's speech at TUCA in 1968, see Fonseca, *Caetano*, 91–92.

35. This live performance of "Caminhando" is featured on the compilation *Geraldo Vandré: 20 Preferidas*.

36. See series of articles in *Correio da Manhã*, Oct. 1, 1968.

37. Quoted by Eli Halfoun, "Caminhando com Vandré," *Última Hora–Rio*, Oct. 5, 1968.

38. More than a decade would pass before Vandré's "Caminhando" was performed before a mass audience. In 1979, the singer-songwriter Simone performed it in one of the watershed cultural events of the *abertura* (opening) process.

39. See anonymous note, "Música e política," *Jornal do Brasil*, Oct. 1, 1968.

40. Bourdieu, "Field of Cultural Production," 30–31.

41. José Ramos Tinhorão, "O dia da eletrônica é a véspera da ópera," *Última Hora–SP*, Nov. 17, 1968; Eli Halfoun, "O festival de imitação," *Última Hora–Rio*, Nov. 15, 1968.

42. See Chico Buarque, "Nem toda loucura é genial, nem toda lucidez é velha," *Última Hora–Rio*, Nov. 30, 1968.

43. See Eli Halfoun, "O vovô," *Última Hora–Rio*, Nov. 30, 1968.

44. See "Caetano quer a música útil," *Correio da Manhã*, Sept. 27, 1968. In subsequent years, Veloso adamantly denied any rivalry between the tropicalists and Chico Buarque, noting that it was largely a product of media sensationalism. See Veloso, *Verdade tropical*, 230–35.

45. See Norma Pereira Rego, "Já falo com as pessoas," *Última Hora–SP*, Dec. 12, 1968.

46. Calado, *Tropicália*, 244. Leonard Theremin, a Russian émigré to the United States, invented this instrument, which was used to great effect in the 1960s by the Beach Boys in their hit song "Good Vibrations."

47. Veloso, *Alegria, alegria*, 24.

48. Dunn, "Tom Zé," 113.

49. See "Censura entrou na parceria," *Ultima Hora–Rio*, Nov. 15, 1968.

50. Hélio Oiticica, "O sentido de vanguarda do grupo baiano," *Correio da manhã*, Oct. 24, 1968.

51. Quoted in Tinhorão, *Música popular: Do gramafone ao rádio e TV*, 185.

52. See unsigned article "Tropicália quer cantar ao ar livre," *Ultima Hora–SP*, Nov. 10, 1968.

53. For more information on festivals in the early 1970s, see Ana Maria Bahiana, "A 'linha evolutiva' prossegue: A música dos universitários," in Bahiana et al., *Anos 70*.

54. See "Sucata: A longa noite de loucuras," *Ultima Hora–Rio*, Oct. 11, 1968.

55. See brief unsigned notes, "Comentarista da Jamaica" and "Bastidores," *Ultima Hora–Rio*, Oct. 14, 1968.

56. See "Show de Caetano pára mesmo," *Última Hora–Rio*, Oct. 17, 1968.

57. See "Seja marginal, seja herói," *Ultima Hora–Rio*, Oct. 17, 1968.

58. These documents were found in the archive of the Department of Political and Social Order of São Paulo state (DEOPS). See Armando Antenore, "O tropicalismo no cárcere," *Folha de São Paulo–Mais!*, Nov. 2, 1997.

59. See "Chega de saudade yê," *Última Hora–Rio*, Oct. 30, 1968.

60. Vilarino, *A MPB em movimento*, 88.

61. Dunn, "Tropicalista Rebellion," 131.

62. Veloso, *Verdade tropical*, 401.

63. A brief explanation of these references may be helpful: Dom Helder and Dom Sigaud represented the progressive and conservative wings of the Catholic Church in Brazil; Rogério Duprat was the premier tropicalist arranger, and Maestro Carioca

was an arranger and band leader of cabaret-style productions; Ché Guevara helped lead the Cuban Revolution and later became a symbol of Latin American liberation, and Kosygin was a Soviet bureaucrat of the Brezhnev era; Jair Rodrigues was a popular performer known for his jazz-bossa stylizations on Elis Regina's program "O Fino da Bossa"; Flávio Cavalcanti hosted televised variety shows that aspired toward "good taste," in contrast to Chacrinha's low-brow spectacle; politicians from the state of Minas Gerais were known for "politics as usual"; Zé Keti was a samba musician featured in the musical showcase "Opinião," and Paulinho da Viola was an emerging singer-songwriter noted for his sophisticated rereading of the samba tradition; Teatro Oficina was the theater group most identified with the tropicalist movement, and the Teatro Copacabana was emblematic of "bourgeois" theater in Rio.

64. For more details on AI-5, see Alves, *State and Opposition in Military Brazil*, 95–96, and Skidmore, *Politics of Military Rule in Brazil*, 81–83.

65. Marisa Alves de Lima, "Marginália: Arte e cultura na idade da pedrada," *O Cruzeiro*, Dec. 14, 1968. This article was reprinted in Lima's documentary volume of the same title in 1996.

66. Veloso writes that he and Gil greatly admired the music of Jorge Ben, citing in particular the song "Se manda" (Get lost) from his 1967 album, *O Bidú*. See *Verdade tropical*, 197.

67. Calado. *A divina comédia*, 165.

68. Ibid., 174.

69. Perrone, *Masters of Contemporary Brazilian Song*, 74–75.

70. See "Entrevista com Chico Buarque," *O Pasquim* 16 (Oct. 9–15, 1970).

71. Maciel published these letters in his book *Geração em transe*, 223–41.

72. Veloso's text about the "Carolina" flap, "Nossa Carolina em Londres Setenta," was never published in *O Pasquim* because he feared that it would also be misunderstood. It was later published in Veloso's *Alegria, alegria* and in Maciel's *Geração em transe*.

73. Gil, *Todas as letras*, 103.

74. A reissue of this album contained in the CD box set *Ensaio Geral* (1998) features Gil's long, unreleased acoustic version of this song.

75. Jameson, "Periodizing the 60s," 180.

76. Ibid., 181.

77. Duarte, "Momentos do movimento," in *Tropicália: 20 anos*, 47.

78. Pereira and Buarque de Hollanda, *Patrulhas ideológicas*, 108.

79. Sovik, "Ponha seu capacete," 60–67.

80. Gil, *Todas as letras*, 110.

81. Vilarino, *A MPB em movimento*, 97–99.

82. In a letter dated November 20, 1967, the director of the museum, Ricardo Cravo Albim, wrote to Governor Francisco Negrão de Lima that the award could be an "authentic 'egg of Columbus'" in terms of publicity, popular repercussion, and originality." This letter is on file at the Museu da Imagem e do Som in Rio de Janeiro.

83. Gil, "Recuso + Aceito = Receito," *O Pasquim* 16 (Oct. 9–15, 1970); reprinted in Gil, *Gilberto Gil*, 43–46.

84. See Claudia de Arruda Campos, *Zumbi, Tiradentes*, 74–76. The production featured white actors who sang popular bossa-sambas by Edu Lobo, such as "Upa Neguinho" (Hey little black boy) and "Tempo de Guerra" (Time of war).

85. Mota, *A ideologia da cultural brasileira*, 48–51.

86. See Timothy Taylor's discussion of "purity" and "authenticity" in relation to contemporary African artists Youssou N'Dour and Angélique Kidjo in *Global Pop*, 125–45.

CHAPTER FIVE

1. Ana Maria Bahiana, "A 'linha evolutiva' prossegue: A música dos universitários," in Bahiana et al. *Anos 70*, 25–39.

2. See Armstrong's discussion of Tropicália and Afro-Brazilian music in *Third World Literary Fortunes*, 205–13.

3. "A crise da cultura brasileira," *Visão*, July 5, 1971. For an analysis of censorship and Brazilian popular music during the early 1970s, see Moby, *Sinal fechado*, 127–43.

4. Wisnik, "O minuto e o milênio," in Bahiana et al., *Anos 70*, 8.

5. See Chico Buarque's interview with Tarik de Souza in *Veja*, Sept. 15, 1971. This interview was reprinted in Souza's *Rostos e gostos*, 61–68.

6. Perrone, *Masters of Contemporary Brazilian Song*, 33–34.

7. Vasconcellos, *Música popular*, 72.

8. For an account of the Médici regime's manipulation of the World Cup victory, see Lever, *Soccer Madness*, 67–69.

9. Later in the decade, Gilberto Gil would parody the patriotic slogan in "O seu amor" (Your love), a simple incantation of affective liberation ("Your love / love it and leave it / free to love") that was featured on the *Doces Bárbaros* album.

10. Johnson, *Cinema Novo X 5*, 148–50.

11. George, *Modern Brazilian Stage*, 73.

12. In 1970, 47 percent of all records manufactured in Brazil featured foreign artists, and many others were Brazilian versions of international hits. See "As duas invasões da música brasileira," *Veja*, Mar. 11, 1970. See also Margarida Autran, "O estado e o músico popular," in Bahiana et al., *Anos 70*, 94.

13. These letters and dispatches were reprinted in 1977 in Veloso's first book of collected writings, *Alegria, alegria*.

14. Veloso, *Alegria, alegria*, 49.

15. Veloso, *Verdade tropical*, 427.

16. Calado (*Tropicália*, 270) has claimed that Gil was greatly influenced by Timothy Leary's *Politics of Ecstasy* and took nearly eighty hits of LSD during his London exile.

17. Chaves, "Memórias do passado no presente," 74–75.

18. Herrera, "Triste Bahia," 24.

19. For an insightful discussion of Pastinha's chant in relation to ironic commentary in capoeira, see Browning, *Samba*, 111–12.

20. Stam, "Palimpsest Aesthetics," 61.

21. Veloso, *Verdade tropical*, 486; Calado, *Tropicália*, 294–95.

22. Perrone, *Masters of Contemporary Brazilian Song*, 77.

23. Risério, "O nome mais belo do medo," 4.

24. Favaretto, *Tropicália*, 45.

25. McGowen and Pessanha, *Brazilian Sound*, 130. For a history of the Novos Baianos, see Luiz Galvão, *Anos 70: Novos Baianos.*

26. Veloso, *Verdade tropical*, 49.

27. McGowen and Pessanha, *Brazilian Sound*, 191.

28. Even after his death in 1989, Raul Seixas continued to appeal to Brazilian youths of all social classes as an avatar of nonconformity and rebellion. See André Barcinski, "O general do exército de malucos," *Folha de São Paulo*, Aug. 16, 1999.

29. Trevisan, *Perverts in Paradise*, 120.

30. "Caetano no templo do caetanismo," *Veja*, Jan. 1, 1972.

31. Gil, *Gilberto Gil*, 161.

32. Gil, *Todas as letras*, 127.

33. Rosnak, *Making of a Counterculture*, 156.

34. Frank, *Conquest of Cool*, 26–33.

35. Martins, "A geração AI-5," 74.

36. Silviano Santiago, "Os abutres," in *Uma literatura nos trópicos*, 134.

37. Buarque de Hollanda, *Impressões de viagem*, 66.

38. Veloso, *Verdade tropical*, 469.

39. Gil, *Todas as letras*, 146.

40. Risério, *Carnaval ijexá*, 23.

41. Reginaldo Prandi, "The Expansion of Black Religion in White Society: Brazilian Popular Music and the Legitimacy of Candomblé." Paper delivered at the 20th Congress of the Latin American Studies Association, Guadalajara, Mexico, 1997.

42. Gil seems to have been aware of the gendered implications of "Chuck Berry Fields," noting that it was reaffirming "popular archetypes" regarding African virility and European rationality. See Gil, *Todas as letras*, 179.

43. Veloso, *Alegria, alegria*, 214.

44. Gil, *Gilberto Gil*, 143.

45. Following his arrest, the *Jornal do Brasil* printed a joke in which Gil informs the arresting officer that drugs have been legalized in California. When the agent retorts, "But we're in Florianopolis," Gil quips, "Yeah, but I thought it was California" (Gil, *Gilberto Gil*, 151).

46. Gilroy, *Black Atlantic*, 74–75.

47. Lipsitz, *Dangerous Crossroads*, 31.

48. See Joseph, "Soul, Transnationalism, and Imaginings of Revolution," and Diawara, "Song of the Griot."

49. See Ana Maria Bahiana, "Enlatando Black Rio," in *Nada será como antes*, 218–19.

50. Quoted in Risério, *Carnaval ijexá*, 31.

51. See Turner, "Brown into Black," 79, and Hanchard, *Orpheus and Power*, 115.

52. Risério, *Carnaval ijexá*, 23.

53. The bibliography on the Afro-Bahian carnival is extensive. For an early account of the emergence of the movement, see Risério, *Carnaval ijexá*. Several essays on the movement through the 1990s can be found in Sansone and Santos, *Ritmos em trânsito*. For a useful history of the movement with excellent photos, see Guerreiro, *A trama dos tambores*. English sources include my essay "The Afro-Bahian Carnival: A

Stage for Protest"; Larry Crook, "Black Consciousness, *samba-reggae*, and the Re-Africanization of Bahian Carnival Music in Brazil"; and Barbara Browning, *Samba: Resistance in Motion*. There are also several relevant essays on the contemporary Afro-Bahian music scene in Perrone and Dunn, *Brazilian Popular Music and Globalization*.

54. Risério, *Carnaval ijexá*, 31.

55. Pereira and Buarque de Hollanda, *Patrulhas ideológicas*, 210.

56. Ibid., 187.

57. See "Rumos às origens," *Veja* (Jan. 19, 1977), 99.

58. The Brazilian government was developing extensive diplomatic and commercial relations with postcolonial Africa (especially the recently independent Lusophone nations) as it ruled a nation marked by pronounced racial inequality and maintained close ties with the apartheid regime of South Africa. See Dzidzienyo, "African Connection," 135–53.

59. Nirlando Beirão, "Baiunos? Baianaves?" *IstoÉ*, Aug. 10, 1977.

60. Reynivaldo Brito, "Caetano desabafa: Sou da patrulha Odara. E daí?" *A Tarde*, Mar. 2, 1979. See also Ridenti, *Em busca do povo brasileiro*, 220.

61. Perrone, *Masters of Contemporary Brazilian Song*, 123–24.

62. See "Gilberto Gil," *Jornegro* 2, no. 7 (1979).

63. Tarik de Souza, "Rebobagem," *Veja*, July 20, 1977; reprinted in Souza, *Rostos e gostos*, 227–28.

64. Pereira and Buarque de Hollanda, *Patrulhas ideológicas*, 209.

65. Gil, *Todas as letras*, 204.

CHAPTER SIX

1. Lucchesi and Dieguez, *Caetano*, 203. Also see Veloso's discussion of this song in Dunn, "Tropicalista Rebellion," 135.

2. Browning, *Infectious Rhythms*, 4.

3. See Rodrigo Leitão, "Errante navegante," *Jornal de Brasília*, Jan. 23, 1991.

4. David Bryne had visited Brazil in 1986 for the Rock in Rio festival and then again in 1988 to film the documentary on Afro-Bahian religion, "The House of Life." By this time, he was in the planning stages for his highly acclaimed and successful compilations of Brazilian music including *Beleza Tropical*, *O Samba*, and *O Forró*. In a record store in Rio de Janeiro, he picked up a reissued copy of Tom Zé's *Estudando o samba*, assuming that it was a conventional samba record.

5. See Julian Dibbell's review, "Tom Zé: 'Massive Hits,'" *New York Times*, Dec. 9, 1990.

6. Silvio Essinger, "A redenção do tropicalista esquecido," *Folha de São Paulo*, Apr. 20, 1999.

7. Pedro Só, "A volta por cima de Tom Zé," *Jornal do Brasil*, Sept. 2, 1993.

8. This quote was taken from an interview with Koellreutter in *Tom Zé, ou quem irá colocar uma dinamite na cabeça do século* (2000), a marvelous video documentary directed by Carla Gallo.

9. Ávila, "Tom Zé," 4–5.

10. Chaui, *Conformismo e resistência*, 33.

11. Vasconcellos, *Música popular*, 75–76.

12. See Perrone and Dunn, "'Chiclete com Banana.'"

13. For a discussion of the *arrastões* and the funk counterculture in Rio de Janeiro, see Yúdice, "Funkification of Rio."

14. Stam, "Palimpsest Aesthetics," 69–70.

15. Author communication with Tom Zé, Nov. 4, 1998.

16. For a more extensive discussion of Tom Zé's *Jogos de armar*, see my article "Tom Zé põe dinamite nos pés do século," *O Estado de São Paulo*, Feb. 25, 2001.

17. I found only one reference to the international projection of Tropicália in the year it occurred. The July 1968 issue of the British magazine *World Pop News* ran a cover story about the movement titled "Tropicália: The New Brazilian Wave!"

18. See, for example, Julian Dibbell's "A Brazil Classic," *Spin*, July 1989, and "Notes on Carmen," *The Village Voice*, Oct. 29, 1991; Chris McGowan's "A Nation of Cannibals," *The Beat* 10, no. 4 (1991); and my articles "It's Forbidden to Forbid," *Américas*, Sept.–Oct. 1993, and "Taking Their Cues from the Cannibals," *Rhythm Music Magazine* 3, no. 9 (1994).

19. Several American bands had discovered tropicalist music years before it garnered so much attention in the U.S. press. As early as the late 1980s, the Boston-based art-rock band Birthday recorded a humorous, nonsensical version of "2001," but it was never commercially released. The L.A.-based group Tater Totz featured a version of "Batmacumba" on their 1988 album *Alien Sleestacks from Brazil*. It has been reported that Kurt Cobain of the band Nirvana became a fan of Os Mutantes after obtaining some of their records during a trip to Brazil in 1993.

20. Harvey, "Cannibals, Mutants, and Hipsters."

21. Polygram issued a five-disc box set that included the tropicalist albums of Veloso, Gil, Costa, and Os Mutantes, as well as the collective concept album of 1968. The label Omplatten reissued the first three recordings of Os Mutantes. In 1999, Luaka Bop also released an Os Mutantes compilation, *Everything is Possible!*, the first in their series of World Psychedelic Classics. In the same year Hip-O Records (an imprint of Universal Records, formally Polygram) produced a marvelous collection, *Tropicália Essentials*, which features the canonical tropicalist recordings.

22. Ben Ratliff, "From Brazil, the Echoes of a Modernist Revolt," *New York Times*, May 17, 1998. For a more extensive analysis of Tropicália with a useful annotated discography, see Ben Ratliff, "The Primer: Tropicália and Beyond," *The Wire* 184 (June 1999).

23. Gerald Marzorati, "Tropicália, Agora!" *New York Times Magazine*, Apr. 25, 1999.

24. Harvey, "Cannibals, Mutants, and Hipsters."

25. Jackson Griffith, "Boogaloo with Beck," *Pulse!* 188 (Dec. 1999): 81; Eric Gladstone, "Musica, Mutato, Muto, Mutante, Mutatio," *Raygun* 63 (Jan. 1999): 42–49.

26. See Brent DiCrescenzo's review of *De Mel, De Melão* in the on-line magazine *Pitchfork* (pitchforkmedia.com).

27. Hermano Vianna, "A epifania tropicalista," *Folha de São Paulo–Mais!*, Sept. 19, 1999.

28. Dunn, "Tom Zé," 120.

29. Xavier, "From the Religious Moral Sense," 193.

30. Veloso later included this song on his live album, *Prenda minha* (1998).

31. See Guerreiro, *A trama dos tambores*, 165–67.

32. Luís Lasserre, "Tropicalismo: Banquete pós-antropofágico," *A Tarde*, Feb. 12, 1998.

33. Baby Consuelo, the former vocalist of the Novos Baianos and a perennial favorite of the Bahian carnival, remarked that "tropicalismo is the root of everything that you see today in the carnival of Salvador." See Christiane González, "Tropicalistas derrubam axé music em Salvador," *Folha de São Paulo*, Feb. 24, 1998.

34. Veloso, *Verdade tropical*, 50.

35. This recording, *Tropicália: 30 anos*, featured "Batmacumba," by Ilê Aiyê, "Domingo no parque," by Margareth Menezes, and "Alegria, alegria," by Daniela Mercury.

36. "A memorável celebração da Tropicália," *A Tarde*, Feb. 25, 1998.

37. Magaldi, "Adopting Imports," 310–11.

38. Vianna, *Mystery of Samba*, 105.

39. See Carlos Calado, "Chico César esquenta debate sobre Tropicália," *CliqueMusic* (cliquemusic.com.br), May 5, 2000.

40. Gilberto Vasconcellos, "Sem mentira não se vive," *Folha de São Paulo–Mais!*, Nov. 2, 1997.

41. Sovik, "Tropicália, Canonical Pop," 114–15.

42. See "Sinceridade Reveladora," *Revista Época* 14 (Aug. 24, 1998), cited in Braga Pinto, "How to Organize a Movement," 109.

43. See special issue of *IstoÉ*, "O brasileiro do século: música," Mar. 1999.

44. Xavier, *Allegories of Underdevelopment*, 27–28.

45. Ridenti, *Em busca do povo brasileiro*, 284–88.

46. See Ben Ratliff, "The Fresh Prince of Brazil," *Spin* 15, no. 6 (June 1999).

47. See Veloso's article "Utopia 2," *Folha de São Paulo: Mais!*, Sept. 25, 1994.

BIBLIOGRAPHY

NEWSPAPERS

Bondinho (Rio de Janeiro)
Correio da Manhã (Rio de Janeiro)
O Estado de São Paulo
Folha de São Paulo
Jornal da Bahia (Salvador)
Jornal da Tarde (São Paulo)
Jornal de Brasília (Brasília)
Jornal do Brasil (Rio de Janeiro)
The New York Times
O Pasquim (Rio de Janeiro)
O Sol (Rio de Janeiro)
Suplemento Literário de Minas Gerais (Belo Horizonte)
A Tarde (Salvador)
Última Hora (editions in Rio de Janeiro and São Paulo)
The Village Voice

MAGAZINES

Américas
The Beat
Billboard
Caros Amigos
O Cruzeiro
Imprensa
IstoÉ
Manchete
The New York Times Magazine
Pulse
Raygun
Rhythm Music Magazine
Spin
Veja
Visão
Wire

BOOKS AND ARTICLES

Adorno, T. W., and M. Horkheimer. "The Culture Industry: Enlightenment as Mass
   Deception" (1944). In Dialectic of Enlightenment, translated by John Cumming,
   120–67. New York: Seabury Press, 1972.
Agrippino de Paula, José. Panamérica. 1967. São Paulo: Max Limonad, 1988.
Aguiar, Joaquim Alves de. "Panorama da música popular brasileira: Da bossa nova ao

rock dos anos 8o." In *Brasil: O trânsito da memória*, edited by Saúl Sosnowski and Jorge Schwartz, 141–74. São Paulo: Editora da Universide de São Paulo, 1994.

Albuquerque, Durval Muniz de, Jr. *A invenção do nordeste e outras artes*. Recife: Fundação Joaquim Nabuco; São Paulo: Cortez Editora, 1999.

Alves, Maria Helena Moreira. *State and Opposition in Military Brazil*. Austin: University of Texas Press, 1985.

Anderson, Robert. "The Muses of Chaos and Destruction of *Arena conta Zumbi*." *Latin American Theater Review* 29, no. 2 (Spring 1996): 15–28.

Andrade, Mário de. *Ensaio sobre a música brasileira*. 1928. São Paulo: Livraria Martins Editora, 1962.

Andrade, Oswald de. *Obras completas*. Vol. 2. Rio de Janeiro: Civilização Brasileira, 1972.

———. *Pau-Brasil*. 1925. São Paulo: Editora Globo, 1990.

———. *O rei da vela*. 1937. São Paulo: Editora Globo; Secretária de Estado da Cultura, 1991.

———. *Serafim Ponte Grande*. São Paulo: Editora Globo; Secretária de Estado da Cultura, 1990.

———. *A utopia antropofágica*. São Paulo: Editora Globo; Secretária de Estado da Cultura, 1990.

Appiah, Anthony, and Henry Louis Gates Jr., eds. *Africana: The Encyclopedia of the African and African American Experience*. New York: Basic Civitas, 1999.

Appleby, David P. *The Music of Brazil*. Austin: University of Texas Press, 1983.

Armstrong, Piers. *Third World Literary Fortunes: Brazilian Culture and Its International Reception*. Lewisburg, Pa.: Bucknell University Press, 1999.

Artaud, Antonin. *Antonin Artaud: Collected Works*. Vol. 4. Translated by Victor Corti. London: Calder & Boyars, 1974.

Avelar, Idelber. *The Untimely Present: Postdictatorial Latin American Fiction and the Task of Mourning*. Durham: Duke University Press, 1999.

Ávila, Carlos. "Tom Zé: Poemúsica." *Minas Gerais Literary Supplement* 8, no. 361 (July 20, 1973): 4–5.

Bahiana, Ana Maria, et al. *Anos 70: Música popular*. Rio de Janeiro: Europa, 1980.

———. *Nada será como antes: MPB nos anos 70*. Rio de Janeiro: Civilização Brasileira, 1980.

Barbosa, Airton Lima, et al. "Que caminho seguir na música popular brasileira?" *Revista Civilização Brasileira* 1, no. 7 (May 1966): 375–85.

Bary, Lelsie. "Civilization, Barbarism, 'Cannibalism': The Question of National Culture in Oswald de Andrade." In *Toward Socio-Criticism: Selected Proceedings of the Conference "Luso-Brazilian Literatures, A Socio-Critical Approach,"* edited by Roberto Reis, 95–100. Tempe: Center for Latin American Studies at Arizona State University, 1991.

Béhague, Gerard. "Bossa and Bossas: Recent Changes in Brazilian Urban Popular Music." *Ethnomusicology* 17, no. 2 (May 1973): 209–33.

———. "Brazilian Musical Values of the 1960s and 1970s: Popular Urban Music from Bossa Nova to Tropicália." *Journal of Popular Culture* 13, no. 3 (Winter 1980): 437–52.

Benjamin, Walter. *The Origin of German Tragic Drama.* 1928. New York: Verso, 1998.

Berlinck, Manoel T. *O Centro Popular de Cultura da UNE.* São Paulo: Papirus, 1984.

Boal, Augusto. "Que pensa você do teatro brasileiro?" *Arte em Revista* 1, no. 2 (May–Aug. 1979): 40–44.

Borheim, Gerd, et al. *Cultura brasileira: Tradição/ contradição.* Rio de Janeiro: Jorge Zahar, 1987.

Bosi, Alfredo. *História concisa da literatura brasileira.* São Paulo: Cultrix, 1970.

Bourdieu, Pierre. "The Field of Cultural Production, or: The Economic World Reversed." In *The Field of Cultural Production: Essays on Art and Literature,* edited by Randal Johnson, 29–73. New York: Columbia University Press, 1993.

Braga Pinto, César. "How to Organize a Movement: Caetano Veloso's Tropical Path." *Studies in Latin American Popular Culture* 19 (2000): 103–12.

Brazil: Nunca Mais. Petrópolis: Editora Vozes, 1985. Translated and edited by Jaime Wright and Joan Dassin as *Torture in Brazil: A Report by the Archdiocese of São Paulo.* New York: Vintage Books, 1986.

Brett, Guy, et al. *Hélio Oiticica.* Rio de Janeiro: Projeto Hélio Oiticica; Paris: Galerie nationale du Jeu de Paume; Rotterdam: Witte de With, 1993.

Browning, Barbara. *Infectious Rhythms: Metaphors of Contagion and the Spread of African Culture.* New York: Routledge, 1998.

———. *Samba: Resistance in Motion.* Bloomington: Indiana University Press, 1995.

Buarque de Hollanda, Heloísa. *Impressões de viagem: CPC, vanguarda e desbunde: 1960/70.* 1980. Rio de Janeiro: Rocco, 1992.

Buarque de Hollanda, Heloísa, and Marcos A. Gonçalves. *Cultura e participação nos anos 60.* São Paulo: Brasiliense, 1986.

Calado, Carlos. *A divina comédia dos Mutantes.* Rio de Janeiro: Editora 34, 1995.

———. *Tropicália: A história de uma revolução musical.* São Paulo: Editora 34, 1997.

Callado, Antônio. *Quarup.* Rio de Janeiro: Editora Civilização Brasileira, 1967.

Campos, Augusto de, et al. *Balanço da bossa e outras bossas.* São Paulo: Editora Perspectiva, 1974.

———. *Música e invenção.* São Paulo: Editora Perspectiva, 1998.

———. *Teoria da poesia concreta.* São Paulo: Livraria Duas Cidades, 1975.

Campos, Claudia de Arruda. *Zumbi, Tiradentes.* São Paulo: Editora Perspectiva and Editora da Universidade de São Paulo, 1988.

Campos, Haroldo. "The Rule of Anthropophagy: Europe under the Sign of Devoration." *Latin American Literary Review* 14 (Jan.–June 1986): 42–60.

Capinan, José Carlos. "Tropicalismo eppur si mueve." *Revista da Bahia* 32, no. 26 (May 1998): 46–59.

Cardoso, Fernando Henrique, and Enzo Faletto. *Dependência e desenvolvimento da América Latina.* Rio de Janeiro: Zahar, 1970.

Carvalho, Martha de Ulhôa. "Tupi or not Tupi MPB: Popular Music and Identity in Brazil." In *The Brazilian Puzzle: Culture on the Borderlands of the Western World,* edited by David Hess and Roberto DaMatta, 159–79. New York: Columbia University Press, 1995.

Castro, Ruy. *Chega de saudade: A história e as histórias da bossa nova.* São Paulo: Companhia de Letras, 1990.

Chaui, Marilena. *Conformismo e resistência: Aspectos da cultura popular no Brasil.* São Paulo: Editora Brasiliense, 1986.

Chaves, Celso Loureiro. "Memórias do passado no presente: A fenomenologia de *Transa.*" *Studies in Latin American Popular Culture* 19 (2000): 73–82.

Corbisier, Roland. *Formação e problema da cultura brasileira.* Rio de Janeiro: Instituto Superior de Estudos Brasileiros, 1960.

Coutinho, Carlos Nelson, and Marco Aurélio Nogueira, eds. *Gramsci e a América Latina.* São Paulo: Paz e Terra, 1988.

Coutinho, Wilson. "Esse teu olhar quando encontra o meu." In *Gerchman*, by Rubens Gerchman. Rio de Janeiro: Salamandra, 1989.

Crook, Larry. "Black Consciousness, *samba-reggae*, and the Re-Africanization of Bahian Carnival Music in Brazil." *The World of Music* 35, no. 2 (1993): 90–108.

Damasceno, Leslie. *Cultural Space and Theatrical Conventions in the Works of Oduvaldo Vianna Filho.* Detroit: Wayne State University Press, 1996.

Diawara, Mantia. "The Song of the Griot." *Transition: An International Review* 75 (1998): 16–30.

Dunn, Christopher. "Afro-Bahian Carnival: A Stage for Protest." *Afro-Hispanic Review* 11, no. 1–3 (1992): 11–20.

———. "Caetano Veloso: Tropicalismo revisitado." *Brasil/Brazil* 11, no. 7 (1994): 99–110.

———. "In the Adverse Hour: The Denouement of Tropicália." *Studies in Latin American Popular Culture* 19 (2000): 21–34.

———. "The Relics of Brazil: Modernity and Nationality in the Tropicalista Movement." Ph.D. diss., Brown University, 1996.

———. "Tom Zé: O elo perdido do tropicalismo." *Brasil/Brazil* 11, no. 7 (1994): 110–20.

———. "Tropicália, Counterculture, and the Diasporic Imagination in Brazil." In *Brazilian Popular Music and Globalization*, edited by Charles A. Perrone and Christopher Dunn, 72–95. Gainesville: University Press of Florida, 2001.

———. "Tropicalism and Brazilian Popular Music under Military Rule." In *The Brazil Reader*, edited by Robert Levine and John Crocitti, 241–47. Durham: Duke University Press, 1999.

———. "The Tropicalista Rebellion: A Conversation with Caetano Veloso." *Transition* 70 (Summer 1996): 116–38.

Dzidzienyo, Anani. "The African Connection and the Afro-Brazilian Condition." In *Race, Class, and Power in Brazil*, edited by Pierre Michel Fontaine, 135–53. Los Angeles: University of California Press; Center for Afro-American Studies, 1985.

Enciclopédia da música brasileira: Erudita, folclórica e popular. 2nd ed. São Paulo: Arte Editora, 1998.

Estevam, Carlos. *A questão da cultura popular.* Rio de Janeiro: Editora Tempo Brasileiro, 1962.

Favaretto, Celso. *A invenção de Hélio Oiticica.* São Paulo: Editora da Universidade de São Paulo, 1992.

———. *Tropicália: Alegoria, alegria.* 1979. São Paulo: Editora Ateliê, 1996.

Ferreira, Nadiá Paulo. "Tropicalismo: Retomada oswaldiana." *Revista de Cultura Vozes* 66, no. 10 (Dec. 1972): 763–77.

Fonseca, Hebert. *Caetano: Esse cara*. Rio de Janeiro: Editora Rivan, 1993.

Frank, Thomas. *The Conquest of Cool: Business Culture, Counterculture, and the Rise of Hip Consumerism*. Chicago: University of Chicago Press, 1997.

Freyre, Gilberto. *Casa-grande e senzala*. 1933. Rio de Janeiro: José Olympio, 1981. Translated by Samuel Putnam as *The Masters and the Slaves*. New York: Alfred Knopf, 1946.

———. *New World in the Tropics*. New York: Alfred Knopf, 1959.

———. *O luso e o trópico*. Lisboa: Commissão Executiva das Comemorações do V Centenário da Morte do Infante D. Henrique, 1961; translation by Helen M. D'O Matthew and F. de Mello Moser as *The Portuguese in the Tropics*.

Gabeira, Fernando, *O que é isso, companheiro?* Rio de Janeiro: Codecri, 1980.

Galvão, Luiz. *Anos 70: Novos Baianos*. São Paulo: Editora 34, 1997.

Galvão, Walnice Nogueira. "As falas, os silêncios (Literatura e imediações: 1964–1988)." In *Brasil: O trânsito da memória*, edited by Saúl Sosnowski and Jorge Schwartz, 185–96. São Paulo: Editora da Universide de São Paulo, 1994.

———. "MMPB: Uma análise ideológica." In *Saco de Gatos*, 93–119. São Paulo: Livraria Duas Cidades, 1976.

García Canclini, Néstor. *Hybrid Cultures: Strategies for Entering and Leaving Modernity*. Translated by Christopher Chiappari and Silvia L. López. Minneapolis: University of Minnesota Press, 1995.

George, David. *The Modern Brazilian Stage*. Austin: University of Texas Press, 1992.

Gerchman, Rubens. *Gerchman*. Rio de Janeiro: Salamandra, 1989.

Gil, Gilberto. *Gilberto Gil: Expresso 2222*. Edited by Antônio Risério. Salvador: Corrupio, 1982.

———. *Songbook*. Vols. 1–2. Edited by Almir Chediak. Rio de Janeiro: Lumiar, n.d.

———. *Todas as letras*. Edited by Carlos Rennó. São Paulo: Companhia das Letras, 1996.

Gilroy, Paul. *The Black Atlantic: Modernity and Double Consciousness*. Cambridge: Harvard University Press, 1993.

Guerreiro, Goli. *A trama dos tambores: A música afro-pop de Salvador*. São Paulo: Editora 34, 2000.

Gullar, Ferreira. *Cultura posta em questão*. Rio de Janeiro: Editora Civilização Brasileira, 1965.

———. *Vanguarda e subdesenvolvimento*. Rio de Janeiro: Civilização Brasileira, 1969.

Hanchard, Michael. *Orpheus and Power: The Movimento Negro of Rio de Janeiro and São Paulo, Brazil, 1945–1988*. Princeton: Princeton University Press, 1994.

Harvey, John. "Cannibals, Mutants, and Hipsters: The Tropicalist Revival." In *Brazilian Popular Music and Globalization*, edited by Charles A. Perrone and Christopher Dunn, 106–22. Gainesville: University Press of Florida, 2001.

Helena, Lúcia. *Totens e tabus da modernidade brasileira: Símbolo e alegoria na obra de Oswald de Andrade*. Rio de Janeiro: Tempo Brasileiro, 1985.

———. *Uma literatura antropofágica*. Fortaleza: Universidade Federal do Ceará, 1983.

Herrera, Antonia. "Triste Bahia: No íntimo de uma cidade quem sabe da alegria?" Exú 5, no. 30 (Nov.–Dec. 1992): 22–27.

Hoisel, Evelina. Supercaos: Os estilhaços da cultura em Panamérica e Nações Unidas. Rio de Janeiro: Civilização Brasileira; Salvador: Fundação Cultural do Estado da Bahia, 1980.

———. "Tropicalismo: Algumas reflexões teóricas." Brasil/Brazil 12, no. 7 (1994): 39–63.

Holston, Mark. The Modernist City: An Anthropological Critique of Brasília. Chicago: University of Chicago Press, 1989.

Homem de Melo, José Eduardo. Música popular brasileira. São Paulo: Editora Melhoramentos, Universidade de São Paulo, 1976.

Huyssen, Andreas. After the Great Divide: Modernism, Mass Culture, Postmodernism. Bloomington: Indiana University Press, 1986.

Ianni, Octávio. O colapso do populismo no Brasil. 1968. Rio de Janeiro: Civilização Brasileira, 1994.

Jameson, Fredric. "Periodizing the 60s." In The 60s without Apology, edited by Sohnya Sayres et al., 178–209. Minneapolis: University of Minnesota Press, 1988.

———. Postmodernism; or, The Cultural Logic of Late Capitalism. Durham: Duke University Press, 1991.

———. "Third World Literature in the Era of Multinational Capitalism." Social Text 15 (1986): 65–88.

Johnson, Randal. "Brazilian Modernism: An Idea Out of Place?" Modernism and its Margins: Reinscribing Cultural Modernity from Spain and Latin America, edited by Anthony L. Geist and José B. Monleón, 186–214. New York: Garland, 1999.

———. Cinema Novo X 5: Masters of Contemporary Brazilian Film. Austin: University of Texas Press, 1984.

———. "The Institutionalization of Brazilian Modernism." Brasil/Brazil 4, no. 3 (1990): 6–23.

———. "Tupy or Not Tupy: Cannibalism and Nationalism in Contemporary Brazilian Literature and Culture." In On Modern Latin American Fiction, edited by John King, 41–59. New York: Hill and Wang, 1987.

Johnson, Randal, and Robert Stam, eds. Brazilian Cinema. 2nd ed. New York: Columbia University Press, 1995.

Joseph, May. "Soul, Transnationalism, and Imaginings of Revolution: Ujamma and the Politics of Enjoyment." In Soul: Black Power, Politics and Pleasure, edited by Monique Guillory and Richard C. Green, 126–38. New York: New York University Press, 1998.

Larsen, Neil. Reading North by South: On Latin American Literature, Culture and Politics. Minneapolis: University of Minnesota Press, 1995.

Leite, J. R. Teixeira, et al. Gente nova, nova gente. Rio de Janeiro: Editora Expressão e Cultura, 1967.

Lemos, Tite de. "A guinada de José Celso." Arte em Revista 1, no. 2 (May–Aug. 1979): 45–50.

Lever, Janet. Soccer Madness: Brazil's Passion for the World's Most Popular Sport. 2nd ed. Prospect Heights, Ill.: Waveland Press, 1995.

Levine, Robert, and John Crocitti. *The Brazil Reader: History, Culture, Politics*. Durham: Duke University Press, 1999.

Lima, Maria Alvarez. *Marginália: Arte e cultura "na idade da pedrada."* Rio de Janeiro: Salamandra, 1996.

Lipsitz, George. *Dangerous Crossroads: Popular Music, Postmodernism, and the Poetics of Place.* New York: Verso, 1994.

Lucchesi, Ivo, and Gilda Korff Dieguez. *Caetano. Por que não?: Uma viagem entre a aurora e a sombra.* Rio de Janeiro: Leviatã, 1993.

McGowen, Chris, and Ricardo Pessanha. *The Brazilian Sound: Samba, Bossa Nova, and the Popular Music of Brazil.* 2nd ed. Philadelphia: Temple University Press, 1998.

Maciel, Luiz Carlos. *Geração em transe: Memórias do tempo do tropicalismo.* Rio de Janeiro: Editora Nova Fronteira, 1996.

Magaldi, Cristina. "Adopting Imports: New Images and Alliances in Brazilian Popular Music of the 1990s." *Popular Music* 18, no. 3 (1999): 309–29.

Maltz, Bina Freidman, et al. *Antropofagismo e tropicalismo.* Porto Alegre: Ed. Universidade/UFRGS, 1993.

Mammí, Lorenzo. "João Gilberto e o projeto utópico da bossa nova." *Novos Estudos Cebrap* 34 (Nov. 1992): 63–71.

Martín-Barbero, Jesus. *Communication, Culture and Hegemony: From the Media to Mediations.* Translated by Elizabeth Fox and Robert A. White. London: Sage Publications, 1993.

Martins, Luciano. "A geração AI-5." In *Ensaios de Opinião.* Rio de Janeiro: Paz e Terra, 1979.

Martins, Wilson. *The Modernist Idea.* New York: New York University Press, 1970.

Mattos, Sérgio. "O impacto da Revolução de 1964 no desenvolvimento da televisão." *Cadernos Intercom* 1, no. 2 (Mar. 1982): 29–43.

Medeiros, Paulo de Tarso Cabral. *A aventura da Jovem Guarda.* São Paulo: Brasiliense, 1984.

Mello e Souza, Gilda. *O tupi e o alaúde: Uma interpretação de Macunaíma.* São Paulo: Duas Cidades, 1979.

Mendes, Gilberto. *Uma odisséia musical: Dos mares do sul expressionista à elegância Pop/Art Deco.* São Paulo: Editora da Universidade de São Paulo, 1994.

Miller, Sydney. "Os festivais no panorama da música popular brasileira." *Revista Civilização Brasileira* 4, no. 17 (Jan.–Feb. 1968): 235–43.

Moby, Alberto. *Sinal fechado: A música popular brasileira sob censura.* Rio de Janeiro: Obra Aberta, 1994.

Moehn, Frederick. "In the Tropical Studio: MPB Production in Transition." *Studies in Latin American Popular Culture* 19 (2000): 57–66.

Moore, Robin D. *Nationalizing Blackness: Afrocubanismo and Artistic Revolution in Havana, 1920–1940.* Pittsburgh: University of Pittsburgh Press, 1997.

Mostaço, Edelcio. *Teatro e política: Arena, Oficina e Opinião.* São Paulo: Proposta Editorial, 1982.

Mota, Carlos Guilherme. *Ideologia da cultura brasileira (1933–1974).* São Paulo: Ática, 1977.

Motta, Nelson. *Noites tropicais: Solos, improvisos e memórias musicais*. Rio de Janeiro: Editora Objetiva, 2000.

Napolitano, Marcos. "A invenção da música popular brasileira: Um campo de reflexão para a história social." *Latin American Music Review* 19, no. 1 (Spring–Summer 1998): 92–105.

Neto, Torquato. *Os últimos dias de Paupéria*. Rio de Janeiro: Eldorado, 1973.

Nunes, Benedito. "Antropofagia ao alcance de todos." In *A utopia antropofágica*, by Oswald de Andrade, 5–39. São Paulo: Editora Globo; Secretária de Estado da Cultura, 1990.

Ortiz, Renato. *A moderna tradição brasileira*. São Paulo: Brasiliense, 1988.

———. *Cultura brasileira e identidade nacional*. São Paulo: Brasiliense, 1985.

Page, Joseph. *The Brazilians*. New York: Addison-Wesley, 1995.

Paiano, Enor. *Tropicalismo: Bananas ao vento no coração do Brasil*. São Paulo: Editora Scipione, 1996.

Pereira, Anthony W. "'Persecution and Farce': The Origins and Transformation of Brazil's Political Trials, 1964–1979." *Latin American Research Review* 33, no. 1 (1998): 43–66.

Pereira, Carlos Alberto M., and Heloísa Buarque de Hollanda, eds. *Patrulhas ideológicas, marca registrada: arte e engajamento em debate*. São Paulo: Brasiliense, 1980.

Perrone, Charles A. "From Noigandres to 'Milagre da Alegria': The Concrete Poets and Contemporary Brazilian Popular Music." *Latin American Music Review* 6, no. 1 (1985): 58–78.

———. *Masters of Contemporary Brazilian Song*. Austin: University of Texas Press, 1989.

———. *Seven Faces*. Durham: Duke University Press, 1996.

Perrone, Charles A., and Christopher Dunn. "'Chiclete com Banana': Internationalization in Brazilian Popular Music." In *Brazilian Popular Music and Globalization*, edited by Charles A. Perrone and Christopher Dunn, 1–38. Gainesville: University Press of Florida, 2001.

Polari, Alex. *Em busca do tesouro*. Rio de Janeiro: Codecri, 1982.

Reily, Suzel Ana. "Macunaíma's Music: National Identity and Ethnomusicological Research in Brazil." In *Ethnicity, Identity, and Music: The Musical Construction of Place*, edited by Martin Stokes, 71–96. Oxford/Providence: Berg Publishers, 1994.

Ricardo, Sérgio. *Quem quebrou meu violão: Uma análise da cultura brasileira na décadas de 40 a 90*. Rio de Janeiro: Record, 1991.

Ridenti, Marcelo. *Em busca do povo brasileiro: Artistas da revolução, do CPC à era da tv*. São Paulo: Editora Record, 2000.

———. *O fantasma da revolução brasileira*. São Paulo: Editora da Universidade Estadual de São Paulo, 1994.

Risério, Antônio. *Avant-garde na Bahia*. São Paulo: Instituto Lina Bo Bardi e P.M. Bardi, 1995.

———. *Carnaval ijexá*. Salvador: Corrupio, 1981.

———. *Caymmi: Uma utopia de lugar*. São Paulo: Perspectiva and Salvador: COPENE, 1993.

———. "O nome mais belo do medo." *Minas Gerais Literary Supplement* 8, no. 360 (July 21, 1973): 4.

———. "Tropicalismo." *Revista da Bahia* 32, no. 26 (May 1998): 8–12.

Rodrigues, Glauco. *Glauco Rodrigues*. Rio de Janeiro: Salamandra, 1989.

Rosnak, Theodore. *The Making of a Counterculture*. 1968. Berkeley: University of California Press, 1995.

Rubim, Albino, et al. "Salvador nos anos 50 e 60: Encontros e desencontros com a cultura." *Rua* 3, no. 4–5 (1990): 30–38.

Salomão, Waly. *Armarinho de miudezas*. Salvador: Fundação Casa Jorge Amado, 1993.

Sansone, Livio, and Jocélio Teles dos Santos. *Ritmos em trânsito: Socio-antropologia da música baiana*. São Paulo: Dynamis Editorial; Salvador: Programa A Cor da Bahia e Projeto S.A.M.B.A., 1997.

Santaella, Lúcia. *Convergências: Poesia Concreta e Tropicalismo*. São Paulo: Nobel, 1986.

Sant'anna, Affonso Romano de. *Música popular e moderna poesia brasileira*. Petrópolis: Vozes, 1986.

Santiago, Silviano. "Fazendo perguntas com o martelo." Preface to *Música popular: De olho na fresta*, by Vasconcellos. Rio de Janeiro: Graal, 1977.

———. *Uma literatura nos trópicos*. São Paulo: Editora Perspectiva, 1978.

———. *Vale quanto pesa: Ensaios sobre questões político-culturais*. Rio de Janeiro: Paz e Terra, 1982.

Santos, Lídia. "Kitsch e cultura de massa no Brasil: Reescrevendo as identidades nacionais." *Studies in Latin American Popular Culture* 19 (2000): 35–50.

Sartre, Jean-Paul. "A Plea for Intellectuals." In *Between Existentialism and Marxism: Sartre on Philosophy, Politics, Psychology and the Arts*, trans. Joan Matthews. New York: Pantheon, 1983.

Schwarz, Roberto. *Misplaced Ideas: Essays on Brazilian Culture*. Edited by John Gledson. New York: Verso, 1992.

———. "Nota sobre vanguarda e conformismo." *Teoria e Prática* 2 (1968): 127–32.

———. *O pai de família e outros estudos*. Rio de Janeiro: Paz e Terra, 1978.

Severiano, Jairo, and Zuza Homem de Melo. *A canção no tempo: 85 anos de músicas brasileiras*. 2 vols. São Paulo: Editora 34, 1998.

Silva, Armando Sérgio da. *Oficina: do teatro ao te-ato*. São Paulo: Editora Perspectiva, 1981.

Skidmore, Thomas E. *Black into White: Race and Nationality in Brazilian Thought*. 1974. Durham: Duke University Press, 1993.

———. *Politics in Brazil, 1930–1964: An Experiment in Democracy*. New York: Oxford University Press, 1967.

———. *The Politics of Military Rule in Brazil, 1964–1985*. New York: Oxford University Press, 1988.

Sodré, Nelson Werneck. *Introdução à revolução brasileira*. Rio de Janeiro: Editora Civilização Brasileira, 1963.

Sosnowski, Saúl, and Jorge Schwartz, eds. *Brasil: O trânsito da memória*. São Paulo: Editora da Universide de São Paulo, 1994.

Souza, Tarik de. *Rostos e gostos da música popular brasileira*. Porto Alegre: L & PM Editores, 1979.

Sovik, Rebecca Liv. "Ponha seu capacete: Uma viagem à tropicália pós-moderna." *Revista da Bahia* 32, no. 26 (May 1998): 60–67.

————. "Tropicália, Canonical Pop." *Studies in Latin American Popular Culture* 19 (2000): 113–28.

————. "Vaca Profana: Teoria pós-moderna e tropicália." Ph.D. diss., Universidade de São Paulo, 1994.

Stam, Robert. "Palimpsest Aesthetics: A Meditation on Hybridity and Garbage." In *Performing Hybridity*, edited by May Joseph and Jennifer Natalya Fink, 59–78. Minneapolis: University of Minnesota Press, 1999.

————. *Tropical Multiculturalism: A Comparative History of Race in Brazilian Cinema and Culture.* Durham: Duke University Press, 1997.

Tatit, Luiz. *O cancionista: Composição de canções no Brasil.* São Paulo: Editora da Universidade de São Paulo, 1996.

Taylor, Timothy. *Global Pop: World Music, World Markets.* New York: Routledge, 1997.

Teles, Gilberto Mendonça. *Vanguarda européia e modernismo brasileiro.* Petrópolis: Vozes, 1982.

Tinhorão, José Ramos. *Música popular: Do gramafone ao rádio e TV.* São Paulo: Ática, 1981.

————. *Música popular: Um tema em debate.* Rio de Janeiro: JCM, 1969.

————. *Pequena história da música popular: Da modinha à lambada.* 6th ed. São Paulo: Art Editora, 1991.

Torgovnick, Marianna. *Gone Primitive: Savage Intellects, Modern Lives.* Chicago: University of Chicago Press, 1990.

Treece, David. "Guns and Roses: Bossa Nova and Brazil's Music of Popular Protest, 1958–1968." *Popular Music* 16, no. 1 (1997): 1–29.

Trevisan, João. *Perverts in Paradise.* London: GMP Publishers, 1986.

Tropicália: 20 anos. São Paulo: SESC, 1987.

Turner, J. Michael. "Brown into Black: Changing Racial Attitudes of Afro-Brazilian University Students." In *Race, Class, and Power in Brazil*, edited by Pierre-Michel Fontaine, 73–94. Los Angeles: University of California Press and Center for Afro-American Studies, 1985.

Unruh, Vicky. *Latin American Vanguards: The Art of Contentious Encounters.* Berkeley: University of California Press, 1994.

Varela, Dailor. "Da tropicália ao lamê." *Revista de Cultura Vozes* 3 (1972): 189–94.

Vasconcellos, Gilberto. *Música popular: De olho na fresta.* Rio de Janeiro: Graal, 1977.

Veloso, Caetano. *Alegria, alegria.* Edited by Waly Salomão. Rio de Janeiro: Pedra Q Ronca, 1977.

————. "Carmen Mirandadada." In *Brazilian Popular Music and Globalization*, edited by Charles A. Perrone and Christopher Dunn, 39–45. Gainesville: University Press of Florida, 2001.

————. *Songbook.* Vols. 1–2. Edited by Almir Chediak. Rio de Janeiro: Lumiar, n.d.

————. *Verdade tropical.* São Paulo: Companhia das Letras, 1997.

Ventura, Zuenir. *1968: O ano que não terminou.* Rio de Janeiro: Nova Fronteira, 1988.

Vianna, Hermano. *The Mystery of Samba.* Chapel Hill: University of North Carolina Press, 1999.

Vilarino, Ramon Casas. *A MPB em movimento: Música, festivais e censura.* São Paulo: Olho d'agua, 1999.

Wisnik, José Miguel. "Um minuto e o milênio ou Por favor, professor, uma década de cada vez." In *Anos 70: Música popular*, by Ana Maria Bahiana et al., 7–23. Rio de Janeiro: Europa, 1980.

Wisnik, José Miguel, and Enio Squeff. *O nacional e o popular na cultura brasileira: Música*. São Paulo: Brasiliense, 1983.

Xavier, Ismail. *Allegories of Underdevelopment: Aesthetics and Politics in Modern Brazilian Cinema*. Minneapolis: University of Minnesota Press, 1997.

———. "From the Religious Moral Sense to the Post-Freudian Common Sense: Images of National History in the Brazilian Tele-Fiction." *Studies in Latin American Popular Culture* 17 (1998): 179–95.

Yúdice, George. "The Funkification of Rio." In *Microphone Fiends: Youth Music and Youth Culture*, edited by Tricia Rose, 193–217. New York: Routledge, 1994.

Zolov, Eric. *Refried Elvis: The Rise of the Mexican Counterculture*. Berkeley: University of California Press, 1999.

DISCOGRAPHY

Arena conta Zumbi (1966). RGE 3206021, 1989.

Beck. *Mutations*. Geffen 25309, 1998.

Ben, Jorge. *O Bidú: Silêncio em Brooklyn* (1967). Beverly 81490, 1991.

———. *Jorge Ben* (1969). Philips 518119, 1993.

———. *A tábua de esmeralda* (1974). Philips 5181112, 1993.

———. *África/Brasil* (1976). Philips 5181162, 1993.

Bethânia, Maria. *Maria Bethânia*. RCA Victor 1339, 1965.

———. *Recital na boite barroco*. Odeon 3545, 1968.

Brown, Carlinhos. *Alfagamabetizado*. EMI 72438, 1996.

Buarque, Chico. *Chico Buarque Vol. 3* (1968). RGE 40302, 1997.

———. *Sinal fechado* (1974). Philips 518217, 1993.

———. *Chico Buarque* (1978). Philips 518220, 1993.

Carlos, Roberto. *Jovem Guarda* (1966). Columbia 850045, n.d.

Chico Science e Nação Zumbi. *Da lama ao caos*. Sony 850224, 1994.

———. *Afrociberdélia*. Sony 850278/2479255, 1996.

Costa, Gal. *Gal Costa* (1969). Philips 514992, 1993.

———. *Gal Costa* (1969). Philips 514993, 1993.

———. *Gal a todo vapor* (1971). Philips 514991, 1993.

Doces Bárbaros (1976). Philips 8429202, 1989.

Duprat, Rogério. *A banda tropicalista do Duprat*. Philips 765048, 1968.

Getz, Stan, and João Gilberto. *Getz/Gilberto* (1964). Verve 314521414-2, 1997.

Gil, Gilberto. *Louvação* (1967). Philips 824681, 1998.

———. *Gilberto Gil* (1968). Philips 518121, 1998.

———. *Gilberto Gil* (1969). Philips 518122, 1998.

———. *Gilberto Gil* (1971). Philips 518123, 1998.

———. *Expresso 2222* (1972). Philips 848939, 1998.

———. *Refazenda* (1975). WEA M995136, 1994.

———. *Refavela* (1977). WEA 994642, 1994.

———. *Realce* (1979). WEA 53068, n.d.

———. *Nightingale*. Elektra/Asylum 6E-167. 1979.

———. *Parabolic* (1991). WEA 76292, 1992.

———. *Quanta*. Warner Brasil 063018644, 1997.

Gil, Gilberto, and Jorge Ben. *Gil e Jorge* (1975). M8464022, 1993.

Gilberto, João. *The Legendary João Gilberto*. World Pacific 93891, 1990.

Leão, Nara (1968). *Nara Leão*. Philips 4320, n.d.

Mendes, Gilberto. *Surf, bola na rede, um pente de Istanbul e a música de Gilberto Mendes*. Eldorado 584008, n.d.

Mutantes. *Os Mutantes* (1968). Philips 829498, n.d.

———. *Mutantes* (1969). Philips 835886, n.d.

———. *The Best of Os Mutantes: Everything is Possible!* Luaka Bop/Warner Bros. 947251, 1999.

Olodum. *O movimento*. Warner Brasil 107800521, 1993.

Portastatic. *De Mel, De Melão*. Merge 180, 2000.

Regina, Elis. *Elis Regina no Fino da Bossa*. Velas 11-V030, vols. 1–3, 1994.

Santtana, Lucas. *EletroBenDodô*. Natasha 789700903112, 1999.

Seixas, Raul. *Gita* (1974). Polygram 838288-2, 1989.

Suely e os Kantikus. "Que Bacana." Philips 365258, 1968.

Tropicália Essentials. Hip-O/Universal 3145469322, 1999.

Tropicália ou panis et circensis (1968). Phillips 512089, 1993.

Tropicália 30 anos. Natasha 289122, 1997.

Vandré, Geraldo. *Canto Geral*. Odeon MOFB 3514, 1968.

———. *20 Preferidas*. RGE 56132, 1997.

Veloso, Caetano. *Caetano Veloso* (1968). Philips 838557, 1990.

———. *Caetano Veloso* (1969). Philips 838556, 1990.

———. *Caetano Veloso* (1971). Philips 838561, 1990.

———. *Transa* (1972). Philips 838511, 1989.

———. *Araça azul* (1972). Philips 824691, n.d.

———. *Jóia*. Philips 6349132, 1975.

———. *Bicho* (1977). Philips 838562, 1989.

———. *Muito* (1978). Philips 836012, n.d.

———. *Cinema Transcendental* (1979). Verve 3145120232, 1989.

———. *Estrangeira*. Elektra 60898, 1989.

———. *Circuladô*. Elektra Nonesuch 79277, 1991.

———. *Circuladô vivo*. Philips 510459, 1992.

———. *Livro*. Philips 536584, 1997.

———. *Prenda minha*. Philips 538332, 1998.

———. *Caetano Veloso: Singles*. Philips 1090, 1999.

Veloso, Caetano, and Chico Buarque. *Caetano e Chico juntos e ao vivo* (1972). Philips 8125222, 1993.

Veloso, Caetano, and Gal Costa. *Domingo* (1967). Philips 838555, 1990.

Veloso, Caetano, and Gilberto Gil. *Tropicália 2*. Philips 518178, 1993.

Zé, Tom. *Tom Zé* (1968). Sony 495712, 2000.

———. *Tom Zé* (1970). RGE 3476007, 1994.

———. *Todos os olhos*. Continental 10121, 1973.

———. *The Best of Tom Zé: Massive Hits*. Luaka Bop/Warner Bros. 26396, 1990.

———. *The Hips of Tradition*. Luaka Bop/Warner Bros. 945118, 1992.

———. *Fabrication Defect: Com defeito de fabricação*. Luaka Bop/Warner Bros. 946953, 1998.

———. *Imprensa cantada*. Trama 149, 1999.

———. *Jogos de armar*. Trama 1112, 2000.

INDEX

Black Power, 2, 131, 178–79
Black Rio, 178–79, 183. *See also* Soul
  music
Bloco afro, 180, 207–8
Boal, Augusto, 52–53, 220 (n. 38); and
  critique of tropicalists, 82–83
Bosi, Alfredo, 14
Bossa nova: and modernity, 7, 28–29,
  89; and jazz, 29–30, 202; and develop-
  mentalism, 30, 33–34; and influence
  on tropicalists, 34–35, 46, 52, 145–46;
  second generation of, 55–58, 160
Bourdieu, Pierre, 4, 138
Brasília, 30–31, 88, 140
Brasilidade: under Vargas, 26; and tropi-
  calists, 73, 158, 209, 212–14; and
  Afro-Brazilians, 178, 210
Brazilian Academy of Letters, 95, 127,
  211
Brown, Carlinhos, 208–9
Brown, James, 99, 131
Brutality garden: significance of, 3,
  97–98
Buarque de Hollanda, Chico, 56, 60, 89,
  109, 111–12, 157, 164, 211–12; and fes-
  tivals, 62–64, 136; and conflict with
  tropicalists, 138, 152–53, 227 (n. 44);
  as leading voice of protest, 162–63
Buarque de Hollanda, Heloísa, 4, 54, 174
Byrne, David, 195, 202, 210, 231 (n. 4)

Cabral, Pedro Alvares, 87–88
"Cademar," 196
Cage, John, 50, 70
Calado, Carlos, 5
"Cálice," 162
Callado, Antônio, 111
Caminha, Pero Vaz, 73, 88, 127
"Caminhando," 135–37, 148, 206
Campos, Augusto de, 4, 31–32, 34, 58,
  64–65, 89, 93, 102, 105, 118, 196
Campos, Haroldo de, 20, 31, 102
Candomblé, 50, 87, 167–68, 174–75, 180,
  182–83, 207
Cannibalism: and Tropicália, 6, 74, 78,

81, 85, 200, 212–13; and *modernismo*,
  17–20. *See also* Manifestos: Cannibalist
Capinan, José Carlos, 47, 118–19, 127–28
Capoeira, 50, 67, 167–68, 191
"Carcará," 53–54
Carlos, Roberto, 109, 150; and Jovem
  Guarda, 58–61; and "Tropicália," 90
Carnival, 16, 25, 75; and tropicalists, 1,
  174–75, 206–8, 233 (nn. 33–34)
"Carolina," 109, 152–53
Carvalho, Martha, 59
Castelo Branco, Humberto, 43
Castro, Ruy, 29, 55, 124–25
"Catecismo, creme dental e eu," 106
Caymmi, Dorival, 47, 50, 151, 164, 166,
  175–76
Caymmi, Nana, 111–12
Celestino, Vicente, 94, 127
Censorship, 81, 137, 142; of tropicalists,
  143–44, 146–47; following AI-5, 157,
  161–63
Centro Populares de Cultura (CPC):
  and national-popular culture, 40–
  42, 46, 53, 218 (n. 9); and critique of
  vanguards, 42–43; dismantling of,
  43–44
"Cérebro Eletrônico," 154
César, Chico, 210
Chacrinha, 125–27, 148, 156
Chamie, Mário, 129, 221 (n. 83)
"Chega de saudade," 29, 35, 145–46
"Chiclete com banana," 199
Chico Science & Nação Zumbi, 209–10
"Chuck Berry Fields Forever," 176, 230
  (n. 42)
Cinema Novo, 50–51, 74–77, 171, 192
"Clever Boy Samba," 51–52, 219 (n. 35)
Cliff, Jimmy, 143, 185–86
Comando de Caça aos Comunistas
  (CCC), 81, 111
"Complexo de épico," 198
Concrete poetry: and developmentalism,
  31–32; and tropicalists, 69, 105, 169,
  192, 196, 200, 213
"Coração materno," 94

CPSIA information can be obtained
at www.ICGtesting.com
Printed in the USA
LVHW030113200121
676902LV00005B/371